Kirtley Library
Columbia College
Columbia, Missouri 65216

the ENCYCLOPEDIA of HOMONYMS
'sound-alikes'

the only
complete comprehensive collection
of 'sound-alike' words
ever published

A REFERENCE BOOK FOR EVERYONE

by Dora Newhouse

Library of Congress Catalog Card Number: 76-27486
ISBN 0-918050-01-4

Copyright © 1976 by Dora Newhouse

All rights reserved. No part of this work covered by the copyrights hereon may be copied or reproduced in any form or by any means - graphic, electronic or mechanical, including photocopying, recording, taping, or information and retrieval systems - without the written permission of the publisher.

current printing (last digit)
10 9 8 7 6 5 4 3 2 1

Published by NEWHOUSE PRESS
P.O. Box 24282 Westwood Village
Los Angeles, California 90024

Printed and bound in the United States of America

HOMOPHONES

Wood you believe that I didn't no
About homophones until too daze ago?
That day in hour class in groups of for,
We had to come up with won or more.

Mary new six; enough to pass,
but my ate homophones lead the class.
Then a thought ran threw my head,
"Urn a living from homophones", it said.

I guess I just sat and staired into space.
My hole life seamed to fall into place.
Our school's principle happened to come buy,
and asked about the look in my I.

"Sir", said I as bowled as could bee,
"My future rode I clearly see."
"Sun", said he, "move write ahead,
Set sail on your coarse. Don't be misled."

I herd that gnus with grate delight.
I will study homophones both day and knight.
For weaks and months, through thick oar thin,
I'll pursue my goal. Eye no aisle win.

George E. Coon

from "The Reading Teacher"-April 1976
Reprinted with permission of the author and the International Reading Association

IN APPRECIATION:

- To Dr. Frank Laubach's method of teaching literacy and 'English to Speakers of Other Languages' (ESOL); his concept of 'Each One, Teach One' and to California Literacy Inc. with their dedicated volunteer tutors who are using his method and who provided impetus for this book.
- To the courteous and knowledgeable staff of the main office of the Los Angeles Public Library and their colleagues at the branch offices.
- To Sue Lewis who spent extraordinary hours guiding and assisting in the project and to Mia Yamaoka whose positive encouragement kept me from faltering.
- To Robert Blake who supplied so many constructive suggestions.
- To the Hagler children, Clifford and Kerry, whose treasured letters and post cards "Dere Ant Dora" and "My mother ohs me money" prompted the condensed and simplified version of this book which will be extremely useful to school systems and bilingual students everywhere.
- To my grandsons, Kam and Damon Santos, who were diligent collectors of homonyms and together with Sue Lewis created several homonym word games that are imaginative, educational and loads of fun.

-Dora Newhouse-

INTRODUCTION

This Encyclopedia is the **only** complete comprehensive collection of 'sound-alike' words that are spelled differently. The English language is constantly changing as words are lost and words are added. Included in these pages are some words that are obsolete or archaic; some that are colloquial or popular slang; some that are recorded in the English classics, the Bible or the literature of Scott and Burns; and some are informal and very up-to-date.

Homophones and homonyms with variant spellings are the subject of this reference book. Although definitions are included, the book is not intended to be a dictionary, and all the meanings of a particular word may not be included. The word definitions are brief and a dictionary should be consulted for more definitive meanings.

This unique reference book is designed, not only to help you master major problems in spelling and pronunciation, but to be of assistance in enlarging and enriching your vocabulary.

If the spelling or pronunciation of a particular word is not known, such as:

| Quay | Gneiss | Colonel |
| Key | Nice | Kernel |

the 'sound-alike' word in the same set will show that quay is pronounced key, gneiss is pronounced nice, and colonel sounds like kernel.

The homonyms are arranged alphabetically, with all the 'sound-alikes' grouped immediately following the alphabetized word set in bold type. The groupings include only words that are pronounced the same. A few words have two pronunciations and the fact that we have used the word in one way does not mean that the other is incorrect. It only means that a 'sound alike' was not found to match it. For example:

Anti-also pronounced antī
Ante
Auntie

Boy
Buoy-also pronounced buī (booey)

A Homonym or Homophone is defined as 'two or more words that are **pronounced alike** but which are different in meaning and usually spelling.'

Dear	Dew	For	There	To
Deer	Do	Fore	Their	Too
Dere	Due	Four	They're	Two

Homographs are homonymous words that are **spelled alike**, but with two or more meanings:

Dear- beloved
Dear- expensive

Organ- functional part of the body
Organ- musical instrument

Address- delivery direction of a letter
Address- a written or spoken speech
Address- to aim or direct, accost

Heteronyms are spelled alike but are **different in both sound and meaning,** usually one syllable words:

Bass- fish
Bass- low note in music

Bow- weapon used with arrow
Bow- bend or nod

Lead- show the way
Lead- the mineral

Row- file, tier
Row- uproar, tumult, melee

Stressonyms, a new word by the author to describe words that are spelled alike but differ in meaning and pronunciation, and **sound different only because of the accent mark.** These multisyllable words are sometimes considered to be heteronyms:

Ab'stract- abridgement, digest, draft, synopsis
Abstract'- remove, purloin, take away from

Ac'cent- tone, pitch, quality of sound, cadence
Accent'- emphasize, stress, speak with an accent

In'valid- sickly person or one disabled
Invalid'- having no force or weight, null

Po'lish- belonging to Poland
Polish'- to clean, wax, brighten

Re'fuse- rubbish, trash, garbage
Refuse'- decline, reject, deny

Synonyms are words that are **similar in meaning** but which do not sound alike and are not spelled the same:

Chatter- prattle, talk, gab
Praise- commend, honor, laud, compliment

Antonyms have **opposite meanings:**

Chatter- silence, quiet
Praise- blame, reprove, censure

—A—

Aar (pr.n)- river in Switzerland
Are- plural of be. Present of verb "to be"

Ab (n)- 5th month of Jewish year corresponding with July and August
Abb (n)- 1. warp yarn. 2. inferior part of edges or skirts of a fleece

Abaissed (adv)- obs. - borne lower than usual. Turned downward
Abased (v)- disgraced, hishonored, shamed

Abel (pr.n)- 1. masc. name. 2. second son of Adam - slain by his brother Cain
Able (adj)- skillful, talented, capable, efficient

Abet (v)- encourage, assist
Abette (v)- foment, connive at

Able- see Abel

Abreast (adv)- side by side
Abrest (adv)- Naut. - over, against, or on a line with vessel's beam

Absinthe (n)- green colored aromatic liquor with licorice flavor
Absinth (n)- wormwood

Accidence (n)- undeveloped form, seed, germ, root
Accidents (n-pl)- mishaps, injuries, hazards, disasters

Accite (v)- Archaic - cite, summon
Acite (v)- obs. - excite

Acclamation (n)- praise, tribute, applause
Acclimation (n)- accustom, inure to new climate

Accoy (v)- obs. - render quiet, soothe
Acoie (v)- Archaic - daunt

Accroach (v)- to usurp, as royal prerogatives
Accroche (v)- obs. - to draw to oneself, as with grappling hook

Accrue (v)- increase, proceed, ensue, result
Acrewe (n)- obs. - sewing extra mesh or stitch added in network

Accurse (v)- curse, revile, damn
Acurse (v)- Dial.- invoke misery upon

Accuse (v)- reproach, censure, blame
Acuse (v)- obs. - to betray

A

Acertein (v)- obs. - to render certain. Make confident
Ascertain (v)- learn by experiment and experience. Get to know

Acetic (adj)- pertaining to vinegar or acetic acid
Ascetic (n)- practice of religious austerity. Monk, hermit

Aches (n-pl)- suffers dull continued pain
Aix (pr.n)- 1. Cathedral City in France. 2. (n) - genus of fresh water duck

Acheve (n)- Feudal law - to do homage on taking the feu
Achieve (v)- obtain, gain, attain

Acholite (n)- rare-Astron. - an attendant body. A satellite
Acolyte (n)- one who assists clergyman in liturgical service

Acker (n)- Eng. Dial. - a ripple, eddy in a river
Acre (n)- 1. field, estate. 2. measure of length

Acor (n)- acidity of the stomach
Acore (v)- obs. - suffering

Acre- see Acker

Acrewe- obs. - see Accrue

Acts (n-pl)- 1. conducts, behaves, does. 2. exploits, deeds
Ax or Axe (n)- sharp tool with handle for chopping

Acurse (v)- Dial. - invoke misery upon
Accurse (v)- curse, revile, damn

Acuse (v)- obs. - to betray
Accuse (v)- reproach, censure, blame

Ad (n)- advertisement
Add (v)- attach, join, increase, annex

Ada (pr.n)- 1. feminine name. 2. city in Oklahoma
Adah (n)- Biblical - ornament

Adaw (v)- Dial. - subdue, daunt
Adawe (adj)- awaken, arouse

Ade (pr.n)- George. Writer, humorist
Aid (v)- assist, help, befriend, support
Aide (n)- attache, right-hand man, assistant officer

Addill (n)- obs. - become muddled and confused
Addle (v)- corrupt, rot, render putrid
Adel (n)- Eng. Dial. - liquid filth, urine, mire
Adill (n)- Eng. obs. - earnings, wages

10

A

Adds (v)- 1. joins, increases. 2. total numbers to find sum
Ads (n-pl)- advertisements
Adze (n)- sharp tool with handle resembling an axe

Adherence (n)- attachments, devotion, fidelity
Adherents (n-pl)- supporters, allies, followers

Adieu (n)- goodbye, farewell - so long, adios
Ado (n)- trouble, fuss, stir

Adolescence (n)- youthful during teens
Adolescents (n-pl)- teenagers

Aegis (n)- Greek myth. Shield of Zeus
Egis (n)- 1. goatskin. 2. sponsorship, auspices

Aeon (n)- gnostic doctrine - one of a class of powers or beings
Eon (n)- age, lifetime

Aerial (n)- antenna
Ariel (n)- African gazelle
Ariel (pr.n)- 1. Shakespeare's 'airy spirit' in Midsummer Nights Dream. 2. (n)- satellite of planet Uranus

Aerie (n)- 1. eagle's nest. 2. elevation, habitation
Airy (adj)- windy, breezy, ventilated

Aes or As (n)- Roman coin
Ass (n)- 1. donkey, onager, burro. 2. dolt, lout, fool, idiot
Asse (n)- caama, South African fox

Aferm (v)- obs. - law - to testify to
Affirm (v)- assert, declare, profess

Afford (v)- give forth, supply
Aford (v)- Archaic - carry out, achieve

Affray (n)- public brawl, noisy quarrel
Afrai (v)- obs. - to startle from quiet, alarm
Afraye (v)- to frighten away
Afrey (v)- Archaic - assault or attack

Affront (v)- insult, abuse, ill treat
Afront (n)- obs. - encounter, friendly or hostile
Afrunt (adj)- Archaic - arrogant

Agate (n)- mineral - variegated quartz. A gem
Agget (n)- obs. - book binders burnisher with an agate tip
Aggot (n)- Archaic - drawplate having drilled eye of agate

Aid (v)- assist, help, befriend, support
Aide (n)- attache, right-hand man, assistant officer

Ail (v)- fall ill, unwell, be sick, suffer, trouble
Ale (n)- beer made from malt liquor

A

Air (n)- wind, breeze, ozone
Aire (n)- person of any rank above the common Freeman (Irish Tribal Society)
Are (n)- metric system - land measure. 160 sq. meters
Ayr (pr.n)- city in Scotland
E'er (adv)- contraction of ever
Eir (n)- 1. sandbank, beach. 2.(pr.n)- Goddess of Healing
Eire (n)- journey, march
Ere (adv)- sooner than, before, previous
Err (v)- misjudge, sin, blunder, mistake
Erre (v)- cause offense by blundering
Eyr (adv)- early
Eyre (n)- itinerant judges who rode circuit to hold court in different countries in England
Heir (n)- beneficiary, inheritor
Ore (n)- Anglo-saxon - honor, respect, reverence, glory (pronounced Ār)

Aired (v)- ventilated
Erred (v)- sinned, blundered, strayed

Airy (adj)- windy, breezy, ventilated
Aerie (n)- 1. eagle's nest. 2. elevation, habitation

Aisle (n)- walk, path, lane, passageway
Isle (n)- small island, key, cay
I'll (contr)- I will
Ile (n)- (n)- obs.- the ileum. Anat. - the last division of the intestine

Ait (n)- small island
Ate (v)- devoured. Past of eat
Eight (n)- number 8

Aix (pr.n)- 1. Cathedral City in France. 2. genus of fresh water duck
Aches (n-pl)- suffers dull continued pain

Ajee (adj)- ajar
Agee (adj)- awry, askew

Alan (n)- 1. large hunting dog, wolfhound. 2. masculine name
Alen (n)- Scandinavian measure
Allen (pr.n)- Ethan. Green mountain hero. Also could be first or last name

Ale (n)- beer made from malt liquor
Ail (v)- fall ill, unwell, be sick, suffer, trouble

Alec (n)- fish sauce, herring
Alec or Aleck (pr.n)- 1. male name - dim. of Alexander. 2. slang- smart aleck- "know it all"

A

Align (v)- to join with others in a cause
Aline (v)- regulate by line, adjust or form in a line

Aline- see Align

All (adv)- sum, total, everyone, whole
Awl (n)- pointed tool for piercing small holes

Allowed (v)- granted, conceded, permitted, let
Aloud (adv)- clamorous, with noise, audible

Alloy (n)- metallic compound. Combination of metals
Aloye (v)- Archaic - reduce purity by less valuable metal - debase by mixture

All ready (phrase)- everything is ready
Already (adv)- before, previously

All together (phrase)- everyone in company
Altogether (adv)- wholly, totally, completely

All ways (phrase)- all ways possible
Always (adv)- eternally, forever, perpetually

Alma (pr.n)- female name
Almah (n)- Egypt - professional dancing girl

Aloud- see Allowed

Altar (n)- communion table, place for worship
Alter (v)- transform, remodel, spay

Amend (v)- mend, repair, improve, correct, better
Amende (n)- penalty of fine, retraction, reparation

Amok (n)- Malay - psychic depression followed by desire to murder
Amuck (adv)- rush about madly

Amour (n)- love affair, intrigue
Amur (pr.n)- river in North East Asia

Amuck- see Amok

Amur- see Amour

An (adj)- one, each, anyone
Ann or Anne (pr.n)- female name

Ana (n)- collection of miscellaneous information
An-na (n)- coin in India
Anna (pr.n)- female name

Analyst (n)- 1. studier, investigator, analyzer. 2. psychiatrist, alienist
Annalist (n)- recorder, compiler, historian

A

Analyze (v)- investigate, question, summarize, study
Annalize (v)- 1. to write annals of. 2. record

Anchor (v)- 1. fasten, attach. 2. of a vessel, hold fast
Anker (n)- Dutch liquid measure

Anchorite (n)- hermit, recluse, monk, nun
Ankerite (n)- mineral resembling dolomite with iron, replacing the magnesia

Aneal (v)- obs. - to give extreme unction
Anele (v)- to annoint
Anneal (v)- to subject to high heat

Ani (n)- bird of cuckoo family
Annie (pr.n)- female name

Anil (n)- indigo plant
Anile (adj)- old - womanish. Feeble-minded
Annil (n)- obs. - law - marriageable years - age of consent to marriage

Animous (adj)- full of spirit. Resolute
Animus (n)- malicious intention or disposition

Anker- see Anchor

Ankerite (n)- mineral resembling dolomite with iron, replacing the magnesia
Anchorite (n)- hermit, recluse, monk, nun

Annalist- see Analyst

Annalize (v)- 1. to write annals of. 2. record
Analyze (v)- investigate, question, summarize, study

Anneal- see Aneal, Aneal

Annil- see Anil, Anile

Ant (n)- insect, emmet, pismire
Aunt (n)- 1. relative, sister of one's father or mother. 2. obs.- prostitute, bawd

Ante (adj)- 1. precede, go before. 2. initial stake in poker
Anti (adj)- against, opposed to. Also pronounced "antī"
Auntie (n)- relative, uncle's wife

Antecedence (n)- priority, precedence, act of going before
Antecedents (n-pl)- family, ancestry, lineage, pedigrees

Apparel (n)- dress, clothes, attire
Apperel (v)- obs. - make or get ready, prepare

A

Apparseive (v)- obs. - psychol. - to adjust new knowledge to what is already known
Appercieve (v)- perceive, comprehend

Appanage (n)- a dependent property or territory
Appennage (n)- Dial. - natural attribute or endowment

Appetence (n)- ardent desire
Appetents (n-pl)- objects of a craving

Aracke (n)- obs. - sweat
Arak (n)- sap of various palms as coconut, date
Arrack (n)- spirituous liquor

Arber (n)- wind pipe of an animal
Arbor (n)- Bot. - a tree
Arbour (n)- Eng. Dial - bower of lattice work supporting vines

Araigne (v)- old Eng. law - to appeal, demand
Araine (n)- Dial. - spider
Arraign (v)- prosecute, to call before court

Arc (n)- bend, curve, part of a circle, crescent
Ark (n)- 1. clumsy boat. 2. chest of sanctity (Holy Box). 3. Noah's Ark

Are- plural of be. Present of verb "to be"
Aar (pr.n.)- river in Switzerland

Argon (n)- inert colorless gas
Argonne (pr.n)- forest in Northern France

Ariel (n)- African gazelle
Ariel (pr.n.)- 1. Shakespeare's airy spirit .2. (n)-satellite of planet Uranus
Aerial (n)- antenna

Arm (v)- 1. weapon of offense or defense. 2. (n)- human upper limb
Arme (v)- obs. - to provide with means of attack or resistance

Armary (n)- closet, chest, safe
Armory (n)- place where weapons of war are deposited

Armer (n)- one who arms or supplies arms
Armor (n)- clothing worn to protect one's person in battle
Armur (n)- obs. - warfare, hostilities

Arnaout (n)- one serving as a soldier in a Turkish Army
Arnaut (n)- inhabitant of Albania

Arrack- see Aracke, Arak

Arraign- see Araigne, Araine

A

Arrant (adj)- notorious, bad, infamous, wicked
Errant (adj)- roving, vagrant, wandering, stray

Arson (n)- criminal setting of fires, incendiarism, pyromania
Arsoun (n)- obs. - a saddlebow

Ascertain (v)- learn by experiment and experience. Get to know
Acertein (v)- obs. - to render certain, make confident

Ascent (n)- upswing, elevation, climb, act of rising
Assent (v)- agree, accept, consent

Ascetic (n)- practice of religious austerity. Monk, hermit
Acetic (adj)- pertaining to vinegar or acetic acid

Asoil (v)- Archaic - expiate, atone
Asoile (v)- obs. - clear up, explanation
Assoil (v)- absolve, acquit, release
Assoyle (n)- Scotch - remove

Asperate (adj)- make rough, harshness, severity
Aspirate (v)- draw or remove by suction

Asperation (n)- making rough
Aspiration (n)- enterprising, desire, ambition

Ass (n)- 1. donkey, onager, burro. 2. dolt, lout, fool, idiot
Asse (n)- caama, South American fox
Aes or As (n)- Roman coin

Assent- see Ascent

Assistance (n)- support, relief, help, aid
Assistants (n)- allies, supporters, helpers

Assoyle- see Asoil, Assoil, Asoile

At (prep)- at, near, by, in
Att (n)- Siamese coin

Ate (v)- devoured. Past of eat
Ait (n)- small island
Eight (n)- number 8

Ate (n)- Greek goddess
Eighty (n)- number 80

Atle (n)- Tamarish salt tree
Atli (pr.n)- Scandinavian myth. King who murders his wife's brothers

Attendance (n)- being there, going to, waiting on
Attendants (n-pl)- companions, escorts, associates, servants

A

Aube (pr.n)- river in France
Ob (pr.n)- gulf in West Siberia, Arctic Sea

Aude (pr.n)- city on South Coast of France
Od (n)- hypothetical force
Ode (n)- lyric poem, song, epode
Owed (v)- past tense of owe. Be indebted, beholden to

Auger (n)- tool for boring holes in wood
Augur (v)- foretell, predict, indicate

Aught (n)- 1. any part, anything. 2. cipher (0), zero
Ought (v)- must, shall, should

Augur- see Auger

Auk (pr.n)- 1. sea bird. 2. tribe of Alaskan Indians
Awk (adj)- perverse, contrary, odd

Aune (n)- old French cloth measure
Own (adj)- possess, have, hold, belonging to oneself

Aunt (n)- 1. relative, sister of one's father or mother. 2. obs.- prostitute, bawd
Ant (n)- insect, emmet, pismire

Auntie (n)- relative, uncle's wife
Anti (adj)- against, opposed to. Also pronounced "antī"
Ante (adj)- 1. precede, go before. 2. initial stake in poker

Aural (adj)- perceived by organs of hearing
Oral (adj)- verbal, spoken, uttered by mouth
Orel (pr.n)- city in central Soviet Union

Aureole (n)- 1. nimbus, halo. 2. ring of life
Oriel (n)- bay window
Oriole (n)- bird of passerine family

Auricle (n)- lobe, outer portion of ear, external ear
Oracle (n)- prophet, seer, fortune teller

Autarchy (n)- absolute, sovereignty, despotism
Autarky (n)- national policy of economic independence

Avale (v)- obs. - descend, dismount
Avail (n)- use, benefit, profit
Availe (v)- Archaic - yield, submit

Away (adv)- absent, not present
Aweigh (adj)- nautical - anchor raised enough to clear bottom

Awful (adj)- bad, unpleasant, gruesome, shocking
Offal (n)- rubbish, waste, dung, sewage

Awk- see Auk

A

Awl (n)- pointed tool for piercing small holes
All (adv)- sum, total, everyone, whole

Axe or Ax (n)- sharp tool with handle for chopping
Acts (n-pl)- 1. conducts, behaves, does. 2. exploits, deeds

Axel (n)- figure skating jump
Axil (n)- angle between side of leaf and branch
Axle (n)- pin, bar or shaft on which wheels rotate

Axes (n)- hatchet, sharp tools with handles for chopping
Axis (n)- shaft, pivot, turning line

Ay (inter)- alas, sound expressing sorrow, distress
Aye (n)- affirmative vote, yes, yea
Ey (n)- an island
Eye (n)- orb, organ of sight
I (pron)- myself, first person, ego

Ayne (adj)- eldest, first born
Eigne (adj)- entailed as of an estate, title to property

B

—B—

Ba (pr.n)- Egypt, religion - soul represented by bird with human head
Baa (n)- cry or bleat of a sheep
Bah (inter)- exclamation of contempt

Babble (n)- idle, talk, senseless prattle
Bable (pr.n)- Bibl.- city and tower in land of Shinar

Baca (v)- Bibl. - weeping
Bacca (n)- Bot. - a berry

Bacchant (n)- a reveler
Bacchante (n)- a man or woman devotee of Bacchus

Bacis (pr.n)- in Greek legend, it's a seer
Bases (n.pl)- baseball- 4 points of the diamond
Basis (n)- stand, support, foundation, base

Bacon (n)- pork
Baken (v)- to cook by dry heat. Baked

Bad (adj)- evil, wicked, poor, defective, inferior
Bade (v)- past tense of verb "to bid"

Badger (pr.n)- burrowing animal with short thick legs
Badgir (n)- Oriental- tower or screen for ventilation

Bail (n)- 1, bond, pledge, security. 2. dip, ladle, scoop
Bale (n)- parcel, bundle, load, package, case

Bailer (n)- one who makes bail
Baler (n)- bundler, loader

Baine (v)- Scot. Dial.- bathe
Bain (n)- Scot.- variant of bone
Bane (n)- 1. poison, woe, harm 2. (v)- do injury to

Bait (n)- temptation, lure, decoy, snare, trail
Bate (v)- lessen, wane, ebb, decrease

Baize (n)- thick woolen fabric or cloth
Bays (n-pl)- 1. bodies of water. 2. reddish-brown horses. 3. (v)- barks

Bald (adj)- without hair, shaven, depilated
Balled (v)- formed into a ball
Bawled (v)- cried aloud

Bale- see Bail

Baler- see Bailer

Ball (n)- 1. dance, party. 2. round body, sphere, globe
Bawl (v)- cry aloud, clamor, wail, weep, sob

B

Balled- see Bald, Bawled

Balm (n)- salve, ointment, lotion
Bomb (n)- grenade, fireball, torpedo, explosive

Banak (pr.n)- Indian of Shoshonean tribe
Bannock (n)- flat, rounded cake or bread made of oatmeal or barley meal

Banc (n)-Law- a bench or seat of justice
Bank (n)- institution for issuing, lending or caring for money

Band (n)- 1. orchestra. 2. crowd, mob, troupe. 3. joining. 4. sash
Banned (v)- prohibited, forbade, excluded

Bands (n)- companies of persons organized to play musical instruments
Banns (n-pl)- announcements in church proclaiming intended marriage
Bans (v)- prohibits, rejects, bars, taboos

Bane- see Baine, Bain

Banian (n)- caste of Hindu merchants
Banyan (n)- loose woolen shirt, gown or jacket worn in India
Banyon (n)- Bot.- a tree

Bank- see Banc

Bannock- see Banak

Banns- see Bands, Bans

Banyon- see Banian, Banyan

Bar (n)- 1. barrier, obstacle. 2. where food or drinks are served. 3. (v)- forbid, prevent
Barr - obs.- make the cry of an elephant

Barb (n)- 1. race of horses related to the Arabs. 2. breed of pigeon
Barbe (n)- short scarf worn at throat or head

Barbary (pr.n)- region in North Africa
Barberry (n)- shrub with red acid fruit- sometimes used for preserves

Barber (v)- to shave, cut or dress the hair or beard of
Barbor (n)- Canada- storm or driving icy spicules formed from sea water
Barbour (n)- Canada- vapor rising from water on a frosty day

Barbet (n)- variety of small poodle having long curly hair
Barbette (n)- 1. war vessel. 2. fixed armour protection a platform from which guns fire over it

B

Barce (n)- Eng. Dial.- a stickle back (small fish)
Barse (n)- common European perch

Bard (n)- composer of poetry, rhymer, poet
Barred (v)- 1. having bars, fastened with a bar. 2. prevented, forbade

Bare (adj)- undressed, naked, unclothed, nude, exposed
Bear (v)- 1. carry, endure. 2. (n)- animal-bruin

Bargain (n)- agreement, contract, purchase
Bargane (n)- Scot.- to contend, struggle

Baring (v)- stripping, uncovering, exposing
Bearing (n)- behavior, comportment, attitude, air
Bering (pr.n)- Strait-name of a sea between Alaska and Siberia

Bark (n)- 1. skin covering, rind of tree. 2. cry of dogs- yelp
Barque (n)- boat or sailing vessel

Barkey (n)- obs.- a sailor's pet name for his ship
Barky (adj)- covered with or containing bark

Barley (n)- cereal grass, also seed or grain obtained from it
Barly (n)- Scot. Dial.- cry for truce among boys at their games

Baron (n)- nobleman
Barren (adj)- sterile, unfruitful, childless

Baroness (n)- Baron's wife
Barrenness (adj)- sterility, infertility

Barr- see Bar

Barred- see Bard

Barren- see Baron

Barrenness- see Baroness

Barry (pr.n)- 1. city near Cardiff, Wales. 2. slang- baritone saxophone
Berry (n)- small fruit
Bury (v)- lay in grave, inter, entomb

Barse- see Barce

Base (adj)- 1. vile, mean. 2. foundation, support
Bass (n)- low deep tone, musical term

Based (v)- put on foundation
Baste (v)- 1. stitch or sew loosely. 2. moisten with fat. 3. thrash, beat, pommel

B

Basel (pr.n)- city in Switzerland
Basil (n)- plant of the mint family
Basil (pr.n)- Saint. Bishop of Caesarea- 379

Bases (n.pl.)- baseball- 4 points of the diamond
Basis (n)- stand, support, foundation, base
Bacis (pr.n)- in Greek legend, it's a seer

Basin (n)- hollow, circular dish or vessel with sloping sides for holding water
Bason (v)- Agric.- to water or irrigate by a basin

Bask (v)- sunbathe, to lie in warmth
Basque (pr.n)- race of people in France or Spain
Basque (n)- fitted tunic

Baste- see Based

Bat (n)- 1. club, stick, mallet, racket. 2. flying mammal
Batt (n)- cotton used to fill mattresses

Bate (v)- lessen, wane, ebb, decrease
Bait (n)- temptation, lure, decoy

Bats (n-pl)- 1. Scot.- a disease in animals
Batts (n-pl)- 1. Scot.- a disease in animals
Batz (n)- coin bearing image of a bear, formerly current in Switzerland

Batt- see Bat

Battel (n)- Eng.- college accounts or charges for board and provisions
Battle (n)- encounter, combat, conflict, fight

Batten (adj)- overeat, devour, fatten, feed
Baton (n)- stick, rod, staff of office

Bawl (v)- cry aloud, clamor, wail, weep, sob
Ball (n)- 1. dance, party. 2. round body, sphere, globe

Bawled - see Bald, Balled

Bay (n)- 1. color. 2. body of water. 3. bark or yelp
Bey (n)- Turkish governor

Bays (n-pl)- 1. bodies of water. 2. reddish-brown horses. 3. (v)- barks
Baize (n)- thick woolen fabric or cloth

Be (v)- have reality, be alive, exist
Bea (pr.n)- Fem. name, dim. for Beatrice or Bernice
Bee (n)- stinging insect, produces honey and wax

Beach (n)- water's edge, sands, seashore
Beech (n)- tree

B

Beak (n)- snout, nozzle, bill, nose
Beek (v)- Scot. 1. bask, warm. 2. season wood by exposing to heat
Beke (v)- Scot.- to shine brightly

Beal (n)- Eng. Dial.- small inflammatory tumor
Beele (n)- Dial.- mining, a pick used to detach ores

Beam (n)- 1. large piece of lumber. 2. a ray or shaft of light
Beme (n)- obs.- a trumpet

Bean (n)- an edible legume of the pea family. 2. coffee bean
Been (v)- p.p. of verb "to be"
Bene (n)- a prayer, a boon

Bear- see Bare

Beardie (n)- 1. common loach (fish) of Europe. 2. Australian ganoid fish
Beardy (adj)- bearded

Bearing- see Baring, Bering

Beat (v)- destroy, master, strike, pound, bruise, batter
Beet (n)- red vegetable
Beete (v)- obs.- mend, correct, relieve

Beatle (n)- 1. slang-ultra modern girl. 2. one of a British singing group
Beetle (n)- 1. insect. 2. heavy wooden mallet. 3. slang- Volkswagon automobile

Beau (n)- 1. fop, dandy. 2. man of dress. 3. boyfriend
Bow (n)- 1. archery term. 2. sling shot, catapult

Beaver (pr.n)- amphibious brown rodent, of the genus castor
Bever (n)- Eng. Dial.- light repast between meals, lunch. drink

Bee- see Be, Bea

Beech- see Beach

Beek- see Beak, Beke

Beele- see Beal

Been (v)- past participle of verb "to be"
Bin (n)- rack, can hamper, container

Been- see Bean, Bene

Beer (n)- lager, ale, malt, liquor, stout, porter
Bere (n)- obs.- clamor, uproar
Bier (n)- coffin, casket, carriage for the dead

B

Beet- see Beat, Beete

Beetle- see Beatle

Beke- see Beak, Beek

Bel (n)- thorny fruit tree of India
Bell (n)- chime, gong, buzzer, whistle, alarm
Belle (n)- beauty, charmer, enchantress

Beme- see Beam

Bendee (n)- obs.- okra
Bendy (adj)- Her.- divided into an even number of bends

Bene- see Bean, Been

Berg (n)- great mass of ice- short for iceberg
Burg (n)- slang- a small town

Bering- see Baring, Bearing

Berm (n)- narrow ledge
Berme (n)- shoulder along side of paved road

Bern or Berne (pr.n)- capitol city in Switzerland
Birn (n)- Scotch- a burden
Burn (v)- scorch, injure by heat, be inflamed

Berry (n)- small fruit
Bury (v)- lay in a grave, inter, entomb
Barry (pr.n)- 1. city near Cardiff, Wales. 2. slang- baritone saxophone

Berth (n)- bed, bunk, sleeping place, lodgings
Birth (n)- origin, start. Act of being born

Better (adj)- superior, surpassing, preferable
Bettor (n)- wagerer, gambler, book maker

Bever (n)- Eng. Dial.- light repast between meals, lunch, drink
Beaver (pr.n)- amphibious brown rodent, of the genus castor

Bey- see Bay

Bi- see Buy, By, Bye

Bier- see Beer, Bere

Big (adj)- bulky, great, large, massive
Bigg (n)- four rowed variety of barley

Bight (n)- 1. part of a rope. 2. inlet, creek
Bite (v)- 1. chew, crunch, eat.

B

Billed (v)- 1. having a beak. 2. furnish with a bill
Build (v)- compose, construct, erect, make

Bin (n)- rack, can hamper, container
Been (v)- past participle of verb "to be"

Binnacle (n)- compass box, housing for compass
Binocle (n)- 1. telescope, binocular. 2. two at a time

Bird (n)- 1. any group of feathered tribe, fowl. 2. warbler, songster. 3. slang- girlfriend. 4. airplane
Burd (n)- lady or young woman
Burred (v)- gutteral pronunciation of letter R
Byrd (pr.n)- Richard. Admiral U.S.N. and polar explorer

Birl (v)- Scot. Dial.- to revolve or cause to revolve
Birle (v)- Dial.- to ply with drink, carouse
Burl (v)- to bubble up, welter

Birn- see Bern, Burn

Birr (n)- make a whirring sound
Buhr (n)- silicious rock, whetstone
Bur (n)- 1. rough or prickly envelope of a fruit. 2. a parasite
Burr (pr.n)- 1. Aaron- vice president of the United States 1801-1805. 2. (v)- trilled pronunciation

Birth- see Berth

Bis (adv)- twice. Used to direct or ask repitition as passage in music
Bisse (n)- Her.- a snake borne as a charge
Byse (n)- obs.- a kind of fur

Bisk (n)- porcelain which undergoes first baking before glazing
Bisque (n)- thick strained creamed soup

Bit (n)- 1. bridle. 2. small piece. 3. short time
Bitt (n)- Naut.- strong post used to secure cables

Bite- see Bight

Blanc (n)- 1. white cosmetic. 2. white sauce
Blank (n)- 1. empty space. 2. (adj)- expressionless, colorless, dull

Blea (n)- obs.- sapwood
Blee (n)- complexion, color, hue

Bleak (n)- small European river fish
Bleeke (adj)- without color, pale
Bleike (adj)- Celt.- yellow

Blear (v)- to have dimmed or watery eyes
Blerr (n)- a disease of the eyes

B

Bleary (adj)- poorly outlined or defined
Bleery (n)- Scot.- 1. fire brand. 2. a thin gruel

Blend (v)- unite, merge, mingle, fuse
Blende (n)- blind, alluding to its dazzling luster

Bleu (n)- cheese
Blew (v)- did blow
Blue (n)- color. Azure, cobalt

Bleume (adj)- Archaic- flower of a seed plant
Bloom (v)- 1. to be rosy, glow. 2. blossom

Bloat (v)- distend, puff, swell, expand, enlarge
Blote (v)- dry by smoke

Bloc (n)- 1. number of persons acting as a unit. 2. assembly, Congress
Block (n)- 1. mass of wood, piece, lump. 2. barrier, obstacle

Blow (v)- 1. send forth current of air. 2. buffet, knock, strike
Blowe (v)- Archaic- boasting, bragging

Blue- see Bleu, Blew

Boar (n)- male hog or swine
Bore (v)- 1. drill, pierce. 2. to make a hole. 3. weary, annoy, tire, irk

Board (n)- 1. billet, feed, lodging. 2. timber, wood, plank
Bored (v)- 1. drilled, pierced. 2. wearied, annoyed, tired
Bord (n)- obs.- Eng.- a shilling

Boarder (n)- lodger, roomer
Border (n)- fringe, lip, edge, rim

Boat (n)- a vessel propelled by power, sail, paddles, oars
Bote (n)- Law- obs.- repair of buildings, fences, etc., or assessment levied for this purpose

Bode (v)- portend, fortell, predict, prophesy
Bowed (adj)- bent, curved, arched

Bogey (n) 1. one strike over par. 2. spirit, ghost, specter
Bogie (n)- wheel supporting tread

Bold (adj)- daring, brave, courageous
Bolled (v)- formed into seed vessels
Bowled (v)- rolled balls

Bolder (adj)- braver, reckless, fearless, foolhardy
Boulder (n)- rounded rock, stone
Boulder (pr.n)- 1. city in Colorado. 2. dam in Nevada also known as Hoover Dam

B

Bole (n)- 1. trunk of tree. 2. earth
Boll (n)- ball of cotton. a pod
Bowl (n)- 1. dish, tureen, basin. 2. roll balls

Bomb- see Balm

Bonce (n)- Eng. Dial. - boy's game played with marbles, also a marble
Bonze (n)- Buddhist priest, monk or nun

Bonne (n)- Fr.- child's nurse
Bun (n)- roll, small bread or cake

Boo (v)- 1. to low as a cow. 2. to hoot
Booh (inter)- exclamation used to startle or frighten

Bood (v)- Scot. and Irish- must, ought
Boud (n)- Eng.- weevil infesting malt or provisions

Boodie (n)- Scot.- hobgoblin
Boody (v)- pout, sulk, mope

Book (n)- 1. written or printed narrative or record. 2. sets of sheets bound into a volume
Bouk (n)- Scot-Eng. Dial.- the trunk of a tree. The body

Boors (n-pl)- rustics, peasants, rude ill-bred persons
Bourse (n)- exchange where merchants, bankers, etc. meet for business

Border- see Boarder

Bore (v)- 1. drill, pierce. 2. to make a hole. 3. weary, annoy, tire, irk
Boar (n)- male hog or swine

Bored- see Board, Bord

Born (v)- brought into life
Borne (v)- brought forth, carried, endured
Bourne (n)- 1. boundary, limit. 2. small stream, brook

Borough (n)- subdivision of a country, incorporated town
Burro (n)- donkey, ass, onager
Burrow (n)- 1. excavate, groove, rut. 2. hole for rabbits

Bote- see Boat

Bots (n-pl)- larvae of botfly especially species infesting horses
Botts (n-pl)- lacemaking- round cushions to weave lace on

Bough (n)- tree limb, twig, branch
Bow (n)- 1. nod, salute. 2. part of a ship

Bouillon (n)- clear soup, broth
Bullion (n)- uncoined silver or gold

B

Boulder- see Bolder

Bourrelet (n)- bridgelike protrusion, a rounded edge
Burlet (n)- hood or roll of cloth formerly worn by women

Bouse (v)- drunk, carouse, booze
Bowse (v)- Naut.- to pull or haul by means of a tackle

Bow (n)- 1. archery term. 2. sling shot, catapult
Beau (n)- 1. fop, dandy. 2. man of dress. 3. boyfriend

Bow- see Bough

Bowed (adj)- bent, curved, arched
Bode (v)- portend, fortell, predict, prophesy

Bowl- see Bole, Boll

Bowled- see Bold, Bolled

Bowse-see Bouse

Boy (n)- lad, youth, male child
Buoy (n)- marker, guide, floating signal- also pronounced Booi (booey)

Brade (v)- obs.- move suddenly and violently
Braid (n)- weave, twist, plait
Brayed (v)- did bray

Brae (n)- slope, hillside
Bray (v)- 1. bleat, call, cry harsh sound. 2. bruise, pound, or mix fine and small
Brey (n)- Her.- a barnacle

Braid- see Brade, Brayed

Brail (n)- net used to haul fish aboard a boat
Braille (n)- system of writing for the blind that uses characters made up of raised dots

Braise (v)- cook, stew
Braze (v)- burn, solder
Brays (v)- donkey's cry

Brake (v)- 1. curb, slow down, retard. 2. device for retardng motion
Break (v)- crack, split, rupture, opening

Brank (n)- Eng. and Scot. Dial.- bridle with side pieces. 2. pillory
Branke (n)- Archaic- sword

Bray- see Brae, Brey

Brayed- see Brade, Braid

28

B

Brays- see Braise, Braze

Breach (n)- division, gap, rift, break, discord
Breech (n)- 1. posterior, hindquarters. 2. part of a gun

Bread (n)- food made of flour, meal
Bred (v)- cultivated, brought up, developed

Breadth (n)- width, scope, span, bulk
Breath (n)- respiration, inhalation, wind

Break- see Brake

Bream (n)- European fresh water fish
Breme (n)- 1. Eng. Dial. - heather. 2. famous, well-known

Breast (n)- bosom, chest, mammary gland
Brest (pr.n)- city in Brittany, France

Bred- see Bread

Brede (n)- 1. Archaic- braid, embroidery. 2. (v)- to roast meat
Breed (v)- produce, beget, engender, generate

Bree (n)- Eng. Dial.- eyelid, eybrow, brow
Brie (n)- soft cheese made in district of Brie, France

Breech- see Breach

Breme- see Bream

Breve (n)- 1. short-tailed bird. 2. (v)- to write down, compose
Brieve (n)- Scot. law- chancery writ directing trial usually by jury.

Brew (n)- 1. North England- a steep incline. 2. (v)- plot, contrive. 3. make ale or beer
Brewe (n)-obs.- a kind of fowl

Brewed (v)- cooked up, concocted, fermented
Brood (n)- litter, offspring, family

Brews (v)- ferments, to make malt liquor
Bruise (v)- disfigure, mar, deface, blemish
Bruzz (n)- a wheel wright's corner chisel

Brey- see Brae, Bray

Briar (n)- a cross cut saw
Brier (n)- a pipe made from brierwood

Bridal (adj)- matrimonial, nuptial, of a wedding
Bridle (n)- strain, hindrance, curb

B

Bright (adj)- lustrous, radiant, sparkling, clear
Brite (v)- Eng. Dial.- to become overripe as wheat, barley

Brighten (v)- polish, shine, light, shed luster
Brighton (pr.n)- seaside resort in England

Brisk (adj)- lively, agile, nimble, sprightly
Brisque (n)- card game as bezique or cinq cents

Brit (n)- young of the herring, as the sprat
Britt (n)- minute marine animals upon which whales feed

Britain (pr.n)- United Kingdom, Great Britain- North Ireland, Scotland, Wales
Briton (pr.n)- native of Britain. Celtic

Brite- see Bright

Broach (v)- 1. mention, express, begin, suggest. 2. tap pierce.
Broch (n)- pointed rod. Fr. cookery- a spit
Brooch (n)- pin, trinket, jewelry, clasp

Broch (n)- one of prehistoric circular stone towers in Shetland and Orkney Islands
Brock (n)- European badger

Brood- see Brewed

Brookie (adj)- Scot.- dirty, sooty
Brooky (adj)- full of brooks

Broom (n)- brush, sweeper, whisk
Brougham (n)- four-wheeled closed carriage, outside driver's perch
Brume (n)- fog, mist

Brows (n)- foreheads, temples
Browse (v)- graze, pasture, to feed

Bruise (v)- disfigure, mar, deface, blemish
Bruzz (n)- a wheel wright's corner chisel
Brews (v)- ferments, to make malt liquor

Bruit (n)- report, rumor, din, noise
Brute (n)- animal, beast, creature, demon
Brut (pr.n)- great grandson or descendant of Eneas

Brume- see Broom, Brougham

Brut- see Bruit, Brute

Bruzz- see Bruise, Brews

Buhr- see Birr, Bur, Burr

B

Build (v)- compose, construct, erect, make
Billed (v)- 1. having a beak. 2. furnish with a bill

Bul (n)- Bibl.- Chesvan, early Hebrew name
Bull (n)- 1. male of any bovine animal. 2. constellation Taurus - one sign of the Zodiac

Bullion- see Bouillon

Bun(n)- roll. Small bread or cake
Bonne (n)- French- child's nurse

Buoy (n)- marker, guide, floating signal- also pronounced Booi (booey)
Boy (n)- lad, youth, male child

Bur- see Birr, Burr, Buhr

Burd- see Bird, Burred, Byrd

Burg (n)- slang- a small town
Berg (n)- great mass of ice- short for iceberg

Burl (v)- to bubble up, welter
Birle (v)- Dial.- to ply with drink, carouse
Birl (v)- Scot. Dial.- to revolve or cause to revolve

Burlet (n)- hood or roll of cloth formerly worn by women
Bourrelet (n)- a ridgelike protrusion, a rounded edge

Burley (n)- fine, light tobacco in plug mostly for chewing
Burly (adj)- large, bulky, stout

Burn (v)- scorch, injure by heat, be inflamed
Birn (n)- Scotch- a burden
Berne or Bern (pr.n.)- capitol city in Switzerland

Burro- see Borough, Burrow

Bury- see Barry, Berry

Bus (n)- motor coach, short for omnibus
Buss (v)- kiss, osculate, smack

But (prep)- however, only, solely, except
Butt (n)- 1. long, barrel, cask. 2. extremity, end. 3. jostle

Buy (v)- pay for, acquire, purchase, obtain
By (prep)- toward, alongside, near, at
Bye (n)- short for goodbye. Secondary or incidental
Bi (adj)- slang- bi-sexual, bi-monthly

Buyer (n)- purchaser, investor, shopper
Byre (n)- cow barn

Bye- see Buy, By, Bi

B

Byrd- see Bird, Burred, Burd

Byre- see Buyer

Byse- see Bis, Bisse

—C—

Caam (n)- heddles of a loom
Calm (v)- still, quiet, placid, tranquil

Cab (n)- vehicle for public hire
Kab (n)- Hebrew measure of capacity, about 2 feet

Cabaya (n)- loose tunic or surcoat worn in the east
Kabaya (n)- cotton garment worn by Malays

Cabbala (n)- secret or esoteric doctrine or science in general
Kabala (n)- mystic art, occultism, mystery

Cache (n)- hoard, deposit, secrete, conceal, hide
Cash (n)- legal tender, coins, money

Cachou (n) obs.- silvered aromatic pastille or pill made of licorice
Cashew (n)- tropical tree chiefly noted for the cashew nut

Cadar (n)- Eng. Dial.- child's cradle
Cader (n)- Eng. Dial.- wooden frame on which a fishing line is wound

Caddice (n)- woolen, cotton or serge cloth
Caddis (n)- any of certain insects, as the worm, fly

Caddie (n)- golf players' attendant, errand boy
Caddy (n)- small box, can or chest used for tea
Cadi (n)- Turkish judge

Caddish (adj)- like a cad. Low bred
Kaddish (n)- Jewish ritual. Mourner's prayer- (Aramaic)

Cain (pr.n)- 1. man's name. 2. son of Adam. 3. (v)- raise cain- violent disturbance
Cane (n)- staff, rod, walking stick
Kain (n)- Scot. duty paid by tenant to landlord as poultry, eggs. Tribute

Caique (n)- Naut.- light skiff or rowboat used on the Bosphorus
Kaik (n)- Maori- village or community

Caird (n)- Scot.- tramp, vagrant. Traveling tinker
Cared (v)- was concerned, felt anxiety or solicitude

Caisse (n)- 1. chest or case. 2. cash box. 3. cashier's desk or office
Case (n)- a box and its contents

C

Calander (n)- large lark of Europe
Calendar (n)- diary, journal, almanac
Calender (n)- machine, hot press
Callander (pr.n)- town in Ontario, Canada- home of Dionne Quintuplets

Calculous (adj)- Med.- calcified mass
Calculus (n)- system of algebraic notation, computation

Calif. (pr.n)- abbreviation for State of California
Caliph (n)- spiritual civil head of a Mohammedan state

Calk (n)- short point projection on shoe to prevent slipping
Cauk or Cawk (n)- limestone, mineral
Caulk (v)- 1. to make airtight, stop leaks. 2. transfer by tracing

Call (v)- cry out, name, summon, invite, visit
Caul (n)- 1. membrane. 2. back of woman's cap. 3. net or network
Cawl (n)- fishbasket or creel

Callander- see Calander, Calendar, Calender

Called (v)- summoned, shouted, announced. Telephoned
Cauld (n)- hard thickened area on skin

Callous (adj)- thick skinned, tough, horny
Callus (n)- hard thickened area on skin

Calow (n)- old squaw
Callow (adj)- immature, lacking adult sophistication

Cam (n)- moving piece of machinery, wheel
Kam (adj)- 1. Gaelic- awry, bent, crooked 2. (n)- masculine name

Came (v)- arrived, reached, approached
Kame (n)- short ridge or mound of stratified drift by glacial melted water

Campaign (n)- organized action to elect a candidate
Campaine (n)- fine white linen lace used for edging on other laces
Campane (n)- Heraldry- a bell

Can (n)- 1. tin or metal container. 2. (v)- be able, possible
Cannes (pr.n)- French city
Khan (n)- Mongol leader. Successor of Genghis Khan

Candid (adj)- frank, free, open. Honest, fair, sincere
Candied (adj)- preserved with sugar

Cane- see Cain, Kain

C

Cangue (n)- portable pillory worn around neck of Chinese criminals
Kang (n)- sleeping structure of bricks or other materials with a place for a fire below

Canions (n)- ornamental rolls worn around lower legs of breeches
Canyons (n)- deep valleys with precipitious sides

Cannon (n)- mounted gun
Canon (n)- 1. decree, test, rule, law. 2. member of a clerical group

Can't - contraction of cannot
Cant (n)- 1. jargon, argot, lingo. 2. (v)- whine, beg, snivel
Kant (pr.n)- Immannuel. Philosopher

Cantel (n)- corner, angle, slanted or tilted position
Cantle (n)- hind part of a saddle

Canter (n)- 1. whiner, vagrant, hobo. 2. (v)- slow gallop, lope, trot
Cantor (n)- soloist in a Synagogue or Temple. Chanter

Canvas (n)- sail cloth, coarse cloth
Canvass (v)- survey, examine, investigate

Canyons- see Canions

Capel (n)- stone composed of quartz, hornblende, etc.
Caple (n)- horse, mare

Capelin (n)- small marine fish
Capeline (n)- armor, small skull cap of steel and iron worn by soldiers in middle ages

Capitaine (n)- French- captain
Capitan (n)- hogfish

Capital (n)- 1. main, chief, principal. 2. fine, excellent. 3. carrying death sentence. 4. money, fund
Capitol (n)- state legislative building. State house
Capitol (pr.n)- building in Washington, D.C., where Congress meets

Capitan- see Capitaine

Caple- see Capel

Caprin (n)- substance found in butter which gives it taste and odor
Caprine (adj)- pertaining to goats. Goatlike

Car (n)- automobile. A vehicle moved on wheels
Carr (n)- Eng. Dial.- a pool, fen, bog or marsh

C

Carack (n)- Archaic- large ship used in east Indian trade
Carrack (n)- obs.- a galleon

Caracole (n)- obs.- winding staircase, a spiral shell
Caracol (n)- small flower

Carat (n)- unit of weight measuring pearls and precious stones
Caret (n)- a mark indicating something to be inserted
Carrot (n)- vegetable
Karat (n)- unit of fineness for gold

Cared (v)- was concerned, felt anxiety or solicitude
Caird (n)- Scot.- tramp, vagrant. Traveling tinker

Careen (v)- tip, heel over; sway from side to side
Carene (n)- a sweet wine boiled down

Caribe (n)- any of several South American fresh water fishes
Caribee (n)- Indian mostly confined to Brazil and Guinea, carib

Caries (n)- decay of teeth
Carries (v)- conveys, transports, endures

Carl (n)- Scot.- robust fellow. Churl. Farmer
Karl (pr.n)- masculine name- also spelled Carl

Carlin (n)- small silver coin struck by Charles of Anjou, King of Naples and Sicily
Carline (n)- Scot.- old woman used contemptuously as of a witch

Carol (v)- 1. chant, warble, sing with joy.
Carol (pr.n)- King of Romania. 1893-1953. Name- Fem. or masc.
Carrel (n)- 1. square tile or dart. 2. short thick weapon
Carrell (n)- small space in library for individual study
Carrol (n)- a study in a cloister

Carr- see Car

Carrack- see Carack

Carrol- see Carol, Carrel, Carrell

Cars (n)- wheeled vehicles. Automobiles
Kars (pr.n)- province in Turkish Asia Minor

Cart (n)- 1. wagon, push cart. 2. (v)- transport, carry, haul
Carte (n)- 1. menu or bill of fare. 2. fencing term
Quart (n)- cards- a sequence of 4 cards
Quarte (n)- fencing- the fourth of eight defensive positions

Case- see Caisse

Cash- see Cache

C

Cashmere (n)- soft wool from hair of goats in Kashmir, Tibet, etc.
Kashmir (pr.n)- native state in Northwest India

Cask (n)- barrel, vat, keg, wooden vessel
Casque (n)- helmet

Cast (v)- toss, pitch, throw, fling
Caste (n)- class, rank, race, social order

Caster (n)- 1. cruet, frame for bottles. 2. small wheel or swivel roller
Castor (n)- beaver
Castor (pr.n)- star in constellation Gemini

Cat (n)- Feline, domesticated. Four-legged mammal. Tabby
Catt (pr.n)- mountain in Canada

Caudal (adj)- tail-like. Near the tail
Caudle (n)- warm drink for the sick
Coddle (v)- 1. caress, pet, fondle. 2. parboil, stew, simmer

Caul- see Call, Cawl

Cauld- see Called

Caulk- see Calk, Cawk

Cauma (n)- Med.- great heat as in fever
Comma (n)- punctuation mark
Kama (pr.n)- Hindu God. River in U.S.S.R.

Cause (v)- bring about, produce, originate
Caws (n-pl)- cries of ravens or crows

Cavel (n) Eng. and Scot.- allotment. A lot or something obtained by a lot
Kevel (n)- hammer, gavel, mallet

Caw (n)- cry made by raven or crow
Kaw (pr.n)- tribe of Siouan Indians, allied to the Osages

Cawl- see Call, Caul

Cedar (n)- evergreen tree
Ceder (n)- yielder, conceder, releaser, resigner
Seeder (n)- person or apparatus for sowing seeds

Cede (v)- yield, concede, surrender, handover
Seed (n)- spore, germ, egg

C

Cee (n)- 1. obs. Eng.- 16th part of a penny. 2. certain quantity of beer
Cie (n)- French- Company
Sea (n)- 1. lake, ocean. 2. billow
See (v)- behold, view, observe, look
Si (adv)- Italian or Spanish for yes

Ceil (n)- overlay wall with wood, plaster
Ciel (n)- furniture- canopy or tester
Seal (v)- 1. brand, label, stamp. 2. mammal- fur seal
Seel (v)- 1. close the eyes. 2. to blind
Sele (n)- Eng. Dial.- a time, a season, an occasion

Ceiling (n)- overhead or a room, topside, interior lining of a room
Sealing (v)- closing, securing, fastening
Seeling (v)- present participle of seel. 2. closing the eyes

Cell (n)- compartment, cage, jail
Sell (v)- vend, offer for sale, peddle, market

Cellar (n)- basement, vault, subterranean room
Seller (n)- one who sells

Cense (v)- perfume with incense
Cents (n)- more than one cent
Scents (v)- smells, detects, gets wind of, inhales
Sense (n)- insight, wisdom, judgement

Censer (n)- container for burning incense
Censor (n)- 1. inspector, examiner, critic. 2. (v)- criticize, review

Cent (n)- penny
Sent (v)- caused to go
Scent (n)- odor, perfume, essence, aroma

Center (n)- middle or central point or place. Midst
Centre (v)- to furnish, form or shape the center

Cere (v)- coat or cover with wax
Sear (v)- parch, scorch, burn, singe
Seer (n)- prophet, oracle, crystal gazer
Sere (adj)- dry, withered, shrunk
Ser (n)- unit of weight in India

Cereal (n)- breakfast food made of grain
Serial (n)- anything published in installments at intervals

Cereus (n)- 1. wax candle. 2. plant bearing fragrant flowers opening at night
Cerous (adj)- chemical containing cerium
Serious (adj)- earnest, thoughtful, grave or solemn character

C

Cerrate (n)- 1. ointment, salve. 2. waxed
Cirrate (adj)- 1. having ringlets. 2. zool.- bearing cirri
Serrate (n)- notched, like edge of saw. Toothed

Cession (n)- surrender, granting, yielding
Session (n)- meeting, assembly, sitting, pow wow

Cetaceous (adj)- species of whale
Setaceous (adj)- bristly

Chagrin (n)- humiliation, shame, despair, dismay
Shagreen (n)- 1. back of horse. 2. rough skin of shark

Chair (n)- 1. seat, bench. 2. professorship, director
Chare (n)- British- chore or job

Chaise (n)- light open carriage- usually with hood
Shays (pr.n)- Daniel. Leader of Shay's rebellion

Champagne (n)- effervescent wine
Champaign (n)- prairie, plateau, meadow

Chance (n)- 1. unplanned, random, accident. 2. gamble, risk
Chants (v)- sings, warbles, serenades, croons

Chanty (n)- a sailor's song
Shanty (n)- lean-to, shed, cabin, shack

Char (v)- burn or reduce to charcoal
Chare (v)- Eng.- to work as at housework. Do odd jobs or chores by the day
Charr (n)- trout- common in Europe

Chark (n)- 1. a fire drill or fire churn. 2. small Russian glass or cup
Shark (n)- a large, voracious, destructive fish

Chased (v)- followed, hunted, pursued, trailed
Chaste (adj)- innocent, spotless, pure, virginal

Chauffeur (n)- paid licensed driver of private motor car
Choffer (n)- Scot.- portable heater or chafing dish
Shophar (n)- curved horn of ram used in Jewish religious services

Cheap (adj)- 1. low priced, inexpensive. 2. worthless, tawdry
Cheep (n)- peep, chirp, tweet

Cheat (v)- trick, swindle, hoax, defraud, dupe
Cheet (v)- 1. Eng. Dial.- cheep as a bird. 2. Scot. (interj) puss- call to a cat

Check (n)- 1. restriction, restraint. 2. (v)- stop, halt, arrest
Cheque (n)- British check
Czech (pr.n)- Czechoslovakia. Slavic language

C

Checker (n)- one of pieces used in game of checkers
Chequer (n)- British checker

Cheek (n)- side of face, below eyes and to the side of the mouth
Cheke (n)- varying weight of Turkey

Cheeky (adj)- slang- audacious, having nerve, rude
Cheki (n)- measure of weight in Arabia

Cheep- see Cheap

Cheer (v)- gladden, encourage, comfort, refresh
Chir (n)- pheasant found in lower Himalaya mountains

Cheet- see Cheat

Cheke- see Cheek

Cheki- see Cheeky

Chews (v)- munches, crunches, masticates
Choose (v)- prefer, single out, select

Chic (n)- 1. stylish, attractive. in style. 2. (adj)- fashionable
Sheik (n)- 1. Arab chief. 2. (v)-slang-tease, deceive

Chick (n)- 1. young chicken or bird. 2. slang- attractive young girl or woman
Tchick (n)- sound máde by pressing tongue against roof of mouth. Cluck

Chile (pr.n)- South American country
Chile (n)- hot pepper, spices, pod
Chilly (adj)- cold, nippy, heatless

Chir - see Cheer

Choffer- see Chauffeur, Shophar

Choir (n)- company of church singers
Quire (n)- paper measure

Choler (n)- bile, anger, ill-temper
Collar (n)- 1. neck band, neck piece. 2. arrest, seize

Choose (v)- prefer, single out, select
Chews (v)- munches, crunch, masticates

Choral (n)- hymn tune sung by the choir
Coral (n)- 1. hard skeleton of sea animals. 2. red color. 3. from the ocean
Corol (n)- floral leaves of a flower. A corolla

C

Chord (n)- 1. string of a musical instrument. 2. right line uniting extremities of an arc
Cord (n)- rope, twin, string
Cored (v)- removed center from fruit

Chronical (adj)- long continuance
Chronicle (n)- account, record, history

Chorea (n)- disease of the nervous system
Korea (pr.n)- country in Southeast Asia

Chou (n)- dynasty in Chinese history
Chow (n)- 1. thick coated muscular dog. 2. slang- food

Chuff (n) rustic, boor, miserly fellow
Chough (n)- bird of crow family

Chute (n)- 1. slide, tube, duct. 2. quick descent, fall
Shoot (v)- to send forth as a bullet, kill, execute
Shute (n)- flume, artificial canal

Cider (n)- juice of pressed apples used as a beverage
Cyder (n)- British- juice of apples used in vinegar
Sider (n)- one who sides with a person or party. Adherent, partisan

Ciel- see Ceil, Seal, Sele, Seel

Cie- see Cee, Sea, See, Sí

Cilicious (v)- hairlike process
Silicious (n)- containing silica

Cimbal (n)- obs.- kind of confectionery or cake
Cymbol (n)- musical instrument
Simball (n)- New England slang- kind of doughnut
Symbol (n)- sign, brand, emblem, mark

Cimon (pr.n)- Athenian general
Simon (pr.n)- Apostle Peter

Cingle (n)- girth for a horse
Single (adj)- solitary, sole, one, separate

Cinque (n)- a five on cards and dice
Sink (v)- 1. subside, drop, wane. 2. (n)- kitchen receptacle attached to drain
Sync (v)- to synchronize

Cion or Scion (n)- 1. young shoot or twig. 2. descendant
Sion or Zion (n)- hill or mount of Jerusalem

Cipher (v)- 1. write in secret characters. 2. add a zero
Sypher (v)- overlap edges of planks to form a smoother joint

C

Circle (v)- 1. encircle, ring. 2. sphere, orb, girdle
Surcle (n)- a twig

Cist (n)- box or chest for sacred utensils
Cyst (n)- saclike structure containing fluid
Sist (n)- Scot.- cite, summon, bring into court

Cit (n)- slang- city person. Short for citizen.
Sit (v)- 1. perch, roost. 2. convene. 3. be situated

Cite (v)- mention, summon, quote, enumerate
Sight (n)- vision, eyesight, view, appearance
Site (n)- position, location, area, situation

Clack (v)- click, clatter, snap, rattle, clink
Claque (n)- set of hired applauders in a theater

Clammer (n)- forceps for obtaining deep-sea specimens
Clamor (n)- outcry, noise, uproar
Clamour (v)- salute or address loudly. Shout

Clause (n)- article, paragraph, condition, stipulation
Claws (n-pl)- nails, talons, paws

Cleek (n)- golf club with iron head or No. 4 wood
Clique (n)- coterie, club, brotherhood, clan

Cleft (n)- space or opening made by splitting. A crack or fissure
Klepht (n)- Greek brigand community in the mountain stronghold of Thessaly

Clew (n)- ball of twine, spool of thread
Clue (n)- solution, cue, key, inkling

Climb (v)- mount, scale, rise, ascend, go up
Clime (n)- climate, weather, temperature.

Clip (n)- 1. sharp blow, rapid pace. 2. (v)- to shear, curtail, hit, pitch
Clype (v)- Scot.- gossip, tattle

Cloak (n)- loose, outer garment
Cloke (v)- hide, conceal

Close (adj)- 1. tight, shut fast. 2. (n)- end, conclusion
Clothes (n)- garments, attire, dress, garb

Clough (n)- a cleft in the hills. A narrow valley
Clow (n)- inclosure. Flood gate as for a lock, water mill, etc.

Clue (n)- solution, cue, key, inkling
Clew (n)- ball of twine, spool of thread

C

Clum (v)- Eng. Dial.- to clutch
Clumme (adj)- obs.- silent, glum

Clype (v)- Scot.- gossip, tattle
Clip (n)- 1. sharp blow, rapid pace. 2. (v)- to shear, curtail, hit, punch

Coak (n)- to unite as two pieces of wood
Coke (n)- solid product from distillation of coal in an oven

Coal (n)- charcoal, ember, combustible mineral substance used as fuel
Cole (n)- cabbage, cole slaw
Kohl (n)-powder used to darken eyelids and eyebrows
Kol (pr.n)- native people from parts of Bengal, India. Mongolo-Dravidian race

Coaled (v)- supplied with coal
Cold (adj)- 1. heatless, frigid, chilly. 2. (n)- virus, infection, cough

Coarse (adj)- harsh, crude, common, rough
Course (n)- direction, path, route
Corse or Corpse (n)- cadaver, body, remains

Coat (n)- jacket, overcoat, garment
Cote (n)- shelter for sheep, pigs, pigeons
Khot (n)- India- farmer of land revenue, contractor

Coax (v)- wheedle, flatter, charm, persuade, cajole
Cokes (n-pl)- coca-colas

Cob (v)- to strike or beat on the buttocks with something flat
Cobb (n)- sea gull- esp. black-backed gull
Kob (n)- African antelope

Cockie (n)- 1. Australian- a small farmer. 2. cockatoo
Cocky (adj)- pert, conceited

Coco (n)- palm tree. Coconut or fruit of this palm
Cocoa (n)- beverage prepared from powder of pulverized cacao seed
Koko (n)- 1. the parson bird. 2. Africa- the taro plant

Cod (n)- soft finned fish
Codde (n)- obs.- stem or stock of a plant

Coddle- see Caudal, Caudle

Coddling (v)- 1. stew, cook slowly, parboil. 2. pamper, petting
Codling (n)- 1. young of the cod. 2. small apple. 3. small moth.

C

Coff (v)- Scot.- to buy
Cough (v)- force air from lungs with short sharp noises
Koph (n)- 19th letter of Hebrew alphabet representing English K or Q

Coffer (n)- container, box, case, chest
Cougher (n)- one who coughs. Hacker

Cog (n)- a tooth on the rim of a wheel or gear
Cogue (n)- broadly built transport

Coif (n)- a cap that fits the head
Quoif (n)- Eng.- white cap worn by lawyers, especially by Sgts. at law

Coiffeur (n)- male hair-dresser
Coiffure (n)- arrangement of dressing of hair. A headdress

Coign (n)- projecting corner
Coin (n)- mint, money, issue, make
Quoin (n)- wedge of wood or metal

Coke (n)- solid product from distillation of coal in an oven
Coak (n)- to unite as two pieces of wood

Cokes- see Coax

Cola (n)- Negro language of West Africa
Kola (n)- extract from the kola nut
Kola (pr.n)- peninsula in northwestern Soviet Union

Colation (v)- straining or purifying liquid
Collation (n)- 1. editing, revision, description. 2. slight meal, lunch, tea

Cold- see Coaled

Cole- see Coal, Kohl, Kol

Collar (n)- 1. neck band, neck piece. 2. arrest, seize
Choler (n)- anger, bile, ill-temper

Colley (n)- European blackbird
Collie (n)- Scottish shepherd dog
Colly (v)- Eng. Dial.- to begrime, sooty

Colleri (n-pl)- Dravidian tribe of South India, formerly noted thieves
Colliery (n)- the place where coal is dug

Colonel (n)- army officer
Kernel (n)- seed in a nut

C

Color (n)- hue, tint, shade, dye, stain
Colour (n)- Brit.- tinge, paint, color
Culler (n)- selector, chooser, gatherer

Comb (n)- toothed piece of metal or bone for arranging hair
Combe (n)- narrow valley, deep hollow
Coom (n)- coal dust, soot
Coomb (n)- liquid measure
Coombe (pr.n)- Welsh valley
Kom (n)- Archeol.- a village
Kome (n)- Geol. division in Greenland

Combel (n)- Her.- a diminutive of the chief
Comble (n)- Archaic- a fillet

Comer (n)- 1. one who comes. 2. one who is promising well
Cummer (n)- 1. Scot.- Godmother. 2. female companion. Girl or woman

Comity (n)- courtesy, civility, respect
Committee (n)- appointed group, council, board, cabinet

Comma (n)- punctuation mark
Kama (pr.n)- Hindu God. River in Soviet Union
Cauma (n)- Med.- Gr.-great heat as in fever

Compear (v)- Scotch law- personally appear in court with lawyer
Compeer (n)- an equal. Person of same rank

Complacence (n)- ease, tranquility, satisfaction, peace of mind
Complaisance (n)- good manners, politeness, respect

Complacent (adj)- serene, composed, self-satisfied
Complaisant (adj)- well-mannered, civil, pleasant, gracious

Complement (n)- 1. supplement, remainder. 2. full amount
Compliment (v)- praise, flatter, commend

Compt (n)- count
Count (v)- assess, value, rank, estimate

Compter (n)- counter
Counter (n)- display table

Con (n)- 1. opposing argument, person. 2. (v)- study, memorize. 3. Swindle
Conn (n)- Naut.- conduct or superintend the steering of a vessel

Conceal (v)- hide, withdraw from observation
Konseal (n)- Med.- capsule for inclosing dose of medicine

C

Concession (n)- compromise, consent, yielding
Consession (adj)- sitting together

Confectionary (n)- a place where confections are kept or made
Confectionery (n)- sweets in general

Confidant (n)- intimate, friend, advisor
Confident (adj)- untroubled, sure, lighthearted, hopeful

Congee (n)- leave to depart, departure
Conjee (n)- water in which rice has been boiled, used in invalid diet

Conn- see Con

Consequence (n)- result, sequel, outcome, effect
Consequents (adj)- following as logical conclusion. Deduction

Consession- see Concession

Consoles (n-pl)- 1. cabinets for radio or television. 2. (v)- soothes, comforts, solaces
Consols (n-pl)- British funded government securities

Consonance (n)- agreement, harmony, concord
Consonants (n)- letters which are not vowels

Coo (v)- soft murmuring sound of pigeons or doves
Coup (n)- 1. unexpected and successful stroke. 2. manuever, achievement

Coolie (n)- East Indian laborer from India, China
Coolly (adj)- without heat. 2. Calm, self-possessed

Coom- see Comb, Combe, Coomb, Kome, Kom

Coop (n)- cage or small enclosure for poultry or small animals
Coup (v)- 1. Her.- to cut off clean. 2. Scot.- capsize or overturn

Cooper (n)- one who makes or repairs barrels, casks, etc.
Couper (n)- a lever in a loom for lifting the harness

Cooter (n)- a fresh water turtle
Couter (n)- Brit. slang- a sovereign (coin)

Cop (n)- policeman. (v)- capture, seize, catch
Kop (n)- 1. South Africa- hill, mountain. 2. Netherlands measure of weight

Copies (n-pl)- 1. transcripts, reproductions. 2. imitates
Coppice (n)- wood or thicket of small trees or bushes

Coppel (n)- small porous vessel used in assaying
Copple (n)- an elevation, conical hill

C

Coquet (v)- philander, trifle in love, vamp
Coquette (n)- vain girl, flirt, golddigger

Cora (n)- gazelle found from Iran to North Africa
Corah (adj)- plain, undyed; applied to Indian silk

Coral- see Choral, Corol

Corbeil (n)- Archaic- a little basket
Corbel (n)- raven

Cord- see Chord, Cored

Core (n)- inner part, hard center of seed fruit as apple, pear
Kor (n)- Hebrew unit of weight
Corps (n)- soldiers, branch of military service

Cornel (n)- dogwood tree
Cornell (pr.n)- University in New York

Correspondence (n)- letter writing, mail, communication
Correspondents (n-pl)- writers, reporters, contributors

Corrie (n)- Scot.- circular hollow in the side of a hill or mountain
Corry (n)- Scot.- in principal mountain lies the dwarfie stone

Corse or Corpse- see Coarse, Course

Cos (pr.n)- one of the Dodecanese Islands
Kos (n)- type of lettuce including romaine

Cosset (n)- a pet lamb
Cossette (n)- one of small chips or slices into which beets are cut for sugar making

Cosy (n)- wadded covering for teapot or other vessel to keep contents hot
Cozy (adj)- snug, comfortable, contented

Cottar (n)- Scot.- peasant tenant occupying small holding in return for services
Cotter (n)- Eng.- a toggle. In United States- called a key

Cough- see Coff, Koph

Cougher- see Coffer

Coul (v)- Eng. Dial.- draw together with a rake or scraper
Cowl (n)- a monks hood usually attached to the gown
Cowle (n)- a grant in writing, safe conduct, amnesty (India)

Council (n)- committee, ministry, assembly, congress
Counsel (v)- advise, instruct, suggest

C

Councillor (n)- member of a council
Counselor (n)- instructor, advisor, tutor, guide

Count- see Compt

Counter- see Compter

Coup- see Coo

Coup- see Coop

Couper- see Cooper

Courant (n)- obs.- a gazette, published newsletter or nespaper
Courante (n)- old fashioned dance with gliding step

Courb (n)- 1. bend or bow. 2. a crook or hump
Curb (n)- 1. check, restraint. 2. raised stone edging along paved street

Courier (n)- express messenger, runner, envoy, emissary
Currier (n)- 1. one who dresses and colors leather. 2. combs horses

Course- see Coarse, Corse, Corpse

Cousin (n)- relative, daughter or son of one's aunt or uncle
Cozen (v)- deceive, cheat

Coutel (n)- obs.- a short knife or dagger
Coutelle (n)- close woven fabric used for mattresses, corsets, etc.

Couter- see Cooter

Covey (n)- 1. a small flock as of quail. 2. a bird with her brood
Cuvey (n)- Archaic- set, bevy, company

Coward (n)- frightened, without courage, fearful
Cowered (v)- crawled, crouched, frightened, flinched

Cowle- see Coul, Cowl

Coy (adj)- modest, shy, blushing, timid
Koi (n)- Japanese carp

Cozy- see Cosy

Cracks (n-pl)- 1. sharp sudden noises. 2. witty or sharp remarks. 3. narrow breaks or openings
Crax (n)- Zool.- genus curassows- large bird of South America

Craisey (n)- Brit.- buttercup
Crazy (adj)- demented, deranged, mad

C

Crape (n)- black material worn as a mourning band on sleeve
Crepe (n)- thin wrinkled cloth of silk, rayon, wool, etc.

Crate (n)- case of slats or hamper to protect goods in transit
Creaght (n)- 1. herd of cattle. 2. to graze

Crawl (v)- drag body across ground. Creep
Kraal (n)- 1. village of South Africa natives. 2. enclosure for cattle

Crax- see Cracks

Crazy- see Craisey

Creaght- see Crate

Creak (v)- grind, grate, squeak, rasp
Creek (n)- small river, stream, brook

Creaker (n)- that which creaks as doors, shoes, etc.
Creeker (n)- spotted sandpiper

Cream (n)- fatty part of milk which rises to surface
Creme (n)- 1. one of various liquors. 2. French cream
Creem (v)- 1. Eng. Dial.- shiver, shudder. 2. crush or squeeze as in wrestling

Crease (n)- line or mark produced by fold, ridge, or furrow
Kris (n)- short sword, heavy dagger

Crecy (pr.n)- town in France
Cressy (adj)- abounding in plants of mustard family. Watercress

Creek (n)- small river, stream, brook
Creak (v)- grind, grate, squeak, rasp

Creeker (n)- spotted sandpiper
Creaker (n)- that which creaks as doors, shoes, etc.

Creem- see Cream, Creme

Crepe- see Crape

Crew (n)- 1. able seamen, sailors. 2. company, band, pack
Crewe (n)- obs.- a pot
Crue (n)- Gaelic- a hut, hovel or cabin
Kroo or Kru (n)- African- tribe of Blacks on western coast of Africa, skilled as seamen

Crewel (n)- yarn used for embroidery
Cruel (adj)- sadistic, savage, fiendish, brutal

C

Crews (n)- 1. ships complement, mariners. 2. gang, squad, team
Cruise (v)- roving voyages, sail, passage, boat trip
Cruse (n)- 1. bottle for liquids. 2. earthen pot

Cric (n)- device for regulating flame on lamp
Crick (n)- painful muscular cramp or spasm

Crizzel (n)- surface of glass clouded in its transparency
Crizzle (v)- roughen or crumple, as water beginning to freeze

Crows (n)- 1. black glossy birds. 2. (v)- boasts, brags, gloats
Croze (n)- tool for cutting grooves in barrel staves

Cruel- see Crewel

Cruise- see Crews, Cruse

Cuck (v)- Eng. Dial.- to sound the cuckoo note. To cuckoo
Kook (n)- slang- screwball, nut

Cuddie (n)- a fish- var. of cuttle. Coalfish
Cuddy (n)- Scot.- blockhead, lout, ass

Cue (n)- clue, hint, intimation
Queue (n)- 1. pigtail. 2. waiting line
Kew (pr.n)- village on Thames, England

Culler (n)- selector, chooser, gatherer
Color (n)- hue, tint, shade, dye, stain
Colour (n)- Brit.- tinge, paint, color

Culet (n)- small flat face forming bottom of a brillant
Cullet (n)- broken or waste glass suitable for re-melting

Cummer- see Comer

Cup (n)- small bowl-shaped vessel, usually with a handle, used for liquids as coffee, tea
Kup or Keup (n)- Siamese measure of weight

Cur (n)- 1. low despicable person. 2. worthless dog
Curr (v)- make a low murmuring sound
Ker (pr.n)- Gr.- religion- ghost or disembodied soul

Curb- see Courb

Currant (n)- fruit, seedless raisin
Current (adj)- 1. present, prevalent, in vogue. 2. a flowing stream

Currie (v)- rub and clean horse with a comb
Curry (n)- East Indian relish made with mixture of spice and seeds
Cury (n)- obs.- cookery- cooked food

C

Currier- see Courier

Cuts (n-pl)- 1. reductions, division, intersects. 2. engraved surfaces for printing
Cutts (n-pl)- Eng.- two pairs of wheels with a long pole between, used as a timbercart

Cuvey- see Covey

Cygnet (n)- a young swan
Signet (n)- 1. small seal, stamp. 2. official seal

Cymba (n)- Zool.- a boat-shaped sponge spicule
Simba (n)- Africa- Swahili, for lion

Cymbal (n)- musical instrument
Simball (n)- New England slang- kind of doughnut
Symbol (n)- sign, brand, emblem, mark
Cimbal (n)- obs.- kind of confectionery or cake

Cymar (n)- loose robe for women
Simar (n)- 1. light outer garment. 2. obs.- under garment or chemise

Cypress (n)- 1. evergreen tree. 2. fine thin black fabric used for mourning
Cypris (n)- small crustacean with light shell
Cyprus (pr.n)- Eastern Mediterranean island south of Turkey

Cyst (n)- saclike structure containing fluid
Cist (n)- box or chest for sacred utensils
Sist (n)- Scot.-cite, summon, bring into court

Czech (pr.n)- 1. Czechoslovakia. 2. (n)- Slavic language
Check (n)- 1. restriction, restraint. 2. (v)- stop, halt, arrest

D

—D—

Dab (n)- flat fish
Dabb (n)- large spiny tailed lizard of Egypt, etc.
Dabbe (v)- Archaic - tap, slap

Dail (n)- Scot. - trough or drain
Dale (n)- low place between hills. A vale or valley

Dain (n)- Eng. Dial. - smell, stink
Dane (pr.n)- native of Denmark
Deign (v)- condescend, vouchsafe, grant, accord

Daire (n)- kind of Oriental tambourine
Dairi (n)- Japan - residence or court of the Mikado

Dal (n)- split pulse esp. of pigeon pea
Dalle (n)- marble slab of decorative character used for flooring and paving

Dam (n)- 1. barrier to stop up flow of water. 2. female animal parent
Damn (v)- doom, curse, find guilty, condemn

Dama (n)- a gazelle of the Sudan
Damas (pr.n)- Francois. French general

Dammed (n)- confined by banks. Obstruction
Damned (v)- doomed, condemned, detestable

Dan (n)- Biblical - Hebrew tribe who migrated to north of Palestine
Dhan (n)- Indian unit of weight

Dandi (n)- a boatman of the Ganges
Dandy (n)- one who gives undue attention to dress. A fop, beau

Dartars (n)- 1. mange affecting the head of sheep. 2. black muzzle
Darters (n-pl)- any small fresh water fishes, related to the perch

Day (n)- time between sunrise and sunset
Dey (n)- Algerian Governor. Ruler in Tripoli

Days (n-pl)- plural of day
Daze (v)- 1. bewilder, confuse, amaze. 2. coma, stupor, shock

Deal (n)- 1. cut and shuffle cards, act of dealing. 2. (v)- apportion, allot, divide
Deel (n)- Archaic - grief
Deil (n)- Scot. - devil

Dean (n)- 1. official in college or university. 2. head of a diocese
Dene (n)- bare sandy, tract, low sandhill near the sea

D

Dear (n)- 1. beloved, sweetheart, darling. 2. (adj) - expensive, costly
Deer (n)- animal of elk, moose, or caribou family
Dere (v)- hurt, harm

Decad (n)- music - group of ten tones of precise pitch relations
Decade (n)- group or division of ten

Decadence (n)- decay, deterioration
Decadents (n-pl)- those exhibiting qualities of degenerating to a lower type

Decarch (adj)- Bot. - having ten protoxylems (wood tissue)
Dekarch (n)- a commander of ten. A decurion

Deckel (n)- obs. - cover, lid
Deckle (n)- paper making - separate thin wooden frame used to form border

Dee (pr.n)- river in Scotland
Di (n)- Music- a tone in the scale between do and re

Deem (v)- form an opinion, judge, think
Deme (n)- administrative division of Greece

Deer -see Dear, Dere

Deflection (n)- a turning or state of being turned
Deflexion (n)- Math.- amount of bending one curve away from another

Deformity (n)- disfigurement, blemish, defect
Difformity (n)- diversity of form

Deign- see Dain, Dane

Deil- see Deal, Deel

Dekarch (n)- a commander of ten. A decurion
Decarch (adj)- Bot. - having ten protoxylems (wood tissue)

Demean (v)- lower in dignity, debase
Demesne (n)- domain, empire, estate, manor

Deme- see Deem

Demivolt (n)- one of 7 artificial motions of a horse. Half vault with forelegs raised
Demivolte (n)- fencing - a half turn

Dense (adj)- 1. stupid, ignorant, inept. 2. close, compact, solid
Dents (v)- 1. marks, scratches, nicks. 2. (n)- depression, cavity

Dental (adj)- pertaining to teeth or dentistry
Dentil (n)- series of small rectangular blocks (archit.)

D

Dentel (n)- a dentil (archit.)
Dentelle (n)- lace or lace-like decoration

Dents- see Dense

Dentine (n)- 1. calcareous matter harder than bone. 2. tooth, ivory
Dentin (n)- Eng. - gauge to test accuracy of handmade screw threads

Dependence (n)- 1. reliance, belief .2. staff, prop, support
Dependents (n-pl)- minors, wards, subordinates

Depravation (n)- 1. deterioration, injury. 2. corruption, vice, evil
Deprivation (n)- 1. loss, bereavement. 2. lack, want

Dere- see Dear, Deer

Dern (adj)- Scot. - underhand, crafty, evil
Derne (v)- Eng. Dial. - to hide, conceal

Descendant (n)- offspring, progeny, family, heir, scion
Descendent (adj)- moving downward, going down

Descent (n)- 1. plunge, drop downward. 2. genealogy, lineage
Dissent (n)- disagreement, contradict, wrangle

Desert (v)- 1. forsake, abandon, evade. 2. run away from military service. AWOL
Dessert (n)- last course of a meal: ice cream, pastry, fruit

Devel (v)- to strike with a heavy blow
Devil (v)- 1. food - to highly season. 2. make fiendish

Deviser (n)- contriver, planner
Devisor (n)- one who bequeaths property
Divisor (n)- term in arithmetic

Devises (v)- prepares, concocts, designs, invents
Devizes (pr.n)- town in Wiltshire, England

Dew (n)- moisture condensed from atmosphere in small drops
Dhu (adj)- Black - used in Celtic names of persons and places
Do (v)- act or perform
Due (adj)- owed, payable

Dewan (n)- India - chief officer or steward. Minister of finance
Diwan (n)- India - royal court, state council, or tribunal of Justice

Dewani (n)- Abbysinian copper coin
Dewanny (n)- office held by Dewan. Jurisdiction to collect revenues

D

Dey (n)- Algerian Governor. Ruler in Tripoli or Tunisia
Day (n)- time between sunrise and sunset

Dhan (n)- Indian unit of weight
Dan (pr.n)- masculine name. Biblical - from Dan to Beersheba: from limit to limit.

Dhole (n)- Asiatic wild dog
Dole (n)- alms, pittance, handout

Dhow (n)- Arab coasting vessel
Dow (v)- to do well or thrive

Di (n)- Music - a tone in the scale between do and re
Dee (pr.n)- river in Scotland

Di (n-pl)- Roman - the Gods
Die (v)- 1. expire, decease, pass away. 2. (n)- cube for gambling
Dye (n)- fluid used for color, tint, hue

Dial (n)- 1. sundial. 2. face of a time piece. 3. slotted disk to manipulate for a telephone call
Dyal (pr.n)- song bird of India. Dial bird

Dike (v)- obstacle
Dyke (n)- ditch

Dine (v)- eat principal meal, feast, banquet, feed
Dyne (n)- physics - unit of force

Dingey (n)- slang- 1. small truck. 2. short train
Dinghy (n)- small boat, rowboat or skiff

Dinkey (n)- Colloq. - locomotive for hauling freight, shunting cars.
Dinky (n)- slang - small, little

Dipped (n)- immersed or plunged into water and withdrawn
Dipt (v)- to lower for an instant than raise as a flag

Dire (adj)- grim, appalling, awful, fatal, deadly
Dyer (n)- a person who colors hair or material

Disc (n)- phonograph record
Disk (n)- 1. plate of cartilage between bones. 2. circular plate, discus

Discous (adj)- flat and circular
Discus (n)- circular plate for throwing disk, quoit
Discuss (v)- argue, debate, talk about

Discreet (adj)- prudent, judicious, careful, wary
Discrete (adj)- separate, detached, distinct

D

Discus (n)- see Discous, Discuss

Dissent (n)- disagreement, contradict, wrangle
Descent (n)- plunge, drop downward, going down

Dissidence (n)- disagreement
Dissidents (n)- one who disagrees or dissents

Divisor (n)- term in arithmetic
Deviser (n)- contriver, planner
Devisor (n)- one who bequeaths property

Diwan- see Dewan

Do- see Dew, Dhu, Due

Do (n)- Music- first note of diatonic scale
Doe (n)- female deer
Dough (n)- 1. soft pasty mass. Unbaked bread. 2. slang - money

Doaty or Doty (adj)- partial decay in certain kinds of timber as oak, birch, beech
Dotty (adj)- composed of or characterized by dots

Dobbie (n)- apparatus for weaving small figures
Dobby (n)- Scot. - stupid fellow, dolt

Doc (n)- slang - doctor. Document
Dock (n)- wharf, pier

Docile (adj)- teachable, pliable, obedient
Dossal (n)- ornamental hanging back of the altar

Dod (n)- an annular die for making drain pipe
Dodd (v)- to lop, cut or clip wool from a sheep's tail

Does (n-pl)- plural of doe - female deer
Doze (v)- sleep, nap, slumber

Dole (n)- alms, pittance, handout
Dhole (n)- Asiatic wild dog

Dom (n)- obs. - a Cathedral Church
Dome (n)- Cupola. Large hemipherical roof or ceiling

Domine (n-pl)- superiors of a nunnery
Domine (n)- obs. - lord, master

Done (v)- 1. finished, completed. 2. cooked.
Dunne (pr.n)- John. English poet
Dun (n)- 1. demand for payment of debt. 2. (adj) - color

Doodle (v)- draw or scribble aimlessly while occupied with something else
Doudle (v)- Scot. - to play bagpipes or doodle sack

D

Dook (v)- Scot. - plunge, bathe. Duck
Douc (n)- Zool. - a monkey of Cochin, China
Duke (n)- reigning prince of less importance than a king

Dop (n)- South African - a superior grape brandy
Dopp (n)- little copper cup in which a diamond is held while being cut

Dor (n)- common European dung beetle
Dore (pr.n)- Monts. - group of mountains in Central France
Dorre (v)- obs. - deceive, make a fool of, mock

Dors (n-pl)- buffoons, practical jokers
Dorse (n)- young of common codfish

Dos (n)- Spanish - two
Dose (n)- measured quantity of medicine

Dos (n)- Eng. Law - property settled by husband upon wife at time of marriage
Doss (n)- Eng. - a place to sleep in. A bed

Dossal (n)- ornamental hanging on back of altar
Docile (adj)- teachable, pliable, obedient

Dost (v)- do - from verb "to be"
Dust (n)- earth in fine particles. Ash, soot, grime

Dottel (n)- Brit. - a plug of half smoked tobacco left in bottom of pipe
Dottle (n)- Scot. - a fool, dotard. Crazy

Dotty (adj)- composed of or characterized by dots
Doaty or Doty (adj)- partial decay in certain kinds of timber as birch, beech, oak

Doubt (n)- uncertainty, mistrust, misgiving
Dought (n)- Scot. - avail
Dout (v)- Eng. Dial. - to put out, extinguish

Doudle (v)- Scot. - to play the bagpipes or doodle sack. To toot
Doodle (v)- draw or scribble aimlessly while occupied with something else

Dough- see Do, Doe

Dow (v)- do well, thrive
Dhow (n)- Arab coastal vessel

Doxie (adj)- Eng. - lazy, slow
Doxy (n)- opinion, doctrine, religious opinion - (ism)

Drachm (n)- monetary unit of Greece. Drachma
Dram (n)- 1. small quantity. 2. unit of weight

D

Draft (n)- drawing, sketch, design
Draught (n)- 1. current of air. 2. a drink or potion

Draftsman (n)- one who draws sketches or plans
Draughtsman (n)- 1. a checker. 2. a man or piece used in the game of draughts

Drain (v)- draw off by degrees, cause to flow gradually out or off
Draine (n)- missel thrush
Drane (n)- Eng. Dial. - drone, bee

Dram- see Drachm

Draught- see Draft

Draughtsman- see Draftsman

Drole (n)- unprincipled or artful person. Rogue
Droll (n)- comical, humorous, laughable

Drool (v)- to talk foolishly. Drivel
Droul (v)- obs. - cry low mourning note

Droop (v)- sag, slouch, stoop, hang listlessly
Drupe (n)- fruit as cherry, peach. Having hard stone or pit

Dual (adj)- double, twofold, composed of two parts
Duel (n)- contest between two persons

Dub (v)- 1. confer dignity, title. 2. slang - clumsy, unskillful person
Dubb (n)- Syrian bear

Ducked (v)- 1. immersed, drenched. 2. avoided, evaded
Duct (n)- 1. chimney flue. 2. canal

Due- see Dew, Do, Dhu

Duke- see Dook, Douc

Dulls (adj)- deadens, clouds, tarnishes. Blunts
Dulse (n)- coarse red seaweeds used as food in Scotland, Iceland and other Northern countries

Dun- see Donc, Dunne

Dust- see Dost

Dyal- see Dial

Dye- see Die, Di
Dyeing (v)- coloring, staining
Dying (v)- expiring, death, demise

Dyer (n)- a person who colors hair or material
Dire (adj)- grim, appalling, awful, fatal, deadly

Dyne- see Dine

E

—E—

Eager (adj)- ardent, earnest, zealous, intense
Eagre (adj)- Brit. - successive waves of great height and movement. Tidal wave

Earn (v)- gain by labor or service, merit, make money
Erne (n)- sea eagle
Urn (n)- 1. vase, ewer, crock. 2. vessel with faucet, samovar

Earnest (adj)- sincere, ardent, eager. Serious in intention
Ernest (pr.n)- masculine name

Eau (n)- spirituous waters, cologne, perfume
Oh (inter)- expression of surprise or pain
Owe (v)- be indebted, bound in gratitude, be under obligation

Eave (n)- projecting edge of roof used to shed rainwater
Eve (n)- night before any date or event as "New Year's Eve"

Eel (n)- elver. Young eel
Ele (n)- 1. fish with long slippery snakelike body. 2.- obs. - oil

Eely (adj)- wriggly, eellike
Ely (pr.n)- town and cathedral in England
Ely (v)- Scot. - to disappear gradually

E'er (contr)- of ever
Eir (n)- 1. sandbank, beach. 2.(pr.n)- Goddess of Healing
Eire (n)- journey, march
Ere (prep)- sooner than, before, previous
Err (v)- misjudge, sin, blunder, mistake
Erre (v)- cause offense by blundering
Eyr (adv)- early
Eyre (n)- itinerant judges who rode circuit court in different counties in England
Are (n)- metric system - land measure, 160 sq. meters
Air (n)- wind, breeze, ozone, ventilation, atmosphere
Aire (n)- Irish person of any rank above freeman (Irish Tribal Law)
Ayr (pr.n)- town in Scotland
Heir (n)- beneficiary, inheritor
Ore (n)- Anglo-Saxon - honor, respect, reverence, glory (pronounced $\bar{A}$r)

Eerie or Eery (adj)- creepy, inspiring fear, unearthly, haunted
Erie (pr.n)- 1. American Indian. 2. Great Lake

Egis (n)- 1. goatskin. 2. sponsorship, auspices
Aegis (n)- Greek myth - shield of Zeus

E

Eight (n)- number 8
Ate (v)- devoured, past of to eat
Ait (n)-small island

Eighty (n)- number 80
Atē (pr.n)- Greek Goddess

Eigne (adj)- entailed - said of an estate. Title to property
Ayne (adj)- eldest, first born

Ele- see Eel

Eleme (n)- superior quality brand of smyrna figs
Elemi (n)- resin obtained from tropical trees, used in making varnish

Elicit (v)- drew out, extract, bring forth, wrest
Illicit (adj)- illegal, unlawful, banned. Immoral, improper

Elision (n)- omission of a vowel in pronunciation
Elysian (adj)- delightful, blissful

Elusion (n)- clever escape, evasion
Illusion (adj)- false impression, fallacy, delusion

Ely- see Eely, Ely

Emerge (v)- appear, issue from, emanate, rise out of
Immerge (v)- to plunge or immerse into fluid

Emersion (n)- act of emerging. Emergence
Immersion (n)- 1. plunging, dipping, bathing. 2. baptism

Enarm (v)- obs. - to lard in cooking
Enarme (v)- armor - strap on set of straps by which shield was held on the arm

Enew (v)- falconry - to drive or plunge into the water
Ennew (v)- to cloud, shade

Eon (n)- age, lifetime
Aeon (n)- gnostic doctrine - one of a class of powers or beings

Equites (n)- Roman members of a military order serving as cavalry
Equities (n-pl)- rights, justice, fairness

Erer (adv)- obs. - before, sooner than
Error (n)- mistake, blunder

Erie- see Eerie

Erne- see Earn, Urn

Ernest- see Earnest

E

Errant (adj)- roving, vagrant, wandering, stray
Arrant (adj)- notorious, bad

Err- see E'er, Air, Heir

Erred (v)- be in error, strayed, mistakes, blundered
Aired (v)- ventilated

Error (n)- mistake, blunder
Erer (adv)- obs. - before, sooner than

Eruption (n)- 1. upheaval, earthquake, blast. 2. breaking out, rash, hives
Irruption (n)- violent invasion, breaking or bursting in

Esthetic (adj)- love of beauty
Aesthetic (adv)- Brit. - pertaining to a sense of the beautiful

Eve- see Eave

Ewe (n)- female sheep
Yew (n)- evergreen tree
You (pron)- person addressed. Yourself

Ewer (n)- pitcher with wide spout, jug decanter
Your're (contr)- you are
Your (pron)- possessive form of you

Ewes (n)- plural of ewe
Use (v)- 1. put into service, apply. 2. manage, handle
Yews (n)- evergreen trees

Expedience (n)- advisable
Expedients (n-pl)- advantageous, profitable

Ey (n)- an island
Eye (n)- orb, organ of sight
Aye (n)- affirmative vote, yes, yea
I (pron)- myself, first person, ego

Eyed (adj)- having eyes
I'd (contr)- I would, I should, I had
Ide (n)- fresh water fish

F

—F—

Facet (v)- to cut small facets upon, as to facet a diamond
Facette (n)- front part of head. The face
Faset (n)- glass making - tool used to carry bottles to annealing furnace

Fade (v)- lose color, pale, blanch, bleach
Fayed (v)- fit closely

Faik (v)- Scot - abate, lessen
Fake (n)- 1. imposter, fraud, cheat. 2. imitation

Faikes (n)- Scot. - mining. A sandstone, fold, stratum of stone
Fakes (n-pl)- 1. persons or things not what it is pretended to be. 2. misrepresents

Faille (n)- ribbed silk or rayon fabric
File (n)- 1. smooth with a file. 2. march in a file. 3. walk in a line
Phial (n)- vial

Fain (adj)- inclined, willing, ready, eager
Fane (n)- place of worship, temple, church
Feign (v)- forge, pretend, invent, imagine

Faint (adj)- giddy, dizzy, light headed
Feint (n)- ruse, trick, wile, stratagem

Fair (adj)- impartial, unbiased, honorable, upright
Fare (n)- 1. price of passage. 2. food and drink

Fairy (n)- sprite, elf, mythical being
Ferry (v)- convey in a boat, pass over water in a boat

Fake- see Faik

Faker (n)- imposter, pretender, quack
Fakir (n)- holybeggar, mendicant, Hindu yogi

Fakes- see Faikes

Falter (v)- halt, hesitate, waiver, flinch
Faulter (n)- offender, commits a fault

Farce (n)- a ridiculous action, display or pretense
Farse (n)- Eccl. - an addition to some part of the Latin service common before the reformation
Fars (pr.n)- province in Southwest Iran

Farl (n)- 1. Irish - small scone or cake. 2. (v)- obs. - to furl
Farls (n)- Scot. - fourth part

Farm (n)- tract of land devoted to agriculture
Pharm (n)- pharmaceutic, pharmacy

F

Faro (n)- gambling game of cards
Pharaoh (n)- ancient Egyptian king

Fars- see Farse, Farce

Fascet- see Facet, Facette

Fast (adj)- 1. rapid, swift. 2. firm, steadfast. 3. abstain from food
Faste (n)- Archaic - pomp, display, ostentation

Fate (n)- lot, doom, destiny
Fete (n)- (also pronounced feet)- festal dam, holiday, celebration

Fated (n)- destined
Feted (n)- honored

Faucet (n)- a fixture for drawing off liquid as a sink, pipe, cask
Fossette (n)- a little hollow. A dimple

Faulter- see Falter

Faun (n)- woodland diety
Fawn (v)- 1. cringe, stoop, creep before. 2. (n)- young deer

Fay (n)- fairy, elf, sprite, pixie
Faye (pr.n)- name - either first name or last name
Feigh (v)- Eng. Dial. - to cleanse, clean, clear away
Fey (adj)- dying, doomed to die

Fayed - see Fade

Fays (n)- fairies, elves, sprites
Faze (v)- worry, discomfort, disturb, embarrass
Phase (n)- situation, condition, aspect

Feal (n)- 1. phrase used chiefly in Scots law. 2. (adj) - Archaic - faithful and loyal
Feel (v)- touch, handle. Search or grope with the fingers

Fear (n)- dread, fright, alarm, panic
Feer (v)- Brit. - to mark off land for plowing by furrows
Pheer (n)- companion

Feat (n)- bold deed, trick, stunt
Feet (n)- plural of foot
Fete (n) (also pronounced Fate)- festal day, holiday, celebration (Fiesta)

Feaze (v)- beat, frighten, punish
Fees (n)- pay for professional service
Feeze (v)- to turn as a screw
Pheese (v)- fume, fret

F

Feed (v)- 1. give food to, supply with nourishment. 2. food for beasts as hay, grain
Feid (n)- Scot. - an enemy, cause of quarrel, a feud

Feet- see Feat

Feid- see Feed

Feigh- see Fay, Faye, Fey

Feign - see Fain, Fane

Feint (n)- use, trick, wile, stratagem
Faint (adj)- giddy, dizzy, light hearted

Felloe (n)- circular rim of a wheel
Fellow (n)- male, mister, man, boy

Feod (n)- tenure, estate held under feudal lord
Feud (n)- quarrel, conflict. Vendetta especially between families

Fere (n)- companion, mate
Fir (n)- tree of evergreen family
Fur (n)- animal hair

Ferm (v)- obs. - blockade, close
Firm (adj)- 1. solid, hard. 2. (n)- company, partnership

Ferrule (n)- 1. bushing for end of a flue. 2. metal rim on end of post
Ferule (n)- rod, cane, switch for punishing children

Ferry - see Fairy

Fete (n)- festal day, holiday, celebration
Fate (n)- lot, doom, destiny

Feted (n)- honored
Fated (n)- destined

Feu (n)- Scot. law - fee
Few (adj)- rare, not many, hardly any, scant
Phew (inter)- exclamation of disgust, impatience, surprise

Feud- see Feod

Fey - see Fay, Faye

Fie (inter)- exclamation expressing disgust
Phi (n)- 21st letter of Greek alphabet

Field (n)- open country
Fyeld (n)- barren plateau on Scandinavian range

F

Fife (n)- musical instrument
Phyfe (pr.n)- Duncan. Furniture maker

File (n)- 1. walk in a line. 2. march in a file. 3. smooth with a file.
Faille (n)- ribbed silk or rayon fabric
Phial (n)- vial

Filet (n)- net or lace with a simple pattern
Fillet (v)- bone and slice meat or fish

Fillip (n)- 1. stroke, blow, knock. 2. (v)- stimulate, spur, urge
Philip (pr.n)- name - masc.

Filter (n)- 1. sieve, strainer, screen. 2. (v)- purify, refine
Philter (n)- love charm, magic potion to induce love

Fin (n)- 1. Fish's tail, flipper, paddlelike process. 2. slang - a five-dollar bill.
Finn (pr.n)- inhabitant of Finland, Native speaker of Finnish

Finary (n)- refinery
Finery (n)- 1. smartness or elegance. 2. showy ornaments or dress

Find (v)- encounter, discover, unearth, dig up
Fined (v)- punished, penalized

Finds (v)- hit upon, uncovers, detects
Fines (n-pl)- money imposed as a penalty for an offense

Finish (n)- end, conclusion, final stage
Finnish (adj)- pertaining to Finland, the Finns or their language

Finn- see Fin

Fir- see Fere, Fur

Firm (adj)- 1. solid, hard. 2. (n)- partnership, company
Ferm (v)- obs. - blockade, close

Fisc (n)- any state or royal treasury- an exchequer
Fisk (v)- Eng. Dial.- run about, frisk

Fisher (n)- 1. fisherman. 2. animal of weasel family
Fissure (n)- crack, break, breech, hole, split

Fits (n)- 1. convulsions, spasms, spells. 2. (v)- adjusts, adapts, fashions
Fitz (n)- a son - surname, especially to illegimate sons and daughters

F

Fizz (n)- bubbling, froth, hissing sound, fizzle
Phiz (n)- face, facial expression
Phizz (adj)- hissing sound

Flair (n)- genius, talent, aptitude
Flare (v)- flash, flame, glare, burn unsteadily
Flayer (n)- fleecer, skinner, swindler

Flask (n)- flattened bottle shaped container
Flasque (n)- cheek of a gun carriage

Flay (v)- 1. to skin or strip off surface. 2. to torture
Fley (v)- to frighten. Put to flight

Flea (n)- insect
Flee (v)- escape, abscond, runaway, decamp

Fleam (n)- Eng. Dial. - a mill stream
Phlegm (n)- mucus secreted in respiratory passages

Fleche (n)- any of the twenty four points on a backgammon board
Flesh (n)- animal food in distinction from vegetable. Meat

Flecks (v)- spots, specks, freckles, patches of color
Flex (v)- bent arm or leg, contract muscles

Flesh- see Fleche

Flew (v)- did fly
Flue (n)- shaft, chimney, smokestack, airpipe
Flu (n)- virus, influenza

Flews (n-pl)- large upper lip of bloodhound
Flues (n)- fishing nets

Fley- see Flay

Flier (n)- small fresh water sunfish
Flyer (n)- 1. aviator. 2. express train. 3. circular for mass distribution

Flight (n)- 1. act of fleeing, hasty departure. 2. act or mode of flying
Flite or Flyte (n)- Scot. obs. - to dispute, especially in words

Flo (pr.n)- name - dim. for Florence
Floe (n)- iceberg, floating ice
Flow (v)- stream, roll along, pour, spurt

Float (n)- 1. something that floats as a raft, cork. 2. (v) - move gently through fluid
Flot (n)- Scot. - scum of boiling broth
Flote (n)- obs. - a number going together, company

F

Flocked (v)- filled with woolen or cotton refuse as a bed
Flocht (n)- Scot. - a flutter

Flocks (n)- herds, roundups, letters, schools
Phlox (n)- showy flower of various colors

Flote- see Float, Flot

Flour (n)- ground meal of grain, wheat, bran
Flower (n)- 1. bloom, posy, blossom. 2. (v) - develop, unfold

Flues (n)- fishing nets
Flews (n-pl)- large upper lip of bloodhound

Flyer- see Flier

Fo (n)- Chinese name for Buddha
Foe (n)- enemy, adversary

Foaled (v)- gave birth to a colt or filly
Fold (n)- 1. enclosure or pen for domestic animals. 2. (v) - to double, pleat or lay in folds

Foehn (n)- warm dry wind of Alpine valley
Fun (n)- merriment, frolic, joke, jest, laughter

For (prep)- in favor of, since, pro, despite
Fore (adj)- first, in front of, former, previous
Four (n)- number 4, between 3 and 5

Forcite (n)- gelatine dynamite in which base is principally sodium nitrate
Foresight (n)- 1. care or provision for the future. 2. prudence

Forel (n)- kind of parchment for book covers
Forrel (n)- Eng. - border or selvage

Foreword (n)- introduction, preface, prologue
Forward (adv)- onward, ahead, before

Fort (n)- fortress, citadel, armed place, stockade
Forte (n)- one's strong point, special gift

Forth (adv)- ahead, forward, in advance, not at home
Fourth (n)- number 4th, between third and fifth

Fossette (n)- a little hollow. A dimple
Faucet (n)- a fixture for drawing off liquid as a sink, pipe, cask

Fou (n)- Scot. - bushel
Fu (n)- department or prefecture in China

Foul (adj)- tainted, contaminated, dirty, filthy
Fowl (n)- birds collectively. Large edible bird

F

Fouler (adj)- defiler, soiler, polluter
Fowler (n)- bird catcher, a person who pursues wild fowl for food and sport

Fraise (n)- 1. a small milling cutter. 2. a ruff for the neck
Frays (n-pl)- 1. quarrels, brawls, fights. 2. (v) - wears away, ravels, tatters
Phrase (n)- word-group, parts of a sentence, passage

Franc (n)- monetary unit of France
Frank (adj)- 1. candid, outspoken, direct. 2. (v) - mail free from postage
Frank (pr.n)- member of ancient Germanic people

Frater (n)- a refractory of a monastary
Freighter (n)- 1. a vessel used mainly to carry freight. 2. one who loads a ship

Fray (n)- 1. terror, fright. 2. attack, assail. 3. collide, clash
Frey (pr.n)- Teut. Myth - God of love, fruitfulness, prosperity

Frays- see Fraise, Phrase

Frees (v)- sets at liberty, rescues, acquits, clears
Freeze (v)- solidify by cold, refrigerate, turn to ice
Frieze (n)- 1. heavy napped woolen cloth. 2. decorative band on a wall

Fret (v)- be vexed, chafed or irritated
Frett (n)- mining - accumulation of ore
Frette (n)- hoop of wrought iron or steel shrunk on casting gun to strengthen it

Friar (n)- brother, padre, monk
Fryer (n)- 1. young chicken. 2. person who fries

Friz (v)- to curl in small curls as of a wig or hair
Frizz (v)- fry, cook or sear with sizzling noise, to sizzle

Fro (adv)- 1. back, away, from. 2. used in phrase "to and fro" meaning back and forth
Froe (n)- an iron splitting tool. a frow
Frow (adj)- Eng. Dial.- brittle, fragile

Frows (n)- cleaving tool
Froze (v)- past tense of freeze

Fu- see Fou

Fuhrer or Fuehrer (n)- leader - used chiefly of leader of German Nazis
Furor (n)- anger, rage, uproar

F

Fun (n)- merriment, glee, frolic, jest, laughter, joke
Foehn (n)- warm, dry southerly wind of Alpine Valley

Fungous (adj)- spongy, fungus like, not substantial
Fungus (n)- morbid growth, group of plants (fungi)

Fur (n)- animal fur
Fir(n)- tree of evergreen family
Fere (n)- companion or mate

Furor- see Fuhrer

Furs (n)- 1. plural of fur. 2. animal hairs
Furze (n)- spiny shrub with yellow flowers

Fuste (n)- offspring of a white and a mestee - West Indies
Fusty (adj)- moldy, musty, ill-smelling

G

—G—

Gab (n)- chatter, prate, idle talk
Gabbe (v)- to mock, deceive, lie

Gabardine (n)- finely ribbed woolen or cotton fabric
Gaberdine (n)- long, loose coat worn in Middle Ages

Gae (v)- 1. Scottish form of go. 2. Scottish for jay bird
Gay (adj)- 1. joyous mood, cheerful, jovial, merry. 2. slang- homosexual

Gael (pr.n)- Scotsman. Person belonging to Gaelic branch of the Celts.
Gale (n)- violent wind, typhoon, monsoon, storm

Gaet (n)- Scot. - manner, way, road
Gait (n)- amble, gallop, trot, pace, canter
Gate (n)- door, turnstile, passageway, entrance

Gage (n)- 1. security, guaranty, pledge, mortgage. 2. fruit - plum
Gauge (n)- standard of measure, scope, size, capacity

Gain (n)- 1. increase, advance. 2. mortise, groove, notch
Gaine (n)- kind of pedestal for holding statue

Gait- see Gaet, Gate

Gaize (n)- Geol. - fine grained micaceous sandstone. Malm rock
Gaze (v)- gape, stare, peer

Gall (v)- irritate, provoke, injure. (n) - malice, spite, bile
Gaul (pr.n)- Frenchman. Native of Gaul
Gaulle (pr.n)- Charles de. French commander

Gamp (n)- umbrella - also pronounced Gimp
Guimpe (n)- wimple, yoke, worn at neck

Gamble (n)- bet, wager, risk, hazard, uncertainty
Gambol (v)- romp, frolic, skip, cavort, prance

Gang (n)- 1. set or company of persons employed or working together. 2. group of boys as in a street gang
Gangue (n)- earthy minerals with metallic ore in a vein or deposit

Gantlet (n)- 1. military punishment. 2. attack from both or all sides
Gauntlet (n)- 1. challenge, dare. 2. cuff, wristband, sleeve

Gaol (n)- British jail
Jail (n)- prison, lock-up, cell; hold in custody

G

Gaoler (n)- British jailer
Jailer (n)- keeper of a jail, warden, turnkey

Garce (n)- measure of weight of East Coast of India
Gars (n-pl)- 1. Eng. Dial. - cause, make, have done. 2. groups of marine fish

Garnet (n)- deep red mineral generally used as a precious gem stone
Garnett (v)- remove foreign substance by passing through machine provided with garnett teeth

Gary (pr.n)- 1. masc. name. 2. large industrial city in Indiana
Gharry (n)- Anglo-Ind. - wheeled vehicle. Cart or carriage

Gast (adj)- Eng. Dial. - barren, not with young - said of animals
Gaste (v)- obs. - to waste

Gate - see Gaet, Gait

Gauge - see Gage

Gaul - see Gall, Gaulle

Gauntlet (n)- challenge, dare, cuff, wristband, sleeve
Gantlet (n)- military punishment. Attack from both or all sides

Gay - see Gae

Gaze (v)- gape, stare, peer
Gaize (n)- Geol. - fine grained micaceous sandstone. Malm rock

Gazelle (n)- small swift antelope of Africa
Ghazal (n)- Persion lyric poem

Gear (n)- movable property, clothing, equipment, trappings
Gere (n)- obs. - outburst or fit of passion or fancy. Frenzy

Gel (n)- short for gelatin. Dispersion of a solid with a liquid
Jell (v)- assume consistency of jelly

Gene (n)- unit of inheritance, transmits hereditary characteristics
Jean (pr.n)- Jeanne, Fem. name - also known as Jane

Genet or Genette (n)- small civetlike carnivore
Jennet (n)- small Spanish horse

Genes (n-pl)- plural of gene
Jeans (n)- clothes made of stout twilled cotton

Gere - see Gear

G

Germ (n)- 1. bit of living matter as organism. 2. source, rudiment
Jerm (n)- small levantine vessel with one or two masts and lateen sails

Gest (n)- 1. exploit, deed. 2. story, tale
Jest (n)- 1. prank, gag, farce. 2. (v) - banter, joke, scoff

Gesture (n)- sign, signal, motion, beckon
Jester (n)- comedian, fool, clown, buffoon

Gharry (n)- Anglo-Ind. - wheeled vehicle. Cart or carriage
Gary (pr.n)- 1. Masc. name. 2. large industrial city in Indiana

Ghazal - see Gazelle

Ghole (n)- ghoul, robber of graves, fiend
Goal (n)- 1. boundary, mark. 2. end or final purpose

Gib (n)- slang - a prison
Jib (n)- Naut. - triangular sail

Gibber (v)- talk volubly and foolishly. Chatter
Jibber (n)- 1. one that backs and shies. 2. a standstill

Gibe (v)- scoff, jeer, ridicule, taunt
Jibe (v)- be in harmony, agree
Gybe (v)- Naut. - to shift suddenly and with force from one side to another

Gig (v)- Scot. - creak
Jig (n)- lively, springy dance

Giggs or Gigs (n)- Vet. - a mouth disease in horses
Jigs (v)- to catch fish with a jig or by jerking a hook into one

Gild (v)- overlay with gold. Electroplate. Gold on surface
Gilled (adj)- provided with gills - as a gilled tadpole
Guild (n)- union, brotherhood, fraternity, corporation

Gilder (n)- one who gilds
Guilder (n)- Dutch coin

Gill (n)- Zool. - an organ for respiration underwater
Gyll (n)- Eng. - a stream in a ravine. A brook

Gill (n)- liquid measure - fixed at one-fourth pint
Jill (n)- a young woman. A sweetheart

Gilt (n)- 1. female swine. 2. (adj)- golden in color
Guilt (n)- misdeed, guilty conduct, wrong, trespass

Gim (adj)- Eng. Dial. - neat, spruce
Gym (n)- short for gymnasium
Jim (pr.n)- Masc. name - dim. for James

G

Gimp (n)- 1. spirit, vim. 2. (v) - indent notch
Guimpe (n)- chemisette worn under a pinafore or jumper

Gin (n)- 1. alcoholic beverage. 2. card game. 3. female kangaroo. 4. slang - street fight or rumble
Jinn (n-pl)- class of spirits, demons, pl. of Jinni

Gip (n)- college servant in Cambridge, England
Gyp (n)- cheat, swindle

Girt (v)- 1. p.p. of gird. Encircled, fastened.
Gurt (n)- Eng. - a trench, a drain

Glair (n)- egg white
Glare (n)- 1. brilliant luster, flare. 2. (v) - scowl, frown, glower

Glassie (n)- 1. glass marble. 2. transparent diamond crystal
Glassy (adj)- resembling glass in its properties or appearance

Glede (n)- European kite or similar bird
Gleed (n)- a coal of fire. Flame. Cinder
Gleyed (adj)- Scot. - cross-eyed, oblique

Gloom (n)- darkness, depression, melancholy
Glume (n)- chaff-like scale of the inflorescence of grasses

Glossed (adj)- 1. polished. 2. translations, explanations
Glost (n)- Ceramics - lead glaze used for pottery

Glows (v)- radiance, emits bright light, flames, ardor
Gloze (v)- cover up, excuse, flatter, humor

Gluten (n)- obtained form white flour by washing out the starch, glue, adhesive
Glutin (n)- 1. chem. - giladin. 2. gelatin

Glutenous (adj)- gluey substance, containing large amounts of gluten
Glutinous (adj)- sticky, viscid, nature of glue
Gluttonous (adj)- given to excessive eating, greedy, voracious

Gnarr (v)- growl, snarl
Knar (n)- a knot on wood or tree

Gnash (v)- grind teeth together
Nash (adj)- Eng. Dial. - hard, stiff, firm

Gnat (n)- small biting insect
Nat (pr.n)- Burmese sprite

Gneiss (n)- rock rich in feldspar and granite
Nice (adj)- tasteful, proper, fine, cultivated, kind

Gnide (v)- 1. rub. 2. break in pieces
Nide (n)- nest or brood of pheasants

G

Gnu (n)- African antelope
Knew (v)- past tense of know. Understood
New (adj)- recent, modern, fresh, untried
Nu (n)- 1. 13th letter of greek alphabet. 2. abbrev. for "name unknown"

Gnus (n-pl)- plural of gnu
News (n)- message, tidings, dispatch, report

Goal (n)- 1. boundary, mark. 2. end or final purpose
Ghole (n)- ghoul, robber of graves, fiend

Gob (n)- 1. mass or lump. 2. Colloq. - a sailor
Gobbe (n)- creeping herb cultivated in tropics for its pods and seeds

Gobi (pr.n)- desert region in Mongolia and East Turkestan
Goby (n)- spiny-rayed fish having ventral fins

Gofor (n)- slang - one who is sent to "gofor" coffee, "gofor" cigarettes, errands, etc.
Gopher (n)- burrowing rodent. North American ground squirrel

Gored (v)- pierced, impaled, stabbed with tusks
Gourd (n)- plant, melon, squash, pumpkin
Gourde (n)- monetary unit of Haiti

Gorilla (n)- animal, ape
Guerilla (n)- underground troop, partisan

Gourd - see Gored

Grail (n)- a cup, chalice. Said to be used at the last supper. The Holy Grail
Graille (n)- a half round single-cut file

Grain (n)- seed of any cereal grass as wheat, corn, oats, rice
Graine (n)- the eggs of the silk worm
Grane (v)- Eng. - choke or strangle

Graft (n)- 1. bribe, plunder, loot. 2. transplant, implantation
Graphed (v)- diagram represented by chart, blueprint, map

Gram (n)- 1. chick pea of East Indies. 2. food used for men, horses, cattle
Gramme or Gram (n)- unit of weight in metric system

Grannie (n)- grandmother. An older woman
Granny (n)- a knot. An imperfect sailor's knot

Grate (v)- 1. rasp, grind, creak. 2. (n) - iron frame
Great (adj)- vast, titanic, bulky, weighty

Grater (n)- wear down with rough friction
Greater (adj)- bigger, larger, vaster

G

Gray (n)- color between black and white
Grey (pr.n)- 1. surname. 2. British spelling for Gray

Grays (n)- colors between black and white
Graze (v)- 1. abrade, scratch, rub. 2. feed on grass, browse

Grease (n)- 1. oily substance, melted fat. 2. (v) - lubricate, oil
Greece (pr.n)- country in Europe

Great - see Grate

Greater - see Grater

Greaves (n)- sediment of animal fat used for fishbait or dog food
Grieves (v)- bewails, mourns, suffers, feels grief

Grede (v)- obs. - cry aloud, shout, proclaim
Greed (n)- 1. selfish, avaricious. 2. excessive appetite for food, drink, money

Greece - see Grease

Greeney (n)- European green finch
Greeny (n)- green or inexperienced person

Grew (v)- past tense of grow
Grue (v)- shudder, shiver, feel horror

Grieves- see Greaves

Griff (n)- 1. a claw. 2. textiles - loom with an arrangement of parallel bars
Griffe (n)- person of mixed Negro and American Indian blood. Mulatto

Grill (v)- 1. broil over a fire. 2. cross examine - interrogate
Grille (n)- griddle, broiler, open grating

Grilles (n-pl)- plural of grille
Grilse (n)- a salmon that has developed into an adult

Grip (n)- clutch, hold fast, iron grip, firm grasp
Grippe (n)- influenza, flu

Grisly (adj)- terrible, horrid, dreadful, shocking
Grizzly (adj)- 1. grayfish, silvery, gray-haired. 2. (n) - bruin, bear

Groan (v)- moan, bellow, howl, complain
Grown (v)- 1. advanced in growth. 2. adult

Grocer (n)- dealer in food commodities
Grosser (adj)- 1. bulkier, larger. 2. crasser, coarser

G

Groin (n)- where thigh joins abdomen in the body
Groyne (n)- 1. structure of timber from bench. 2. barrier against the tide

Groop (n)- Scot. - trench or drain especially in the stable
Group (n)- company, assembly, flock

Gros (n)- old silver coin of England or France
Grows (v)- cause to spring up, mature, flourish

Grosser - see Grocer

Group (n)- company, assembly, flock
Groop (n)- Scot. - trench or drain especially in the stable

Grows - See Gros

Grown - see Groan

Groyne - see Groin

Grue - see Grew

Guerilla (n)- underground troop, partisan
Gorilla (n)- ape

Guessed (v)- conjectured, estimated
Guest (n)- 1. person entertained at house or club. 2. person who pays for food and lodging

Guide (n)- pilot, steer, lead, escort
Guyed (n)- rope used to steady or secure

Guild (n)- union, brotherhood, fraternity, corporation
Gild (v)- overly with gold. Electroplate
Gilled (adj)- provided with gills, as a gilled tadpole

Guilder- see Gilder

Guilt (n)- misdeed, wrong, trespass, guilty conduct
Gilt (n)- 1. female swine. 2. (adj)- golden in color

Guimpe - see Gamp or Gimp

Guise (n)- semblance, disguise, shape, look
Guys (n)- 1. men or boys. 2. teases, ridicules

Gul (n)- Persian - a rose
Gull (n)- 1. aquatic bird. 2. slang - a dupe, one easily cheated

Guyed - see Guide

Guys - see Guise

Gybe- see Gibe, Jibe

Gyll- see Gill

G

Gym (n)- dim. for gymnasium
Gim (adj)- Dial. Eng. - neat, spruce
Jim (pr.n)- man's name - dim. for James

Gyp- see Gip

Gyve (n)- shackle, fetter especially for legs
Jive (n)- swing music, talk of swing enthusiasts

H

—H—

Haak (v)- Eng. - to wander
Haik (n)- outer garment used by Arabs (also pronounced hike)
Hake (n)- any of several fishes allied to the cod

Haik(n)- outer garment used by Arabs (also pronounced hake)
Hike (v)- 1. move, draw. 2. (n)- march, tramp or walk

Hail (n)- 1. greeting, salute, hello. 2. frozen rain, snow pellets
Hale (v)- 1. tug, haul. 2. (adj) - healthy, vigorous

Hailes (n-pl)- boundaries or goals in Scottish game called clackens
Hails (v)- pour down small roundish masses of ice
Hailse (v)- obs. - greet, salute

Hair (n)- curls, ringlets, locks, tresses
Haire (n)- Archaic - sackcloth. Haircloth worn next to the skin in penance
Hare (n)- rodent like mammal with long ears
Herr (n)- German title of respect

Hairy (adj)- 1. shaggy, bristly, whiskered, bearded. 2. slang - dangerous, exciting
Harry (pr.n)- 1. man's name. 2. (v) - Scot. - to steal, take in a raid, plunder

Hake - see Haak, Haik

Hall (n)- entry of a house, corridor, passageway, lobby
Haul (v)- 1. carry, tote, take. 2. (n) - heave, drag. 3. booty, spoil

Ham (n)- 1. thigh of a hog, pork. 2. performer who overacts
Hamm (pr.n)- city in West Germany

Hance (n)- Naut. - sudden fall or break as of fife rail down to the gangway
Hanse (n)- Arch. - small arch joining a straight lintel to a jamb

Handsome (adj)- comely, fair, good looking, attractive
Hansom (n)- two wheeled horse drawn vehicle

Haras (n)- obs. - horse breeding establishment. Stud farm
Harass (v)- irritate, distress, gall, trouble

Hare- see Hair, Haire, Herr

Harl (n)- filaments of flax or hemp
Harle (n)- Scot. - red breasted merganser (duck-like water bird)

H

Haro (inter)- ancient hue and cry. Exclamation of distress. Help!
Harrow (n)- farm implement for leveling plowed ground

Harold (pr.n)- 1. Masc. name. 2. King of England in 1035
Herald (n)- messenger, announcer, proclaimer

Harry- see Hairy

Hart (n)- male of the deer. Stag
Heart (n)- 1. bosom, breast, seat of life. 2. core, hub, center

Haul (v)- 1. carry, tote, take. 2. (n) - heave, drag. 3. booty, spoil
Hall (n)- entry of a house, corridor, passageway, lobby

Hauld (n)- Scot. - a place of resort. A refuge
Hauled (v)- pulled or dragged by force. Transported by force

Haw (inter) - command to a horse
Haugh (n)- hedge, enclosure, meadow

Haws (n)- 1. fruit of the Hawthorne. 2. (inter)- hesitation of speech
Hawse (n)- part of ships bow having holes for cables

Hay (n)- mowed grass, forage grass, fodder, feed
He (n)- fifth letter of Hebrew alphabet equiv. to English "H"
Hey (inter)- to call attention, exclamation of surprise

Hays (v)- cures grass for hay, cuts and dries grass
Haze (n)- 1. fog, mist, cloud. 2. (v) - abuse, tease, initiate
Hayes (pr.n)- Rutherford. 19th President of U.S. (1877-1881)

Heal (v)- cure, remedy, repair, help get well
Heel (n)- 1. hind of foot. 2. scoundrel. 3. end of loaf of bread
Hele (v)- to cover over, as a roof with tiles
He'll (contr)- he will

Healed (v)- cured, returned to a sound state
Heald (n)- weaving - a harness or heddle

Hear (v)- perceive by ear, hark, listen
Heer (n)- old yarn measure of about 600 yds. or 1/24 of a spindle
Here (adv)- in this place, nigh, near at hand

Heard (v)- did hear. Past tense of hear
Herd (n)- 1. animals - group, pack, drove. 2. assemble, gathering, team

Hearse (n)- funeral vehicle
Hers (pron)- belonging to her. Form of possessive her
Herse (n)- 1. lattice. 2. harrow, implement

H

Heart- see Hart

Heaume (n)- armor - large helmet reaching to shoulders. Coif of mail
Holm (n)- 1. small island. 2. evergreen tree. 3. holly
Home (n)- shelter, residence, lodgings

He'd (contr)- he would, he had
Heed (v)- pay attention, take notice, listen to

Heel- see Heal, Hele, He'll

Heigh (inter)- exclamation used to call attention
Hi (inter)- greeting
Hie (v)- hurry, run, hasten, scurry
High (adj)- 1. lofty, tall, elevated. 2. expensive, dear, costly

Height (n)- altitude, elevation, summit
Hight (adj)- 1. name, call. 2. promise, command
Hyte (adj)- Scot. - mad

Heir (n)- beneficiary
Air (n)- wind, breeze, ozone, ventilation, atmosphere
Aire (n)- person of any rank above common freeman (Irish tribal law)
Are (n)- metric system - land measure - 160 square rods
Ayr (pr.n)- town in Scotland
Eir (n)- 1. sandbank, beach. 2.(pr.n)- Goddess of Healing
Eire (n)- march, journey
Ere (adv)- before, sooner than, previous
E'er (contr)- of ever
Err (v)- misjudge, blunder, sin, mistake
Erre (v)- cause offense by blundering
Eyr or Ear (adv)- early
Eyre (n)- itinerant judges who rode circuit to hold court in different counties in England
Ore (n)- Anglo-saxon - honor, respect, reverence, glory ($\bar{A}r$)

Hel (pr.n)- Scand. Myth. Daughter of Loki
Hell (n)- inferno, a bode of the dead, evil and condemned spirits

Hend (v)- to take hold of, to grasp
Hende (adj)- 1. obs. - near, convenient. 2. (adv) - kindly, courteously

Herald- see Harold

Herd- see Heard

Here (adv)- in this place, nigh, near at hand
Heer (n)- old yarn measure of about 600 yards of 1/24 of a spindle
Hear (v)- perceive by ear, hark, listen

H

Herl (n)- barbs of feathers used in dressing angler's flies
Herle (n)- Scot. - a heron
Hurl (v)- throw, sling, cast, toss

Heroin (n)- a poisonous, habit-forming drug
Heroine (n)- a woman admired for her bravery, female hero

Herr- see Hair, Hare, Haire

Hers (pron)- belonging to her, possessive
Hearse (n)- funeral vehicle
Herse (n)- 1. lattice. 2. harrow, implement

Hertz (n-pl)- unit of frequency
Hurts (n)- 1. causes body injury, damages, harms. 2. aches, pains

Hery (v)- Archaic - to glorify, extol, praise
Herry (v)- Eng. Dial. - make a hostile invasion of or raid upon

Hew (v)- 1. cut, hack, chop. 2. form, shape, fashion
Hue (n)- 1. color, tint, shade. 2. outcry, tumult, uproar
Hugh (pr.n)- male name
Hu (n)- Chinese measure

Hey- See Hay, He

Hi, Hie, High, Heigh- See Heigh

Hide (v)- 1. secret, suppress, conceal. 2. (n) - skin of animals, pelts
Hied (v)- hastened, sped, hurried
Hyde (pr.n)- name - Dr. Jekyll's other self

Higher (adj)- taller, more elevated, loftier
Hire (n)- 1. wages, salary, stipend. 2. (v)- engage services of

Hight- see Height

Hike (v)- 1. move, draw, jerk. 2. (n)- a march, tramp, walk
Haik (n)- outer garment used by Arabs

Him (pron)- he, himself, that man
Hymn (n)- sing praises, psalm, sacred song

Hipe (n)- wrestling - lift opponent, swing to one side, raise and throw him on his back
Hype (n)- 1. deception, put on. 2. slang - hypodermic

Hire- see Higher

Ho (inter)- exclamation of surprise
Hoe (n)- 1. dig, scrape, weed. 2. long handled tool
Whoa (imperative)- stop, stay, wait a minute. (also pronounced wo)

H

Hoar (adj)- 1. gray or white with age. 2. frost, rime
Hor (n)- Biblical - mountain
Hore (adj)- 1. musty, moldy. 2. (n) - dirt, mud
Hors- French - out of
Whore (n)- prostitute

Hoard (v)- accumulate, stockpile, stowaway, amass
Horde (n)- crowd, multitude, tribe
Whored (v)- corrupted, seduced, debauched

Hoarse (adj)- shrill, husky, grating, rough
Horse (n)- mount, steed, equine, stallion, mare

Hoc (n)- old card game in which holder of certain cards could give them any value wanted
Hock (n)- 1. slang - pawn, pledge. 2. joint in hind limb of a horse corresponding to an ankle

Hocks (n-pl)- 1. Archaic - caterpillars. 2. long handled hooks
Hox (v)- Eng. Dial - to worry, annoy. Pester by following

Hoe- see Ho, Whoa

Hoes (n)- 1. digs, weeds. 2. tools for digging and weeding
Hose (n)- 1. stockings. 2. pipe, tubing

Hoey (n)- Chinese secret society
Hooey (n)- slang- nonsense, bunk
Hui (n)- Hawaiian - a uniting. Firm, partnership

Hold (v)- 1. contain, keep, retain. 2. cargo space below decks
Holed (v)- slitted, cut, perforated

Hole (n)- opening, aperture, breach
Whole (n)- everything, all, intact

Holey (adj)- full of holes
Holy (adj)- sacred, hallowed, blessed
Wholly (adv)- entirely, altogether, fully

Hollo (v)- call with a loud voice, shout, yell
Hollow (adj)- empty, void, vacant

Holm (n)- 1. small island. 2. evergreen tree. 3. holly
Home (n)- shelter, fixed residence, lodgings
Heaume (n)- Armor - large helmet reaching to shoulders worn over close fitting steel cap

Holmes- see Homes, Homs

Holy- See Holey, Wholly

Home- see Holm

H

Homes (n)- dwellings, abodes, living quarters
Homs (pr.n)- city in Syria
Holmes (pr.n)- Sherlock, or Oliver Wendell
Holmes (n)- obs.- a German fustian made at Ulm

Honorary (adj)- given for honor only
Onerary (adj)- carrying of burdens

Hoop (n)- band, ring, circlet, wheel
Houp (n)- Scot. - a mouthful of drink
Whoop (v)- yell, shout, holler, cry out loud

Hor, Hore, Hors- see Hoar, Whore

Horde - see Hoard, Whored

Horn (n)- 1. musical instrument. 2. animal - tusk, antler
Horne (pr.n)- 1. surname. 2. Archaic- cuckold

Horse (n)- mount, steed, equine, stallion, mare
Hoarse (adj)- shrill, husky, grating, rough

Hose- see Hoes

Hostel (n)- lodging place for young. Inn
Hostile (adj)- at war, militant, antagonistic, unfriendly

Houp - see Hoop, Whoop

Hour (n)- unit of time, 60 minutes, interval
Our (pron)- belonging to us

How (adv)- in what manner. To what extent
Howe (adj)- obs. - hollow, deep, low concave

Hox- see Hocks

Hu, Hue (n)- see Hew, Hugh

Huck (v)- obs. - to haggle, bargain
Huk (n)- Philippine island guerilla

Hui- see Hoey, Hooey

Huk- see Huck

Humerus (n)- long bone in arm extending from shoulder to elbow
Humorous (adj)- funny, pleasant, droll, witty

Hurl (v)- throw, sling, cast, toss
Herl (n)- barbs or feathers used in dressing angler's flies
Herle (n)- Scot. - a heron

Hurts (n)- 1. aches, pains. 2. damages, harms
Hertz (n-pl)- unit of frequency

H

Hyde- see Hide, Hied

Hymn (n)- sing praises, psalm, sacred song
Him (pron)- he, himself, that man

Hype (n)- 1. deception. Put on. 2. slang - hypodermic
Hipe (n)- wrestling. Lift opponent, swing to one side, raise and throw him on his back

Hyte- see Height, Hight

I

—I—

I (pr.n)- myself, first person, ego
Ey (n)- an island
Eye (n)- orb, organ of sight
Aye (n)- affirmative vote, yes, yea

I'd (contr)- I would, I should, I had
Id (n)- fresh water fish
Ide (n)- one of the ides - certain day of ancient Roman month. (the ides of March)
Eyed (adj)- having eyes

Idle (adj)- lazy, unemployed, not kept busy
Idol (n)- 1. beloved, darling. 2. graven image, pagan deity
Idyl or Idyll (n)- pastoral composition of rural life, poem

Igniter (n)- one that kindles or sets on fire
Ignitor (n)- device for igniting explosive charge of internal combustion engine

Ile (n)- obs. - the ileum. Anat. - the last division of the small intestine
I'll (contr)- I will
Isle (n)- small island, key, cay
Aisle (n)- walk, path, lane, passageway

Illicit (adj)- illegal, unlawful, banned, immoral, improper
Elicit (v)- draw out, extract, bring forth, wrest

Illusion (adj)- false impression, fallacy, delusion
Elusion (n)- clever escape, evasion

Immerge (v)- plunge or immerse into fluid
Emerge (v)- to appear, issue from, emanate, rise out of fluid

Immersion (n)- 1. plunging, dipping, bathing. 2. baptism
Emersion (n)- act of emerging. Emergence

Impassable (adj)- 1. closed, airtight, watertight. 2. unattainable
Impassible (adj)- incapable of feeling, insensible, unmoved

Impi (n)- body of Kafir warriors or native armed men
Impy (adj)- impish, mischievous

Impressed (adj)- 1. pressed in or upon. 2. imprinted, stamped
Imprest (v)- to draw money, by way of an advance

In (prep)- on the inside of, within, among, amidst
Inn (n)- small hotel, hostel, lodging place, tavern

I

Incense (v)- 1. inflame with wrath, provoke. 2. sweet aroma, perfume with incense
Insense (v)- instruct, inform

Incide (v)- obs. - to cut or cut into. To break up
Inside (n)- inner side or surface. The part within

Incidence (n)- range of occurence, scope, direction, trend
Incidents (n)- occurences, events, episodes, affairs

Incite (v)- instigate, goad, spur, arouse
Insight (n)- mental vision, intuition, power of understanding
Insite (adj)- obs. - ingrafted, implanted

Indict (v)- accuse, arraign, charge with a crime
Indite (v)- compose, write, transcribe, record

Indicter (n)- one who brings charges of an offense
Inditer (n)- writer, composer, author

Indiscreet (adj)- reckless, rash, headstrong, unwise
Indiscrete (adj)- not discrete or separated. Compact, homogeneous

Indol (n)- chemical substance of indigo and phenol, etc.
Indole (adj)- Archaic - without guile

Indraft (n)- 1. drawing or pulling in. 2. inward attraction
Indraught (n)- an opening from the sea into the land. An inlet

Ingenious (adj)- clever, inventive, resourceful, talented
Ingenous (adj)- frank, candid, free from guile

Ink (n)- fluid of various colors, commonly black, used for writing and printing
Inke (n)- falconry - the neck of a bird

Inlaik (n)- Scot. - shortcoming, lack
Inlake (v)- to make a lake

Inn (n)- small hotel, hostel, lodging place, tavern
In (prep)- on the inside of, within, among, amidst

Innocence (n)- 1. freedom from sin. 2. chastity, purity, clean hands
Innocents (adj)- childlike, honest, unworldly

Insense- see Incense

Inside- see Incide

Insight- see Incite

Instance (v)- cite as example, illustrate, explain
Instants (n-pl)- specific moments. Points of time

I

Intense (adj)- energetic, powerful, vigorous, extreme
Intents (n-pl)- purposes, aims, projects, design

Intension (n)- determination, absorption
Intention (n)- purpose, object, aim, ambition

Intents (n-pl)- purposes, aims, projects, design
Intense (adj)- energetic, powerful, vigorous, extreme

Intern (v)- confine or impound especially during a war
Interne (n)- Med. - resident physician or surgeon in a hospital

Invade (v)- intrude upon, trespass, raid, violate
Inveighed (v)- attacked, denounced, blamed

Irruption (n)- violent invasion, breaking or bursting in
Eruption (n)- 1. upheaval, earthquake. 2. breaking out in hives or rash

Isle- see Ile, I'll, Aisle

Its (adj)- belonging to
It's (contr)- it is

—J—

Jab (v)- 1. thrust quickly or abruptly. 2. poke
Jabb (n)- a kind of small fish net

Jack (n)- 1. worker at odd jobs. 2. man or boy. 3. male donkey or rabbit
Jak (n)- East Indian tree like the bread fruit tree

Jadd (n)- Scot. - a mare
Jade (n)- 1. precious gemstone, usually green. 2. vicious woman

Jag (n)- 1. sharp projecting point. 2. spree
Jagg (n)- Scot. - leather bag or wallet. Saddlebag

Jail (n)- prison, lock-up, hold in custody, cell
Gaol (n)- British jail

Jailer (n)- keeper of a jail, warden, turnkey
Gaoler (n)- British jailer

Jak- see Jack

Jam (n)- 1. thick preserve of crushed fruit, jelly. 2. crowd, pack, crush
Jamb (n)- upright column, doorpost, pillar, side of door
Jambe (n)- Heraldry - a leg, a gamb

Jambeau (n)- medieval armor - a leg piece
Jambo or Jamboo (n)- East Indian trees and their fruits as roseapple, java plum

Jan (n)- obs. - a purse
Jann (n)- Moham. Myth - supernatural being. Genii or jinn

Jean or Jeanne (pr.n)- fem. name also called Jane
Gene (n)- unit of inheritance. Transmits hereditary characteristics

Jeans (n)- clothes made of stout, twilled cotton
Genes (n-pl)- plural of gene

Jell (v)- assume consistency of jelly
Gel (n)- short for gelatin

Jennet (n)- small Spanish horse
Genet or Genette (n)- small civet-like carnivore

Jerk (n)- 1. short quick pull or twist. 2. twitch. 3. slang - foolish, eccentric person
Jerque (v)- to examine or search papers of a vessel for unentered goods

J

Jerker (n)- 1. one who jerks. 2. North American chub
Jerquer (n)- Eng. - custom house officer who searches vessels

Jerm (n)- small levantine vessel with one or two masts and lateen sails
Germ (n)- 1. bit of living matter as organism. 2. source, rudiment

Jesse (pr.n)- Masc. name - Biblical - the father of King David
Jessie (pr.n)- Fem. name

Jest (n)- 1. prank, gag, farce. 2. (v)- banter, joke, scoff
Gest (n)- 1. exploit, deed. 2. story, tale

Jester (n)- comedian, fool, clown, buffoon
Gesture (n)- sign, signal, motion, beckon

Jewel (n)- precious stone, gem, brilliant treasure
Joule (n)- physics. - unit of energy

Jewry (n)- 1. Jewish people. 2. land of Judea. 3. ghetto
Juri (n-pl)- tribe of Indians in Northwest Brazil - now nearly extinct
Jury (n)- body of persons sworn to render a verdict

Jib (n)- Naut. - triangular sail
Gib- slang - a prison

Jibber (n)- 1. one that balks or shies. 2. a standstill
Gibber (v)- talk volubly, foolishly. Chatter

Jibe (v)- be in harmony, agree
Gibe (v)- scoff, sneer, jeer, ridicule, taunt
Gybe (v)- Naut. - to shift suddenly and with force from one side to another

Jig (n)- lively, springy dance
Gig (v)- Eng. - creak

Jigs (v)- to catch fish with a jig or by jerking a hook into one
Giggs or Gigs (n)- Vet. - a mouth disease in horses

Jill (n)- young woman. A sweetheart
Gill (n)- liquid measure fixed at ¼ of a pint

Jim (pr.n)- Masc. name - dim. for James
Gim (adj)- Eng. Dial. - neat, spruce
Gym (n)- dim. for gymnasium

Jingal (n)- a large musket mounted on a carriage
Jingle (n)- 1. Light clinking sound. 2. comic poem or verse

J

Jinn (n-pl)- plural of jinni. Demons, spirits
Gin (n)- 1. alcoholic beverage. 2. card game. 3. snare, trap. 4. Female kangaroo. 5. slang - street fight or rumble

Jo (n)- 1. a sweetheart. 2. Scot. - for my friend, my joy. 3. Japanese unit of measure
Joe (pr.n)- nickname for Joseph. 2. G.I. Joe - American soldier

Joll (n)- head and parts of certain fish as salmon, sturgeon for the table
Jowl (n)- under jaw. Fold of flesh hanging from the jaw

Jollie (n)- a potters machine
Jolly (adj)- 1. full of life, mirth. 2. (n)- slang - a marine in the English Navy

Jordan (n)- 1. bottle of water from Jordan brought back by pilgrims. 2. almond from Malaga
Jorden (n)- Eng. Dial. - chamber pot

Joule (n)- physics - unit of energy
Jewel (n)- precious stone or possession, gem, brilliant treasure

Joust (v)- to join battle especially on horseback
Just (adv)- 1. exactly, precisely. 2. honest, upright

Juneau (pr.n)- capital of Alaska
Juno (pr.n)- ancient Roman Goddess. Wife of Jupiter

Juri- see Jewry, Jury

Just- see Joust

K

—K—

Kab (n)- Hebrew measure of capacity - about 2 qts.
Cab (n)- vehicle for hire

Kabala (n)- mystic art, occultism, mystery
Cabbala (n)- secret or esoteric doctrine or science in general

Kabaya (n)- cotton garment worn by the Malays
Cabaya (n)- loose tunic or surcoat worn in the East

Kaddish (n)- Aramaic - Jewish ritual. Mourner's prayer
Caddish (adj)- like a cad. Lowbred

Kaik (n)- Maori - village or community
Caique (n)- Naut. - light skiff used on the bosphorus

Kail (n)- Scot. - greens used in soup for vegetables
Kale (n)- plant of the cabbage family

Kaim (n)- Eng. - ridge or mound of worn away material
Kame (n)- Scot. - stratified drift deposited by glacier melted water
Came (v)- past of come. Arrived, reached, approached

Kain (n)- Scot. - duty paid by tenant to landlord as poultry, eggs. Tribute
Cain (pr.n)- 1. son of Adam who killed his brother Abel. 2. (v)- raise cain, cause a violent disturbance
Cane (n)- staff, rod, walking stick

Kam (adj)- Gaelic - awry, bent, crooked wheel
Cam (n)- moving part or piece of machinery

Kama (pr.n)- Hindu God. River in Soviet Union
Comma (n)- punctuation mark
Cauma (n)- Med. - great heat as in fever

Kame - see Kaim, Came

Kang (n)- sleeping structure of brick or other material with a place of a fire underneath
Cangue (n)- portable pillory worn around neck of Chinese criminals

Kant (pr.n)- Immanuel. Philosopher
Can't- contraction of cannot
Cant (n)- 1. jargon, argot, lingo. 2. (v)- beg, whine, snivel

Karat (n)- unit of fineness for gold
Carat (n)- unit of weight measuring precious stones and pearls
Caret (n)- mark indicating something to be inserted ∧
Carrot (n)- vegetable

K

Karl (pr.n)- 1. Masc. name. 2. (n)- obs. - hemp
Carl (n)- Scot. - robust fellow, churl, farmer

Kars (pr.n)- province in Turkish Asia Minor
Cars (n)- wheeled vehicles, automobiles

Kashmir (pr.n)- native state in No. West India
Cashmere (n)- soft wool from hair of goats from Tibet, Kashmir

Kat (n)- shrub cultivated by Arabs - the leaves are used for brewing beverage like tea
Khat (n)- Turkish unit of weight

Kauri (n)- timber tree of Australia
Cowry (n)- small species of shell once used for money in Africa
Cowrie (n)- marine shell of genus cypraea

Kaw (pr.n)- tribe of Siouan Indians, allied to the Osage
Caw (n)- the cry made by a crow or raven

Keen (adj)- ardent, eager, intense, sharp
Keene (adj)- obs. - of language - sharp, severe, incisive

Keel (v)- 1. turn over, capsize, upset. 2. (n)- center board
Kiel (pr.n)- seaport city in North Baltic

Keir (n)- Scand. - a tub
Kier (n)- large boiler or vat

Keno (n)- form of lotto or bingo used in gambling in which numbered balls are used
Kino (n)- E. Ind. - dried red juice or gum of tropical plants used in medicine or the arts

Ker (n)- Gr. Religion - ghost or disembodied soul
Cur (n)- 1. mongrel or inferior dog. 2. worthless fellow
Curr (v)- make a low murmuring sound

Kern (v)- 1. Eng. - to harden, to granulate. 2. (n)- kernel, corn
Kerne (n)- light - armed foot soldier of Celtic population used in Medieval times
Kirn (n)- Scot. - merrymaking at end of harvest

Kernel (n)- 1. center of seed or nut. 2. marrow, center
Colonel (n)- army officer. Military rank

Kevel (n)- hammer. Gavel, mallet
Cavel (n)- Eng. or Scot. - allotment

Kew (pr.n)- village on Thames, Eng.
Cue (n)- clue, intimation, hint
Queue (n)- 1. pigtail. 2. waiting line

K

Key (n)- opener, latchkey, opening device, pass
Quay (n)- dock, pier, wharf, anchorage
Chi (n)- 22nd letter in Greek alphabet

Khan (n)- Mongol leader. Successor of Genghis Khan
Can (v)- 1. do, be able, be possible. 2. (n)- tin or metal container
Cannes (pr.n)- French city

Khas (n-pl)- tribes of Laos states in Indo-China
Khass (adj)- India - designating an estate managed directly by the state

Khat- see Kat

Khot (n)- India - farmer of land revenue. Contractor
Cote (n)- shelter for sheep, pigs, pigeons
Coat (n)- jacket, overcoat, garment

Kid (v)- 1. tease, banter, jest. 2. (n)- young goat
Kyd (v)- obs. - to know

Kiel- see Keel

Kil (n)- Irish church - monk's cell
Kill (v)- slay, slaughter, murder, assassinate
Kiln (n)- furnace or oven for baking, burning or drying something
Kyl (n)- Himalayan Ibex

Kino- see Keno

Kip (n)- hide or leather from calf. Kipskin
Kyp (n)- Eng. and Scot. - gristly prolongation on male salmon's lower lip in breeding season

Kirn- see Kern, Kerne

Kissed (v)- osculated, embraced, caressed, fondled
Kist (n)- chest, box, casket, container

Kite (n)- bird of the hawk family
Kyte (n)- Scot. - belly, stomach

Klepht (n)- Greek brigand community in the mountain stronghold of Thessaly
Cleft (n)- space or opening made by splitting. A crack

Knacker (n)- buyer of old houses, ships for materials
Nacker (n)- buyer of useless horses for slaughter

Knag (n)- prong of deer's horns
Nag (n)- 1. horse, equine, steed. 2. (v)- torment, tease, pester

K

Knap (n)- summit, hill, knoll, elevation, height
Nap (n)- 1. sleep, rest, repose, doze, drowse. 2. short fibers on surface of materials
Nappe (n)- whole or continuous part of a conic surface

Knape (n)- Eng. Dial. - a boy, a young man.
Nape (n)- back part of the neck

Knappery (n)- a place where chipping or knapping, as of flints, is carried on
Napery (n)- household linen esp. table linen

Knar (n)- rough rock or stone
Narr (v)- Eng. Dial. - to growl or snarl as a dog

Knark (n)- Eng. slang - a hard-hearted man
Nark (n)- Eng. - informer, stool pigeon, spy employed by police

Knarred (adj)- knotty, gnarled
Nard (n)- 1. ointment made partly from nard. 2. spikenard

Knave (n)- rascal, scoundrel, bad man, cheat
Nave (n)- hub, center, central part

Knead (v)- 1. mix, stir, work into shape. 2. rubdown
Kneed (v)- having knees
Need (v)- require, want, crave, lack, have use for

Knees (n-pl)- patellar region, joints. Plural of Knee
Neeze (v)- to sneeze

Kneel (v)- bow, bend the knee, genuflect, curtsy
Neal (n)- tempered by heat
Neele (n)- darnel. A weedy grass
Neil (n)- 1. Gael. and Irish- champion, chief. 2. (pr.n)- Masc. name

Knell (v)- death bell, peal, toll, funeral bell
Nell (pr.n)- Fem. name, dim. for Eleanor or Helen

Knew (v)- understood, past tense of know
New (adj)- recent, modern, fresh, up to date
Nu (n)- 1. 13th letter of Greek alphabet. 2. Abbrev. for "name unknown"
Gnu (n)- African antelope

Knicker (n)- small ball of clay, baked hard and oiled, used as a marble
Nicker (n)- 1. a water sprite. 2. (obs.) - a devil. 3. (v) - to neigh

Knight (n)- soldier, horseman, brave, warrior, defender
Night (n)- darkness, bedtime, dark, nighttime

K

Knit (v)- weave, twist, interweave, stitch
Nit (n)- egg of a louse. Young insect

Knitch (n)- obs. - a bundle, a burden
Nitch (v)- to connect, to join together
Niche (n)- 1. hollow or recess. 2. (v)- to settle, cuddle or nestle down in a niche

Knob (n)- handle, grip, hold, hump
Nob (v)- in boxing, to beat or strike on the head

Knock (n)- 1. rap, slap, clap, blow. 2. criticism, blame
Nock (v)- set an arrow into the bowstring

Knocks (n-pl)- plural of knock
Knox (pr.n)- 1. fort in Ill. where U.S. gold is stored. 2. Henry- 1st Secty of War - 1789-1800
Nox (pr.n)- Roman Myth - Goddess of Night

Knoll (n)- hillock, knob, mound, bulge
Noll (n)- the head

Knot (n)- 1. web, interlacement, braid, plait. 2. a wading bird
Not (adj)- 1. know not. 2. word of refusal
Nott (v)- to shear

Know (v)- recognize, realize, see, notice
No (adj)- 1. none, not any. 2. (v)- deny, contradict, oppose

Knowe (n)- Scot. - knoll, hillock
Now (n)- present time or moment, immediately, at once, yet

Knows (v)- is aware of. Understands
Nose (n)- 1. organ of smell. 2. muzzle, beak, nozzle, snout
Noes (n-pl)- negative votes. Plural of no

Knub (n)- lump or protuberance. A swelling
Nub (n)- 1. point or gist of a story. 2. (v)- Eng. - nudge or push gently

Kob (n)- African antelope
Cob (v)- beat or strike on the buttocks with something flat
Cobb (n)- sea gull - esp. black-backed gull

Kohl (n)- powder used to darken eyelids
Kol (pr.n)- native people from parts of Bengal, Ind. Mongolo - Dravidian race
Coal (n)- charcoal, ember, combustible
Cole (n)- cabbage, coleslaw

Koi (n)- Japanese carp
Coy (adj)- modest, shy, timid, blushing

K

Koko (n)- 1. the parson bird. 2. Africa - the taro plant
Coco (n)- palm tree. Coconut or fruit from this palm
Cocoa (n)- beverage prepared from powder of pulverized cacao seed

Kola (n)- extract from kola nut
Kola (pr.n)- peninsula in No. W. Soviet Union
Cola (n)- Negro language of W. Africa

Kom (n)- Archeol.- a village
Kome (n)-Geol.- division in Greenland
Comb (v)- draw, disentangle or cleanse with a comb
Combe (n)- narrow valley, deep hollow
Coom (n)- coal dust, soot
Coomb (n)- liquid measure
Coombe (pr.n)- Welsh valley

Konseal (n)- med. - capsule for inclosing dose of medicine
Conceal (v)- hide. Withdraw from observation

Kook (n)- slang - screwball
Cuck (v)- Eng. Dial. - to sound the cuckoo note. To cuckoo

Kop (n)- 1. So. Africa - hill, mountain. 2. Netherlands unit of weight
Cop (n)- 1. policeman. 2. (v)- capture, seize, catch

Koph (n)- 19th letter of Hebrew alphabet, representing English K or Q
Coff (v)- Scot. - to buy
Cough (v)- to expel air or irritating matter from lungs or air passages

Kor (n)- Hebrew measure of weight
Corps (n)- soldiers. Branch of military service
Core (n)- 1. inner part. 2. hard center of seed fruit as apple, pear

Korea (pr.n)- country in S.E. Asia
Chorea (n)- disease of the nervous system

Kos or Cos (n)- type of lettuce including romaine
Cos (pr.n)- one of the Dodecanese Islands

Kraal (n)- 1. village of South African natives. 2. enclosure for cattle
Crawl (v)- drag body across ground. Creep

Kris (n)- short sword, heavy dagger
Crease (n)- mark produced by fold, ridge, or furrow

K

Kroo or Kru (n)- tribe of Blacks on West Coast of Africa skilled as seamen
Crue (n)- Gaelic - a hut, hovel or cabin
Crewe (n)- obs. - a pot
Crew (n)- 1. able seamen, sailors. 2. company, band, pack

Kup or Keup (n)- Siamese Measure of weight
Cup (n)- small bowl-shaped vessel, usually with a handle, used for liquids as coffee, tea

Kyl - see Kil, Kill, Kiln

Kyp - see Kip

Kyte - see kite

L

—L—

La (inter)- exclamation of wonder, surprise
Law (n)- statue, regulation, rule

Label (n)- identification, sign, brand, stamp, countermark
Labile (adj)- unreliable, unstable, uncertain

Lac (n)- resinous substance deposited by an insect
Lack (n)- 1. need, want, requirement. 2. (v)- be short, be deficient
Lakh (n)- monetary unit of India

Lacks (n)- wants, needs, essentials
Lax (adj)- 1. loose, slack, careless. 2. soft. pliable, relaxed

Lade (v)- 1. load, burden, freight, stow. 2. dip, draw, scoop
Laid (v)- placed, put. Past tense of lay

Lai (n)- Fr. - medieval type of short tale
Lay (n)- 1. song, poem. 2. not professional. 3. (v)- place, put, deposit
Lei (n)- wreath of flowers. Leaves for neck and head
Leu (n-pl)- Romanian monetary unit

Lai (pr.n)- member of Mongoloid tribe in Chin Hills, Burma
Lie (n)- 1. tell a falsehood, prevaricate, fib. 2. (v)- recline
Lye (n)- strong alkaline solution

Laid- see Lade

Laigh (n)- Scot. - lowland or bottom. A hollow
Lake (n)- pond, lagoon, brook, stream

Lain (v)- reclined, rested
Lane (n)- alley, passage, path, roadway

Lair (n)- den or resting place of wild animals
Layer (n)- 1. stratum, thickness. 2. one who lays

Lait (n)- 1. Scot. - the pollack (fish). 2. (v)- to search, examine
Late (adj)- 1. not on time, tardy. 2. (adv)- not long ago, recently

Lakh- see Lac, Lack

Lakie (n)- Scot. - temporary movement of the tide observed in the frith of forth
Laky (adj)- pertaining to lake-colored pigment

Lam (n)- escape, flee, run off or away
Lamb (n)- 1. young sheep, kid, ewe. 2. meat - spring lamb, mutton

L

Lama (n)- Tibetan monk. High priest
Llama (n)- South American mammals related to the camel but smaller and without a hump

Lane- see Lain

Lant (n)- stale urine used for various manufacturing purposes
Lante (v)- Eng. - obs. - past tense of lend

Lapps (pr.n)- Finnic people of No. Norway, Sweden, Finland, Laplanders
Laps (v)- 1. folds, wraps. 2. take liquids with the tongue, licks as cats and dogs
Lapse (v)- fail, slip, backslide, decline. 2. (n)- error, flaw

Lari (n)- dialect of Sindhi (India)
Larree (n)- Persian hook money in 17th Century

Lask (v)- obs. - lessen, relax
Lasque (n)- flat, thin diamond much used in native Hindu work

Latchet (n)- thong, strap or shoelace for fastening shoe or sandal
Latchett (n)- sapphire gurnard (fish)

Late- see Lait

Latin (n)- Roman language, classical language
Latten (n)- brasslike alloy. Tin plate

Law (n)- statute, regulation, rule
La (inter)- exclamation of surprise, wonder

Lax- see Lacks

Lay (n)- 1. song, poem. 2. not a professional. 3. (v)- place, put, deposit
Lai (n)- Fr.- Medieval type of short tale
Lei (n)- wreath of flowers. Leaves for the neck and head
Leu (n-pl)- Romanian monetary unit

Layer- see Lair

Lays (n)- 1. songs, poems. 2. (v)- puts in place, put down
Laze (v)- be idle, shiftless, sleepy, inert

Lea (n)- meadow, pasture, grass, field
Lee (n)- away from the wind. Sheltered side, haven

Leach (v)- 1. dissolve, remove, wash out. 2. (n)- edge of a sail
Leech (n)- parasite, blood sucker, worm

Lead (n)- element, mineral, ore, metal
Led (v)- guided, conducted. Past tense of lead

L

Lead (v)- begin, open, be first
Lede (n)- obs. - a people, a nation, a person
Leed (n)- Scot. - song, tune, tale

Leads (n)- 1. directs, guides. 2. leading roles, performer's parts
Leeds (pr.n)- town in England

Leaf (n)- 1. frond, blade, part of a plant. 2. page, insert, folio
Leif (pr.n)- Norse name
Lief (adv)- willingly, gladly

Leak (v)- 1. ooze, run out. 2. reveal, disclose, inform
Leek (n)- onion like vegetable

Lean (v)- 1. incline forward, point. 2. depend or rely on. 3. not fat.
Lien (n)- legal claim, legal right

Leap (v)- jump, bounce, hop, spring, vault
Leep (v)- Scot. to boil, scald. (as milk)

Lear (adj)- empty, unoccupied, without contents
Lear (pr.n)- king in Shakespeare's 'King Lear'
Leer (n)- ogle, sly look, smirk, evil eye
Lere (v)- obs. - to learn, study, teach, guide

Leas (n-pl)- meadows, fields, pastures
Lease (v)- 1. let, rent, sublet. 2. (n)- contract for houses or buildings
Lees (n-pl)- dregs, sediment, remains
Leese (v)- obs. - to loosen, release

Leased (v)- rented. Past tense of lease
Least (adj)- smallest, slightest, lowest in consideration
Lest (conj)- for fear that. If, perhaps

Leat (n)- Eng. - artificial water trench esp. one to or from a mill
Leet (n)- Scot. - a list of those eligible or candidates for an office

Leave (n)- 1. permission, concession. 2. furlough, rest
Leve (n)- raise, lift
Lieve (adv)- 1. willing. 2. dear

Leaver (n)- one who leaves
Lever (v)- pry up, force in a given position
Levir (n)- a husband's brother or one who assumed his place in the custom of the Levirate
Livre (n)- a former French monetary unit

L

Lectern (n)- choir desk from which lectures or scripture lessons are read
Lecturn (n)- Scot. - reading or writing desk. Escritoire

Led- see Lead

Lede- see Lead, Leed

Ledger (n)- an account book in which recording business transactions are kept
Leger (adj)- lying or remaining in a place, stationary

Lee (n)- away from the wind, sheltered side, haven
Lea (n)- meadow, pasture, grass, field

Leech- see Leach

Leeds (pr.n)- city in England
Leads (n)- 1. guides, directs. 2. leading roles, performers parts

Leefang (n)- Eng. Naut. - rope fastened to a cringle of a sail
Leefange (n)- obs. naut. - horse on a deck which travels the sheets of a fore & aft sail

Leek (n)- onion like vegetable
Leak (v)- 1. ooze, run out. 2. reveal, disclose, inform

Leep (v)- Scot. - to boil, scald (as milk)
Leap (v)- jump, bounce, hop, spring, vault

Leer- see Lear, Lere

Lees- see Leas, Lease, Leese

Leet- see Leat

Leger (adj)- lying or remaining in a place, stationary
Ledger (n)- an account book in which recording business transactions are preserved

Lei (n)- wreath of flowers. Leaves for neck and head
Leu (n-pl)- Romanian monetary unit
Lay (n)- 1. song, poem. 2. not professional. 3. (v)- place, put, deposit
Lai (n)- Fr. - Medieval type of short tale

Leif- see Leaf, Lief

Lends (v)- advances, accredits, trusts, extends credit
Lens (n)- eyeglass, optical magnifier, field glasses

Lessen (v)- wither, ebb, become less, reduce, abate
Lesson (n)- something to be learned or study, homework instruction

L

Let (v)- allow, permit, cause
Lett (pr.n)- people closely related to Lithuanians. Lettish language

Lettice (n)- white or gray fur worn up to middle of 16th century
Lettuce (n)- salad plant

Leucifer (n)- Zool.- genus of free swimming crustaceans
Lucifer (pr.n)- fallen rebel, arch angel. Devil. Satan

Levee (n)- 1. embankment, dike, terrace. 2. reception, party, assembly
Levi (pr.n)- Bible- Son of Jacob and Leah. Ancestor of Levites
Levy (n)- assessment, taxation, conscription

Lever (v)- pry up. Force in a given position
Leaver (n)- one who leaves
Levir (n)- a husband's brother or one who assumes his place in the custom of the levirate
Livre (n)- former French monetary unit

Lew (adj)- Eng. Dial. - lukewarm, tepid
Lieu (n)- place, stead. Instead of
Loo (n)- game of cards
Loup (pr.n)- 1. Indian of Pawnee tribe. 2. French - a wolf
Lue (v)- Eng. - mining - to sift or bolt

Lewd (adj)- bawdy, unclean, lurid, offensive
Looed (v)- forfeit at game of loo

Lewis (pr.n)- Masc. name. 2. (n)- kind shears used in cropping cloth. 3. gun
Louis (pr.n)- 1. Masc. name. 2. (n)- in literature- a famous warrior

Liar (n)- fibber, prevaricator, falsifier, story teller
Lier (v)- be horizontal, recliner, sprawler
Lyre (n)- musical instrument of ancient Greece

Lichen (n)- 1. fungus growth on trees and rocks. 2. eruptive skin disease
Liken (v)- compare, to represent as like, relate

Licker (n)- animal or person who licks
Liquor (n)- 1. fluid, water, beverage. 2. alcohol, spirits, booze

Lickerish (adj)- obscene, filthy, lustful, carnal
Licorice (n)- sweet tasting dried plant used in candy or medicine

Lide (n)- 1. Eng. Dial. - the month of March. 2. flower as daffodil or lily
Lied (v)- told an untruth, deceived

L

Lie (n)- 1. tell a falsehood, prevaricate, fib. 2. (v) - recline
Lye (n)- strong alkaline solution
Lai (n)- member of Mongoloid tribe in Chin Hills, Burma

Lied- see Lide

Lief- see Leaf, Leif

Lien(n)- legal claim, legal right
Lean (v)- 1. incline toward, point. 2. depend or rely on. 3. not fat

Lier- see Liar, Lyre

Lieu (n)- place, stead. Instead of
Lew (adj)- Eng. - tepid, lukewarm
Loo (n)- game of cards
Loup (pr.n)- 1. Indian of Pawnee tribe. 2. French - wolf
Lue (v)- Eng. - mining. To sift or bolt

Lieve- see Leave, Leve

Lift (v)- move or raise to a higher position. Elevate
Lyft (n)- Scot. - the sky, heavens, atmosphere

Lightening (v)- 1. becoming lighter, brightening. 2. lessen the weight of
Lightning (n)- thunderbolt, flash in the sky, bolt from the blue

Light (adj)- 1. bright, luminous. 2. (v) - set fire, ignite, kindle. 3. illuminate
Lite (n)- Eng. Dial. 1. - little, few, small. 2. delay, wait

Liken (v)- compare, relate, to represent as
Lichen (n)- 1. fungus growth on trees and rocks. 2. eruptive skin disease

Limb (n)- 1. arm or leg. 2. large or main branch of a tree
Limn (v)- paint, design, draw, describe, sketch

Limey (n)- slang - an English sailor or soldier
Limy (adj)- containing, resembling, or covered with lime

Limn- see Limb

Lin (n)- female sex hormone obtained from cattle and sheep
Linn (n)- lind or the linden tree
Lyn (n)- 1. Scot. - waterfall. 2. precipice or ravine

Linch (v)- insertion with linch pin to hold wheel
Lynch (v)- put to death without process of law. Hang, murder

Lingoe (n)- weaving pieces of round lead hanging at end of each coupling to keep twine in tension
Lingo (n)- 1. language, speech, dialect. 2. Malay tree

L

Links (v)- connects, unites, couples, merges, yokes
Lynx (n)- member of cat family. Wild beast

Lion (n)- large cat native in Africa and South Asia. Wild beast
Lyon (n)- Scot. Her. - dim. for lyon, king-of-arms

Lippie (n)- Scot. - the fourth part of a peck
Lippy (adj)- slang - saucy, impudent

Liquor (n)- 1. fluid, water, beverage. 2. alcohol, spirits, booze
Licker (n)- animal or person who licks

Lis (n)- Irish - circular inclosure with an earth wall
Liss (n)- Eng. - peace, rest
Lisse (v)- Scot. - relieve, assuage - of care or pain

Lisa (pr.n)- Fem. name- dim. for Elizabeth or Melissa
Lyssa (n)- Med. - hydrophobia

Lite - see Light

Literal (adj)- exact meaning, faithful, true to fact
Littoral (adj)- pertaining to the sea - existing on or near shore

Livre- see Leaver, Lever, Levir

Llama(pr.n)- South American mammal related to the camel, but smaller and without a hump
Lama (n)- Tibetan monk. High priest

Lo (exclamation)- look, see, behold
Low (adj)- 1. dejected, sad. 2. not high. 3. quiet, not loud. 4. sound of cattle - moo

Load (n)- 1. cargo, bale, mass. 2. burden, onus, millstone
Lode (n)- 1. road, way, watercourse. 2. mining - veinlike deposit
Lowed (v)- characteristic sound of cattle, mooed

Loan (v)- credit, mortgage, to lend
Lone (adj)- isolated, unaccompanied, solitary

Loath (adj)- unwilling, averse, reluctant
Loathe (v)- hatred, disgust, intense aversion

Loch (n)- lake
Lock (n)- fastening, belt, padlock, hook, clasp
Lough (n)- Irish - an arm of the sea

Locks (n-pl)- 1. bolts, clasps, fastenings. 2. hair of the head, tresses
Lox (n)- 1. smoked salmon. 2. (L)iquid (Ox)ygen

Lode - see Load, Lowed

L

Lone (adj)- isolated, unaccompanied, solitary
Loan (v)- credit, mortgage, to lend

Longe (n)- halter, guide rope used to lead a horse in exercise or training
Lunge (n)- 1. sudden thrust or pass. 2. leap

Loo- see Lew, Lieu, Lue, Loup

Loob (n)- tin mining - slimes washed from ore in dressing
Lube (n)- lubricant. Grease used to oil machinery

Looed (v)- forfeit at game of loo
Lewd (adj)- bawdy, unclean, lurid, offensive

Look (v)- see, seem, observe, inspect, examine
Louk (v)- Eng. Dial. - to pull up, uproot, weed
Louke (n)- obs. - an accomplice. A pal

Loon (n)- 1. fish eating diving bird. 2. lazy, stupid fellow
Lune (n)- 1. crescent or half moon. 2. line for holding a hawk

Loop (n)- noose, circle, ring, bend, curve
Loupe (n)- magnifying glass used by jewelers

Loor (n)- 1. Eng. Dial. - footrot. 2. Bot. - disease affecting sweet orange when growing on its own roots
Lour (n)- Asiatic - sardine valued for its oil
Lure (n)- 1. decoy, bait. 2. allure

Loose (adj)- 1. free, liberated, unattached. 2. immoral, lewd, lawless
Lose (v)- 1. misplace, mislay, be deprived of. 2. fail, be defeated

Loot (n)- booty, spoils, plunder, steal, pillage
Lute (n)- stringed musical instrument

Lorain (n)- obs. - a bridle strap
Loran (n)- device by which navigator can locate position. (**Lo**)ng (**Ra**)nge (**N**)avigation
Lorane (n)- Scot. - laurel

Lori (n)- Loris - small nocturnal slow moving lemurs
Lorry (n)- British motor car
Lory (n)- small bright colored parrot

Lose (v)- 1. misplace, mislay, deprived of. 2. be defeated, fail
Loose (adj)- 1. free, liberated, unattached. 2. immoral, lawless, lewd

Losenge (v)- obs. - deceive, flatter
Lozenge (n)- 1. diamond-shaped figure, rhomb. 2. small flat candy often medicated

L

Losh (v)- Eng. Dial. - to splash, as water running over stones
Loshe (n)- obs. - an elk

Lota (n)- 1. Zool.- genus burbot. 2. fresh water fish
Lotah (n)- India - small brass or copper globular vessel for water

Lough (n)- Irish - an arm of the sea
Loch (n)- a lake
Lock (n)- 1. bolt, clasp, fastening. 2. hair of the head, tress

Louk- see Look, Louke

Loupe- see Loop

Louis (pr.n)- 1. Masc. name. 2. (n)- in literature- a famous warrior
Lewis (n)- 1. military- small automatic machine gun named after inventor Col. Lewis. 2. shears. 3. Masc. name

Lour (v)- frown, scowl, look sullen
Lower (v)- 1. decrease, diminish. 2. humiliate

Lour- see Loor

Low (adj)- 1. dejected, sad. 2. not high. 3. quiet, not loud. 4. sound of cattle-moo
Lo (exclamation)- look, see, behold

Lowed - see Load, Lode

Lower (v)- 1. decrease, diminish. 2. humiliate
Lour (v)- frown, scowl, look sullen

Lox (n)- smoked salmon. (L)iquid (Ox)ygen
Locks (n-pl)- 1. bolts, clasps, fastenings. 2. hair of the head, tresses

Lozenge- see Losenge

Lube (n)- lubricant. Grease used to oil machinery
Loob (n)- tin mining - slimes washed from ore in dressing

Lucern (n)- obs. - a hunting dog
Lucerne (n)- 1. clover, alfalfa, forage plant. 2. (pr.n) city in Switzerland.
Lusern (n)- lynx. Lynx fur

Lucifer (pr.n)- fallen arch angel. Devil. Satan
Leucifer (n)- Zool. - genus of free swimming crustaceans

Luckie (n)- Scot. - elderly woman shown in context as grandmother, midwife
Lucky (adj)- fortunate. Favored by luck

L

Lue- see Lew, Lieu, Loo, Loup

Lumbar - 1. pertaining to the loins. 2. artery, lumbar vertebra
Lumber - 1. move clumsily. 2. planks, timber, boards, wood

Lune (n)- 1. crescent or half moon. 2. line for holding a hawk
Loon (n)- 1. fish eating diving bird. 2. lazy, stupid fellow

Lunge (n)- 1. sudden thrust or pass. 2. leap
Longe (n)- halter. Guide rope used to lead a horse in exercising or training

Lure (n)- 1. decoy, bait. 2. allure
Lour (n)- Asiatic sardine noted for its oil
Loor (n)- Eng. Dial. - footrot. Bot. - disease affecting sweet orange when growing on its own roots

Lusern- see Lucern, Lucerne

Lute (n)- stringed musical instrument
Loot (n)- 1. booty, spoils. 2. plunder, sack, steal

Lyddite (n)- high explosive, chiefly picric acid
Lydite (n)- mining - touchstone, allied to flint, basanite

Lye (n)- strong alkaline solution
Lie (n)- 1. fib, prevaricate, tell a falsehood. 2. (v) - recline
Lai (n)- member of Mongoloid tribe in Chin Hills, Burma

Lyft (n)- Scot. - sky, heavens, atmosphere
Lift (v)- move or raise to a higher position. Elevate

Lyn- see Lin, Linn

Lynch (v)- to put to death without process of law. Hang. Murder
Linch (v)- insertion with linch pin to hold wheel

Lynx (n)- member of cat family. Wild beast
Links (v)- connects, unites, merges, couples

Lyon (n)- Scot. Her. - short for lyon king-of-arms
Lion (n)- large cat native in Africa & So. Asia. Wild beast

Lyre (n)- musical instrument of ancient Greece
Liar (n)- fibber, prevaricator, falsifier, story teller
Lier (v)- 1. be horizontal. 2. (n)- recliner, sprawler

Lyssa (n)- Med. - hydrophobia
Lisa (pr.n)-Fem. name - dim. for Elizabeth, Melissa

M

—M—

Ma (n)- childish form of mama

Mah (n)- "the fish on which the universe if fabled to rest" from Omar Khayyam

Mac (n)- a prefix in names of Scotch, Gaelic, Irish origin signifying son

Mack (n)- 1. an old card game. 2. (adj)- Scot.- neat, tidy

Macassar (n)- an oil used in hair dressing obtained from sandalwood tree

Makassar (pr.n)- district of Celebes

Mackinac (pr.n)- pronounced mackinaw. Strait joining lakes Michigan and Huron. World's longest suspension bridge

Mackinaw (n)- short, heavy, plaid coat

Madam (n)- 1. lady, mistress. 2. woman in charge of a brothel

Madame (n)- French title of respect for married women or woman of rank

Made (v)- prepared, invented, created, manufactured

Maid (n)- 1. lass, damsel, young unmarried woman. 2. female servant

Mag (n)- 1. Eng. Dial, - European magpie. 2. long tailed titmouse

Magg (v)- Scot. - to steal, mangle

Maggot (n)- legless worm like larva of a two-winged fly

Magot (n)- 1. the barbary ape. 2. small grotesque figure of Oriental style and workmanship

Mah- see Ma

Maid- see Made

Mail (n)- 1. system of transmission of letters. 2. postal service. 3. armor

Maill (n)- obs. - rent, tribute, tax

Maille or Maile (n)- Scotch gold coin of Robert II and his successors

Male (n)- man, boy, fellow. Masculine

Main (adj)- head, principal, chief, primary

Mane (n)- long hair on back of neck of some animals

Maine (pr.n)- state in N.E. United States

Maize (n)- corn, cereal plant, Indian corn, grain

Maze (n)- 1. winding course, labyrinth. 2. state of confusion

Malay (adj)- pertaining to Malays, their country or language

Melee (n)- confused general hand to hand fight

M

Male- see Mail, Maill, Maille

Mall (n)- promenade, shaded public walk, arcade
Maul (n)- 1. heavy wooden hammer, bat or club. 2. (v)- batter, beat
Moll (n)- 1. prostitute. 2. unmarried female companion of gangster or thief

Mallow (n)- European species of flowers used for medicine
Malo (n)- Hawaiian - a breech cloth

Man (n)- human creature. Male, masculine
Mann (pr.n)- Horace. Educator

Manchet (n)- Archaic - finest kind of a wheat bread. Small wheat roll or muffin
Manchette (n)- an ornamental cuff

Mandril (n)- Eng. mining - a miner's pick
Mandrill (pr.n)- large West African baboon

Mane- see Main, Maine

Manila (pr.n)- capitol of Philippine Islands
Manilla (n)- ring of metal, as silver, worn on arm and used as money on West Coast of Africa

Manks (v)- obs. - impairs, spoils, maims
Manx (adj)- 1. pertaining to the isle of man. 2. (n)- Celtic Dialect

Mann (pr.n)- Horace. Educator
Man (n)- human creature. Male, masculine

Manner (n)- 1. conduct, behavior. 2. method, style, type
Manor (n)- rural domain, mansion of a lord, landed estate

Mantel (n)- shelf or projecting ledge above fireplace
Mantle (n)- cloak, cape, shawl, covering

Mara (n)- 1. Bibl. - bitter. 2. name Naomi claimed for herself
Marah (n)- Bibl. - first halting place of Israelites after passing Red Sea

Maratha (pr.n)- member of Hindu division in S.W. and central India
Mahratta (n)- Sanskritic language of West India

Marc (n)- residue of grapes after juice is extracted
Mark (v)- 1. stamp, imprint. 2. designate, signify. 3. regard, notice
Mark (pr.n)- evangelist - considered author of Second Gospel
Marque (n)- 1. seizure by way of reprisal. 2. token of pledge

M

Marcor (n)- obs. - a wasting away. Marasmus
Markhor (n)- species of wild goat inhabiting mountainous regions from Northern India to Afghanistan

Mare (n)- female horse, filly, foal, jenny
Mare (pr.n)- island in Northern California
Mayor (n)- principal officer of a municipality. City manager

Marian (adj)- pertaining to Virgin Mary
Marion (pr.n)- city in Ohio and Virginia

Mark- see Marc, Marque

Marks (n.pl)- letters, signs, traces, characteristics
Marx (pr.n)- Karl - German socialist, revolutionary, writer

Marli (n)- gauze used as a ground for embroidering lace, etc.
Marly (adj)- abounding with marl, fertilizer, manure

Marque - see Marc, Mark

Marquee (n)- rooflike shelter projecting over sidewalk or terrace
Marquis (pr.n)- French nobleman below a duke - above an Earl or Count

Marry (v)- wed, espouse, join together. Make one
Mary (pr.n)- female name. Bibl. - mother of Jesus
Merry (adj)- gay, joyous, blithe, full of cheer

Marshal (n)- military commander. Chief officer of arms
Marshall (pr.n)- George. Secretary of State 1947-1949 and Secretary of Defense 1950-51
Martial (adj)- armed, warlike, hostile

Marten (n)- fur bearing animal
Martin (n)- large bird of the swallow family
Martin (pr.n)- 1. first or last name. 2. (n)- obs - a dupe

Marter (n)- obs. - a trafficer. Receiver of stolen goods
Martyr (n)- one who sacrifices his life station, etc. for sake of a principle or to sustain a cause
Martyre (n)- Archaic - torture, havoc

Martial- see Marshal, Marshall

Martyr- see Marter

Marx (pr.n)- Karl- German socialist, writer, revolutionary
Marks (n.pl)- letters, signs, traces, characteristics

Mary- see Marry, Merry

Mashie (n)- golf club like the iron, with a shorter head
Mashy (adj)- produced by crushing or bruising

M

Masjid (n)- Mosque. Moslem place of worship
Musjid (n)- Mohammedan Temple

Mask (n)- covering for the face
Masque (n)- entertainment, revel, masquerade

Masqat (pr.n)- seaport in S.E. Arabia
Muscat (n)- sweet grape much used for making wine
Musket (n)- 1. gun. 2. kind of hawk

Massed (v)- heaped, piled, accumulated
Mast (n)- 1. spar, flagstaff. 2. vertical pole

Massif (n)- Geol. - principal mountain mass defined by valleys
Massive (adj)- bulky, weighty, heavy

Mat (n)- become entangled. Formed tangled masses
Matt (n)- without luster. Dim.
Matte (n)- unfinished metallic product of smelting

Maul (n)- 1. heavy wooden hammer, bat or club. 2. (v)- batter, beat
Mall (n)- promenade, shaded public walk, arcade
Moll (n)- 1. prostitute. 2. unmarried female companion of gangster or thief

Mayor (n)- principal officer of a municipality. City manager
Mare (n)- female horse, filly, foal, jenny
Mare (pr.n)- island in Northern California

Maze (n)- winding course, labyrinth, state of confusion
Maize (n)- corn, cereal plant, grain, Indian corn

Mead (n)- alcoholic liquor made by fermenting honey and water
Mead (pr.n)- lake in Nevada - near Hoover Dam
Mede (pr.n)- 1. native in Media. 2. ancient kingdom of Asia
Meed (n)- reward or recompense for service

Mealies (n)- So. Afr. - maize or Indian corn
Meles (n)- genus of old world badger

Mean (v)- 1. intend, design, aim at. 2. (adj)- stingy, miserly, penurious
Mien (n)- air, aspect, appearance, look, conduct

Meant (v)- p.p. of mean. Intended, aimed at
Ment (pr.n)- Egypt Myth. - Egyptian hawk - headed deity

Mear (n)- Scot.-a mare
Meer (n)- a boundary, landmark
Mere (adj)- 1. bare, plain, pure and simple. 2. (n)- pond, pool
Mir (n)- Russian community village
Mire (n)- Astron. - meridian mark

M

Measel (n)- contagious disease with eruptive red spot
Mesel (n)- obs. - leprosy, leper

Meat (n)- flesh of animals, nutriment. Food in general
Meet (v)- 1. confront, come face to face. 2. (adj)- fitting, proper
Mete (v)- apportion, allot, measure out, distribute

Meaux (pr.n)- town in France
Mho (n)- Elec. (anagram) a unit of conductivity being the reciprocal of the Ohm
Mo (n)- Japanese measure of weight
Mot (n)- 1. word, motto. 2. pithy or witty saying. 3. witticism
Mow (v)- to cut down grass or grain
Mowe (n)- Archaic - to make mouths or grimaces

Medal (n)- decoration, reward, citation, testimonial
Meddle (v)- interfere, pry, snoop

Meddler (n)- busy body, snooper, interferer
Medlar (n)- fruit tree

Mede- see Mead, Meed

Medlar- see Meddler

Meer- see Mear, Mire, Mere, Mir

Meet- see Meat, Mete

Meeting (n)- assemblage, encounter, convention, gathering
Meting (v)- alloting, dispensing, sharing, assigning

Meiler (n)- 1. mound of wood to be charred. 2. ore to be roasted. 3. coal to be coked
Miler (n)- racing - one trained to race a mile

Mel (n)- Latin - honey
Mell (n)- 1. Scot or Eng. - hammer or mallet. 2. (v)- strike or beat severely. 3. to hammer

Melee (n)- confused general hand to hand fight
Malay (adj)- pertaining to Malays, their country or language

Meles (n)- Zool. - genus of old world badger
Mealies (n-pl)- So. Afr. - maize or Indian corn

Ment (pr.n)- Egypt. myth. - Egyptian hawk - headed deity
Meant (v)- p.p. of mean. Intended, aimed at

Mercy (n)- leniency, compassion, pity, tolerance, pardon
Mersy (pr.n)- river in England

Mere- see Mear, Meer, Mire, Mir

112

M

Merk (n)- Scot. - former monetary unit
Murk, Mirk (adj)- darkness, gloom

Merkin (n)- 1. slang - obs. - the female pubes or false hair for it (wig). 2. cannon mop
Mirkin (v)- obs. - to make dusk, dim, gloomy
Murken (v)- obs. - to murmur

Merry- see Marry, Mary

Meros (n)- 1. anatomy - thigh. 2. Zool. - meropodite
Meroz (n)- Bibl. - refuge

Mersy- see Mercy

Mesel- see Measel

Metal (n)- ore. Gold, silver, lead, copper, etc.
Mettle (n)- pluck, stamina, spirit, grit, nerve

Mete (v)- apportion, allot, measure out. Distribute
Meet (v)- 1. confront, come face to face. 2. (adj)- fitting, proper
Meat (n)- flesh of animals, nutriment. Food in general

Meter (n)- 1. unit of length. 2. instrument that measures
Metre (n)- Brit. - poetic measure, verse

Meting (v)- alloting, dispensing, sharing, assigning
Meeting (n)- assemblage, gathering, convention, encounter

Metre- see Meter

Mettle- see Metal

Meuse (n)- 1. gap or hole in wall through which a wild animal is accustomed to pass. 2. a Muset
Mews (n)- 1. set of stables around a court. 2. (v)- to confine in pens, coops
Muse (v)- 1. reflect, meditate. 2. (n)- Goddess (myth)

Mew (v)- to confine in a pen or hutch
Mue (v)- to shed feathers, molt

Mewl (v)- purr, whine, cry, bawl
Mule (n)- 1. beast of burden. 2. hybrid between donkey and horse. 3. bedroom slipper

Mews- see Meuse, Muse

Mica (n)- group of minerals that separate into thin elastic laminae
Micah (pr.n)- Hebrew prophet

M

Mien (n)- 1. air, aspect, appearance. 2. look, conduct
Mean (v)- 1. intend, design, aim at. 2. (adj)- stingy, miserly, penurious

Might (n)- strength, vigor, power, energy
Mite (n)- 1. very small insect or creature. 2. very small object

Mighty (adj)- sturdy, strong, powerful, robust
Mity (n)- full of insects. Infested with mites

Mil (n)- unit of length
Mill (v)- 1. grind, pulverize. 2. jostle, push. 3. (n)- factory, foundry, plant

Milch (adj)- milk giving animal as a goat or cow
Milk (n)- white fluid secreted from female mammary glands

Miler (n)- one specially trained or qualified to go a mile
Meiler (n)- 1. mound of wood to be charred. 2. ore to be roasted. 3. coal to be coked

Millenary (adj)- aggregate of a thousand, thousand years
Millinery (n)- hats made and sold by milliners

Milk- see Milch

Mimer (n)- Norse legend - the Smith who reared Siegfried
Mimir (n)- Norse myth - giant who abode is a spring flowing from the roots of the world ash

Mina (n)- ancient Greek unit of weight
Myna (n)- various Asiatic birds of the starling family

Mince (v)- 1. chop fine, hash, dice. 2. simper, lisp, pose
Mints (n-pl)- 1. places where coins are made. 2. invents, creates. 3. aromatic plants

Mind (n)- 1. intellect, reason, intent. 2. object to. 3. notice. 4. obey
Mined (v)- excavated, tunneled. Dug in the earth

Miner (n)- 1. worker in the mines. 2. layer of military mines
Minor (n)- 1. under legal age. 2. inferior, subordinate, less

Minks (n-pl)- weasel like animal with valuable lustrous hair
Minx (n)- impudent, pert, flirtatious girl

Mino (n)- Japan - kind of cape or overcoat of straw or rushes worn by laborers
Minot (n)- old French dry measure

Minor- see Miner

Mints- see Mince

M

Minx- see Minks

Mire- see Mear, Mere, Meer, Mir

Mirabel (n)- libertine, gay rake
Mirabelle (n)- superior kind of European plum

Mirk, Murk - see Merk

Mirkin (v)- obs. - to make dark, dim, or gloomy
Merkin (n)- 1. obs. - slang - the female pubes or false hair for it (wig). 2. cannon mop.

Mirky (adj)- dark, obscure
Murky (n)- Music - composition for the harpsichord with a bass in broken octaves

Miscall (v)- call by wrong name, mis-name, mispronounce
Miskal (n)- Persian and Arabian measure of weight

Miser (n)- 1. person who hoards his money. 2. (adj) - covetous, miserly
Mizer (n)- well boring and mining - a boring tool

Misericord (n)- thin bladed medieval dagger
Misericorde (n)- compassion, mercy, pity

Mishmee (n)- bitter root of an Asiatic herb used in medicine as a tonic
Mishmi (pr.n)- India - primitive mongoloid hill tribe and their language

Misread (v)- 1. to misinterpret in reading. 2. (n)- one who reads wrong
Misrede (v)- obs. - to advise badly

Missal (n)- book of common prayer. Mass book, breviary
Missel (n)- large European thrush. Bird
Missile (n)- bullet, projectile, bomb, spear, harpoon

Missed (v)- 1. omitted, passed by, failed. 2. (n) - lost, blundered, erred
Mist (n)- 1. haze, fog, cloud, smog. 2. confusion, uncertainty

Missel- see Missal, Missile

Mist- see Missed

Mite (n)- 1. small insect, particle, piece. 2. very small amount
Might (n)- strength, power, vigor, energy

Miter (n)- a butting surface or bevel of joined pieces
Mitre (n)- headdress. Headband

Mity- see Mighty

M

Mixed (adj)- mingled, blended
Mixt (n)- obs. - a compound

Mizer- see Miser

Mo (n)- Japanese measure of weight
Mot (n)- 1. word, motto. 2. pithy or witty saying. 3. witticism
Mow (v)- to cut down grass or grain
Mowe (n)- Archaic - to make grimaces or mouths
Mho (n)- Elec. (anagram) unit of conductivity being the reciprocal of Ohm
Meaux (pr.n)- town in France

Moan (v)- mourn, lament, groan, weep for
Mon (pr.n)- dominant race of Pegu in Burma
Mown (adj)- cut as if mowed

Moaner (v)- groaner, complainer, bewailer
Moner (n)- Zool. - one of the monera (class of protoza)

Moar (n)- Irish Law - former parish officer who collected rents and fines for the lord
Mohr (n)- West African gazelle
More (n)- greater quantity, number or amount. Additional amount

Moat (n)- ditch, channel, deep trench
Mote (n)- particle, speck, spot. Scrap, fragment

Moco (n)- rock cavy. Brazilian rodent allied to the guinea pig
Moko (n)- Maori - kind of tattooing or a pattern of it

Mod (n)- Gael. - yearly meeting for literary and musical competitions of Highland Association of Scotland
Mode (n)- 1. fashion, vogue, style. 2. method, manner, process
Mowed (n)- 1. cut down grass, grain, etc. 2. cut down or killed in battle

Mohr- see Moar, More

Mold (n)- 1. fungi forming on vegetable or organic matter. 2. Anat - the top of the head
Mould (n)- loose earth rich in organic matter

Molder (n)- maker of molds for casting in a foundry, one who molds bricks
Moulder (n)- crumble away, waste away

Moll- see Mall, Maul

Mollie (n)- Naut. - social meeting of captains of icebound whaler ships on one of the ships
Molly (n)- 1. slang - effeminate man or boy. 2. large basket of fruit

M

Molt (v)- cast skin or feathers, slough
Moult (v)- Brit. - shed feathers in process of renewal

Mon- see Moan, Mown

Moner- see Moaner

Monion (n)- stump of amputated limb, the upper arm
Munnion (n)- 1. a mullion. 2. Arch. - upright member of a framing

Montjoy (n)- obs. - a pile, a heap as of stones or refuse
Montjoye (n)- 1. French battle cry. 2. "Montjoye St. Denis," apostle of the French

Moo (v)- utter characteristic cry of a cow. Low
Moue (n)- pouting, grimace
Mu (n)- 12th letter of the Greek alphabet

Mooch (v)- slang - skulk, sneak. Hang or rove about
Mouch (v)- get without paying, at another's expense

Mood (n)- temper, frame of mind, disposition
Mooed (v)- made a mooing sound. Lowed

Moodir (n)- Turkish governor of a city or district
Mudir (n)- governor of a province in Egypt

Moody (adj)- gloomy, sullen, capricious, subject to moods
Moudie (n)- Eng. and Scot. Dial. - a mole. Mole catcher

Moolah (n)- slang - money
Mullah (n)- learned teacher of the laws and dogmas of Islam

Moor (pr.n)- 1. No. African people of Arab and Berber ancestry. 2. (v) - make fast with lines, cables
Muir (n)- refuse of fruit after juice has been expressed
Mure (v)- 1. to inclose in walls. 2. to immure, to shut up

Moose (n)- large animal of the deer family
Mousse (n)- preparation of whipped cream, eggs, gelatine, sweetened

Moot(adj)- 1. open to question, disputed. 2. (v)- bring up for discussion. Debate
Mut (pr.n)- (Egypt.Mother) Egypt. Religion - consort of Amon-ra - the sun mother of Chonsu - the moon
Mute (v)- 1. deaden or muffle sound of. 2. (adj) utter no sound or word. Silent

Morat (n)- ancient drink of honey flavored with mulberries
Morate (adj)- obs. - mannered esp. of good manners or morals

M

More (n)- greater quantity, number or amount. Additional amount
Mohr (n)- West African gazelle
Moar (n)- Irish Law- former parish officer who collected fines and rents for the lord

Morel (n)- edible fungus considered superior to most mushrooms
Morelle (n)- 1. the black nightshade. 2. the morello cherry

Morgan (n)- breed of carriage and saddle horse
Morgan (pr.n)- 1. first or last name. 2. name applied to the ox-eye daisy
Morgen (n)- Dutch unit of measure

Morn (n)- daybreak, morning, dawn
Morne (n)- obs. - the head of a lance rebated for tilting
Mourn (v)- express sorrow or grief, bewail, bemoan
Mourne (v)- to be seized with a contagious disease, said of animals

Morning (n) - sun up, early part of the day, forenoon
Mourning (n)- outward tokens of sorrow as black garments

Morphea (n)- skin disease which leaves scarlike markings upon their disappearance
Morphia (n)- Morphine. Opiate to induce sleep and reduce pain

Mors (pr.n)- Roman relig. - death as a deity, identified with Greek Thanatos
Morse (n)- 1. metal clasp to fasten garments. 2. the walrus

Mosel (pr.n)- river flowing from France into the Rhine, Germany
Moselle (n)- light white wine

Mossi (n)- Black nation west of Central Sudan
Mossy (adj)- overgrown, covered or edged with moss

Mot (n)- brief strain of a bugle, horn
Motte (n)- small patch of woods in prairie land

Mote (n)- particle, spot, speck. Scrap, fragment
Moat (n)- ditch, channel, deep trench

Moter (n)- attachment to a cotton gin that removes motes from cotton
Motor (n)- 1. source of mechanical power. 2. convey, transport or drive a motor car

Moton (n)- old armor - plate protecting shoulder and arm
Motoun (n)- mutton. Sheep, ram

Mouch- see mooch

M

Moudie- see Moody

Moue- see Moo, Mu

Mould (n)- loose earth rich in organic matter
Mold (n)- 1. fungi forming on vegetable or organic matter. 2. Anat. - the top of the head

Moulder (n)- crumble away, waste away
Molder (n)- 1. maker of molds for casting in foundry. 2. one who molds bricks or makes dough into bread

Moult- see Molt

Montour (n)- altitude, elevation. Angle of elevation
Mounture (n)- a structure for mounting on

Mourn- see Morn, Morne, Mourne

Mourning (n)- outward tokens of sorrow as black garments
Morning (n)- forenoon, early part of day. Sun up

Mousse (n)- preparation of whipped cream, eggs, sugar, gelatin
Moose (n)- large animal of deer family

Mow- see Mo, Mowe, Mót, Mho, Meaux

Mowed (n)- 1. cut down grass, grain, etc. 2. cut down or killed in battle
Mode (n)- 1. fashion, vogue, style. 2. method, manner, process
Mod (n)- Gael.-yearly meeting for literary and musical competitions of Highland Assoc. of Scotland

Mown (adj)- cut as if mowed
Mon (pr.n)- dominant race of Pegu in Burma
Moan (v)- mourn, lament, groan, weep for

Mu- see Moo, Moue

Mucic (adj)- pertaining to a dibasic acid
Music (n)- melody or harmony generally

Mucous (adj)- slimy. Like mucus
Mucus (n)- secretion of mucous membranes

Much (n)- great quantity, great deal
Mutch (n)- 1. Scot. and Eng. - woman's or childs cap. 2. man's head covering

Mud (n)- slimy or pasty mixture of earth and water
Mudd (n)- Tangier measure of weight

Mudde (n)- Netherlands measure of weight
Muddy (v)- to soil with mud, to dirty, render turbid

M

Mudir- see Moodir

Mue- see Mew

Mug (v)- 1. drinking cup with handle and no lip. 2. slang - human face
Mugg (v)- 1. waylay or assault from behind. 2. Scot. - breed of teeswater sheep

Muggar (n)- East Indian crocodile
Mugger (n)- one who beats and robs a person from behind. A thug

Muir- see Moor, Mure

Mule (n)- 1. beast of burden. 2. hybrid between horse and donkey. 3. bedroom slipper
Mewl (v)- purr, whine, cry, bawl

Mullah (n)- learned teacher of the laws and dogmas of Islam
Moolah (n)- slang - money

Mullar (n)- die for stamping an ornament in relief as upon metal
Muller (n)- a vessel in which wine, etc. is mulled over a fire

Mullein (n)- plant. Tall herbs having coarse leaves
Mullen (v)- obs. - pulverize, bruise

Mum (adj)- silent, not speaking
Mumm (v)- go merry making and acting in disguise. To mask

Munnion (n)- a mullion. Arch. - upright member of a framing
Monion (n)- 1. stump of an amputated limb. 2. the upper arm

Mur (n)- Eng. Dial. - a dormouse
Murr (n)- obs. - a catarrh. A cold with hoarseness
Murre (n)- diving bird. Razor-billed auk
Myrrh (n)- spiny shrub used for incense, perfume

Mure- see Moor, Muir

Murk, Mirk (adj)- darkness, gloom
Merk (n)- Scot. - former monetary unit

Murken- see Merkin, Mirkin

Murky- see Mirky

Mus (pr.n)- Zool. - genus of rodents. Mice, rats
Muss (n)- a state of disorder. (v) - make untidy, disarrange

Muscarin (n)- violet oxazine dyestuff which with tannin dyes cotton blue
Muscarine (n)- crystalline alkaloid - tasteless, odorless, very poisonous

M

Muscat (n)- sweet grape much used for making wine
Musket (n)- 1. gun. 2. kind of a hawk
Musqat (pr.n)- seaport in S.E. Arabia

Muscle (n)- 1. muscular strength, brawn. 2. animal flesh
Mussel (n)- member of fresh water clam family. Shell fish

Muse (v)- 1. reflect, meditate. 2. (n) - myth - goddess
Mews (n)- 1. set of stables around a court. 2. (v) - confines in cages, coops
Meuse (n)- hole in wall through which a wild animal is accustomed to pass. A muset

Musjid (n)- Mohammedan temple
Masjid (n)- mosque. Moslem place of worship

Musket- see Muscat

Mussel- see Muscle

Mustard (n)- 1. a plant. 2. pungent powder or paste seasoning from plant
Mustered (v)- gathered together. Assembled

Mute- see Moot

Mutch (n)- 1. Scot. and Eng. Dial. - woman or childs cap. 2. man's head covering
Much (n)- great quantity, great deal

Myna (n)- various Asiatic birds of starling family
Mina (n)- ancient Greek unit of weight

Myrrh- see Mur, Murr, Murre

N

—N—

Nab (v)- seize, capture, grab, snare
Knab (v)- to nab

Nabble (v)- obs. - gnaw, nibble
Knabble (v)- Eng. Dial. - bite gently

Nacker (n)- buyer of useless horses for slaughter
Knacker (n)- buyer of old houses, ships for materials

Nacre (n)- mother of pearl
Naker (n)- kettle drum

Nae (adj)- no, not
Nay (adv)- refusal, denial
Nee (adj)- 1. born. 2. used to introduce maiden name of married women
Neigh (v)- whinny. Cry of a horse

Nag (n)- 1. old horse, equine. 2. (v) - torment, tease, pester
Knag (n)- prong of deer's horns

Nagged (v)- tormented, complained, irritated, pestered
Knagged (adj)- knotted

Naker- see Nacre

Nap (n)- 1. rest, sleep. repose. 2. surface of cloth
Nappe (n)- whole or continuous part of a conic surface
Knap (n)- summit, hill, elevation, height

Nape (n)- back part of the neck
Knape (n)- 1. Eng. Dial. - a boy, a young man. 2. obs. - a knave

Napery (n)- household linen, esp. table linen
Knappery (n)- a place where chipping or knapping, as of flint is carried on

Nard (n)- 1. ointment made partly from nard. 2. spikenard
Knarred (adj)- gnarled, knotty

Nare (n)- a nostril
Ne'er- contraction of never

Nark (n)- Eng. - informer, stool pigeon. Spy employed by police
Knark (n)- Eng. slang - a hard hearted man

Narr (v)- Eng. Dial. - to growl or snarl as a dog
Knar (n)- rough rock or stone

Nash (adj)- Eng. Dial. - hard, stiff, firm
Gnash (v)- grind teeth together

N

Nat (n) - Burmese native Demon or Devil
Gnat (n) - small biting insect

Naught (n) - worthless, useless. Regard as of no importance
Naut (n) - Australia - sea mile used as a measure for submarine cables
Nought (n) - cipher, zero, nothing

Naut- see Naught

Naval (adj) - pertaining to ships, belonging to a navy
Navel (n) - depression in middle of belly. Umbilicus

Nave (n) - hub, center, central part
Knave (n) - rascal, scoundrel, bad man, cheat

Navel- see Naval

Navvy (n) - Brit. laborer employed in making canals and railroads
Navy (n) - body of warships. Fleet of ships

Nay- see Nae, Nee, Neigh

Neal (v) - temper by heat
Neele (n) - darnel. A weedy grass
Neil (n) - 1. Gael. and Irish - champion, chief. 2. (pr.n) - Masc. name
Kneel (v) - bow, bend the knee, genuflect, curtsy

Neap (adj) - 1. designating tides. 2. pole or tongue of a wagon
Neep (n) - Scot. and Brit. turnip

Near (adv) - 1. at, within, almost. 2. (adj) - closely related, intimate. 3. stingy
Neer (n) - Scot. - a kidney

Neck (n) - portion of the body between head and shoulders
Nek (n) - South African - a saddle or neck between two hills

Need (v) - require, want, crave, lack, have use for
Kneed (v) - having knees
Knead (v) - 1. mix, stir, work into shape. 2. rub down

Neep- see Neap

Neer- see Near

Neeze (v) - to sneeze
Knees (n-pl) - having knees

Ne'er- contraction of never
Nare (n) - a nostril

Neigh- see Nae, Nee, Nay

N

Neil- see Neal, Kneel

Nek- see Neck

Nell (pr.n)- female name
Knell (v)- death bell, peal, toll, funeral bell

Nellie (pr.n)- Fem. name, dim. of Ellen, Helen or Eleanor
Nelly (n)- the sooty albatross. The giant fulmar (sea bird)

Neuss (pr.n)- suburb of Dusseldorf, West Prussia
Noise (n)- clamor, din, racket, hubbub

New (adj)- recent, modern, fresh, untried
Nu (n)- 1. 13th letter of Greek alphabet. 2. Abbrev. for "name unknown"
Gnu (n)- African antelope
Knew (v) -understood, past tense of know

News (n)- message, tidings, dispatch, report
Nous (n)- 1. the highest intellect. 2. the reason. 3. mental quickness
Gnus (n-pl)- plural of gnu, African antelope

Nice (adj)- tasteful, proper, fine, cultivated, kind
Gneiss (n)- rock rich in feldspar and granite

Niche (n)- 1. a hollow or recess. 2. (v) - to cuddle, settle or nestle down in a niche
Nitch (v)- to connect, to join together
Knitch (n)- obs. - a bundle, a burden

Nicker (n)- 1. a water sprite. 2. obs. - a Devil. 3. (v) - to neigh
Knicker (n)- small ball of clay, baked hard and oiled, used as a marble

Nicks (n-pl)- cuts, dents, scars, mars
Nix (n)- slang - nothing, no one
Nyx (pr.n)- Goddess - Greek myth

Nide (n)- nest or brood of pheasants
Gnide (v)- rub. Break in pieces

Nigh (adj)- 1. nearly, almost. 2. short or direct
Nye (n)- Eng. Dial. - of pheasants, a brood

Nimb (n)- Archaic - a nimbus or halo
Nym (pr.n)- a rogue and follower of Falstaff in Shakespeare's plays

Night (n)- darkness, bedtime, nighttime, dark
Knight (n)- soldier, horseman, brave, defender

Nil (n)- nothing, no part, none
Nill (v)- to be unwilling

N

Nipah (n)- Malay - drink made from juice of East Indian palm
Nypa (n)- bot. - genus of tropical Asiatic palms

Nit (n)- egg of a louse. Young insect
Knit (v)- twist, weave, stitch, interweave

Nitch - see Niche, Knitch

Niter (n)- salt peter, nitrate of potassium
Nitre (n)- sodium carbonate - natron

Nix (n)- slang - nothing, no one
Nyx (pr.n)- Greek myth - Goddess
Nicks (n-pl)- cuts, dents, scars, mars

No (adj)- 1. none, not any. 2. (v)- deny, contradict, oppose
Noh (n)- Japanese drama and ancient religious dance
Know (v)- recognize, realize, see, notice

Nob (n)- 1. head, pate, cranium. 2. (n)- personage, celebrity
Knob (n)- handle, grip, hold, hump

Nobel (pr.n)- Alfred. Swedish inventor of dynamite. Established Nobel prize
Noble (adj)- 1. great, goodly, grand. 2. (n) - personage, nobility

Nock (v)- set an arrow into the bowstring
Knock (n)- 1. rap, clap, blow, slap. 2. blame, criticism

Noel (n)- Christmas
Nowel (n)- Archaic - Christmas carol

Noes (n-pl)- negative votes. Denials, disapprovals
Nose (n)- 1. organ of smell. 2. prow, bow. 3. beak, stem
Knows (v)- is aware of. Understands

Nog (n)- wooden peg or block built into the wall as a hold for nails
Nogg (n)- Eng. Dial. - strong ale formerly brewed in Norfolk

Noggen (adj)- Eng. - hempen, clumsy, rough
Noggin (n)- 1. small mug or cup. 2. small quantity of drink

Noise (n)- sound, clangor, ado, roar
Neuss (pr.n)- suburb of Dusseldorf, West Prussia

Noll (n)- the head, pate
Knoll (n)- hillock, mound, bulge

Nome (n)- 1. deal out. 2. akin to
Nome (pr.n)- 1. seaport city in Alaska. 2. province in ancient Greece
Gnome (n)- troll, goblin, diminutive being

N

Nominee (n)- person named or designated by others, for any office, position or duty
Nominy (n)- Eng. Dial. - a riming doggerel, a wordy tale, a rigmarole

Nonet (n)- music - composition for nine instruments
Nonett (n)- obs. - titmouse
Nonette (pr.n)- little nun

None (pro)- not one, not any. No one
Nun (n)- religious woman, female devotee, sister. Bride of Christ

Noon (n)- middle of the day. Mid day. Twelve o'clock in the daytime
Nun (n)- 14th letter of Hebrew alphabet. Numerical value is 50

Noop (n)- Scot. - a rounded prominence of the elbow
Noup (n)- Scot. - a high, steep promotory

Noot (contraction)- obs. - to know not
Nut (pr.n)- Egypt. Myth. - Goddess whose winged image was painted on outside of coffins

Nose- see Noes, Knows

Not (adj)- know not, word of refusal
Nott (v)- to shear
Knot (n)- 1. web, interlacement, plait. 2. wading bird

Nought- see Naught, Naut

Noup- see Noop

Nous- see News, Gnus

Now (n)- present time or moment. Immediately, at once
Knowe (n)- Scot. - a mound. Hillock

Nowel- see Noel

Nox (pr.n)- Roman myth - Goddess of the night
Knocks (n-pl)- raps, claps, slaps. Criticizes, blames
Knox (pr.n)- 1. Henry. First secretary of War 1789-1800. 2. Fort in Ill. where U.S. gold is stored

Nu- see New, Knew, Gnu

Nub (n)- 1. point or gist of a story. 2. (v)- Eng. - nudge or push gently
Knub (n)- lump or protuberance. A swelling

Nud (v)- Eng. Dial. - move or butt with head as suckling calf
Nude (adj)- bare, unclothed, naked

N

Nuke (n)- obs. - the spinal cord
Nuque (n)- back of the neck, nape

Nun (n)- religious woman, female devotee, sister. Bride of Christ
None (pro)- not one, not any. No one.

Nun (n)- 14th letter of Hebrew alphabet. Numerical value is 50
Noon (n)- middle of the day, mid day. Twelve o'clock daytime

Nuque- see Nuke

Nut- see Noot

Nut (n)- hard shelled dry fruit or seed
Nutte (v)- obs. - to make use of. To enjoy

Nye (n)- Eng. Dial. - of pheasants, a brood
Nigh (adv)- closely, nearly, almost. Imminent, future

Nym (pr.n)- rogue, follower of flagstaff, in Shakespeare's plays
Nimb (n)- Archaic - a nimbus or halo

Nypa (n)- Bot. - genus of tropical Asiatic palms
Nipa (n)- Malay - drink made from juice of East Indian palm

Nyx- see Nicks, Nix

O

—O—

Oak (n)- hardwood tree bearing acorns as fruit
Oke (n)- unit of weight in Turkey

Oam (n)- Scot. - steam, warm air
Ohm (n)- unit of electrical resistance
Om (n)- mystical word used in Hindu worship

Oar (n)- 1. paddle, scull, pole. 2. (v) - row, propel, steer
Or (conj) 1. alternative, otherwise, else. 2. (n) - Heraldry - yellow or gold color
Ore (n)- metal bearing mineral or rocks
O'er- contraction of over

Oared (adj)- furnished with or propelled by oars
Ord (pr.n)- military fort in California
Ord (n)- a point or a weapon with a point

Ob (n)- obs. - a sorcerer. Hebrew - a necromancer (magician)
Ob (pr.n)- gulf in West Siberia
Obe (n)- ancient Laconia, a subdivision of a clan
Aube (pr.n)- river in France

Obe (n)- 1. sorcery practiced in West Indies. 2. charm or fetish
Obi (n)- silken sash worn by Japanese women

Oblat (n)- obs. - disabled soldier quartered in a monastary
Oblate (v)- 1. to offer, bring forward. 2. (n) - geom. - spheroid, ellipsoid

Oca (n)- South American wood sorrel
Oka (n)- Bulgarian liquid measure

Ocher (n)- natural earths from yellow to orange and red
Ochre (adj)- dye or tinge with other pigments

Od (n)- hypothetical force
Ode (n)- song, lyric, poem
Owed (v)- be indebted, under obligation
Aude (pr.n)- south coast of France

Odds (n)- not even, advantage or disadvantage, variation, difference
Ods (inter)- God - used in oaths

Oder (pr.n)- river in Germany
Odor (n)- bouquet, smell, scent, aroma, stink

Ods- see Odds

O

Oe (n)- atmospheric disturbance
Oh (inter)- expression of surprise or pain
Eau (n)- perfume, cologne. (French) - water
Owe (v)- bound in gratitude, be indebted, be obligated

O'er- see Oar, Ore, Or

Off (adj)- away, apart, removed, distant
Offe (n)- obs. - crumb, bite, morsel

Offal (n)- rubbish, waste, dung, sewage
Awful (adj)- bad, unpleasant, gruesome, shocking

Ohm (n)- unit of electrical resistance
Om (n)- mystical word used in Hindu worship
Oam (n)- Scot. - steam, warm air

Oka (n)- Bulgarian liquid measure
Oca (pr.n)- South American wood sorrel

Oke (n)- unit of weight in Turkey
Oak (n)- hardwood tree bearing acorns as fruit

Okie (n)- slang - migrant worker from Oklahoma - one who lost his land or was forced to move
Oki (n)- Iroquoian term equivalent to the Algonquian "manito" (powers or spirits)

Oleo (n)- cooking and table fat. Oleomargarine
Olio (n)- mixture, medley, potpourri, miscellany

Om- see Ohm, Oam

Omar (pr.n)- Arabian caliph
Omer (n)- Hebrew measure

One (n)- single person or thing, someone, unit, something
Won (v)- gained, succeeded, prevailed

Onerary (adj)- carrying of burdens
Honorary (adj)- given for honors only

Ooze (n)- soft mud or slime, marsh or bog, exude
Ouse (pr.n)- river in England

Or- see Oar, Ore, O'er

Oracle (n)- prophet, seer, fortune teller
Auricle (n)- lobe, outer portion of ear

Oral (adj)- verbal, spoken, uttered by mouth
Orel (pr.n)- city in Central Soviet Union
Aural (adj)- perceived by organs of hearing

Ord- see Oared

O

Ordennance (n)- arrangement of parts in pictures and bldgs.
Ordinance (n)- rule, law, decree, statute, edict
Ordnance (n)- military supplies, arms, guns, artillery

Order (n)- 1. society, brotherhood, club. 2. (v) - regulate, arrange, bid
Ordure (n)- filth, dung, excrement

Orf (n)- Scot. - obs. - cattle
Orphe (n)- sea fish. Domesticated variety of the id fish

Orfray (n)- obs. - the osprey
Orphrey (n)- elaborate embroidery, esp. of gold

Oriel (n)- bay window
Oriole (n)- bird of Passerine family
Aureole (n)- nimbus, halo, ring of life

Orphe- see Orf

Orphrey- see Orfray

Oscin (n)- chemical - scopoline. A crystalline tertiary base
Oscine (n)- Zool. - one of the oscines (passerine birds)

Osiris (pr.n)- Egypt. Relig. - great God of the underworld & judge of the dead
Osyris (n)- Bot. - shrub with stiff, fleshy leaves, small flowers, fruit

Ought (v)- must, shall, should
Aught (n)- 1. any part, anything. 2. cipher, zero, 0

Our (pro)- belonging to us
Hour (n)- 60 minutes. Unit of time, Interval

Ouse- see Ooze

Outby (adv)- Scot. Outdoors. At a short distance
Outbye (n)- mining - toward the shaft or entry

Outcoat (n)- obs. - overcoat
Outcote (v)- Archaic - surpass

Outcast (n)- an exile. One who has been cast out or expelled
Outcaste (n)- India - one who has been denied all ordinary social rights

Outray (v)- Eng. Dial. - to vanquish, overcome
Outre (adj)- exaggerate. Extravagant. Bizarre

Owe (v)- bound in gratitude. Be indebted
Oh (inter)- expression of surprise or pain
Oe (n)- atmospheric disturbance
Eau (n)- perfume, cologne. (French) - water

O

Owed (v)- under obligation. Indebted
Ode (n)- lyric, poem
Od (n)- hypothetical force

Oxstar (n)- Scot. - an arm or the arms
Oxster (n)- the armpit

P

—P—

Pa (n)- Colloq. of papa
Pah (inter)- exclamation of disgust
Pas (n)- movement in dancing esp. in ballet

Pac (n)- 1. moccasin. 2. heavy boot worn by loggers
Pack (n)- 1. group, bunch, quantity, number. 2. deck of cards
Paque (n)- Archaic - Passover or Easter

Paced (v)- strode, counted or measured by paces
Paste (n)- glue, adhesive, gum, mastic

Pacha (n)- high civil or military official
Pasha (n)- title of rank or honor placed after a name

Pack- see Pac, Paque

Packed (v)- tied up, wrapped, done up, stuffed
Packt (pr.n)- Egypt. Myth. - Goddess
Pact (n)- treaty, contract, agreement, deed

Packs - 1. crams, binds, parcel, package. 2. crowds, throngs
Pax (pr.n)- Roman myth. Goddess of Peace

Pact- see Packed

Paean (n)- praise, hymn of joy, jubilation, hosanna
Paeon (n)- foot of 4 syllables - one long, 3 short
Peon (n)- 1. day laborer. 2. India foot soldier

Pagle (n)- Brit. Dial. - primrose plant
Paigle or Pagil (n)- Botanical - cowslip

Pah- see Pa

Pail (n)- bucket, tub, container, receptacle
Pale - 1. blanch, fade, whiten. 2. region, area. 3. enclosure, fence

Paillasse (n)- mattress of straw
Pallaise (n)- Brit. - excelsior or moss

Pain (n)- suffering, hurt, ache, twinge, discomfort
Pane (n)- window glass, glass panel, light
Peine (n)- severe and hard punishment

Pained (adj)- tortured, ached, twinged
Paned (adj)- having panes

Pair (n)- brace, team, couple, duo
Pare (v)- peel, skin, shell, strip
Pear (n)- edible fruit

Pairing (v)- act of making a pair
Paring (v)- act of cutting off rind or skin

132

P

Pais (n)- Law- The people from among whom a jury is taken
Pay (n)- 1. salary, wages, fee. 2. (v)- refund, redeem. 3. be punished, suffer
Pei (pr.n)- river in China

Palace (n)- official residence of sovereigns or exalted personages
Pallas (pr.n)- name of Athena

Palate (n)- 1. roof of the mouth. 2. taste, savor, appetite
Palette (n)- oblong tablet used by painters to mix colors
Pallet (n)- cot, couch, bed, bunk, berth
Pallette (n)- armor - small armpit plate

Palay (n)- Tagalog, p.1. - rice in the husk
Palli (pr.n)- India - member of Low Sudra caste

Pale- see Pail

Pall (n)- 1. shroud, grave clothes. 2. cloy, satiate, glut
Paul (pr.n)- 1. Saint, Christian Missionary. 2. Man's name
Pawl (n)- ratchet, lever, catch, clasp

Palli- see Palay

Palliasse- see Paillasse

Pallas- see Palace

Pallet- see Palate, Pallette, Palette

Palm (n)- 1. inner surface of hand. 2. subtropical tree of plant
Paum (v)- obs. - conceal in palm of hand, as cheating in cards

Palped (adj)- 1. Zoology - jointed feeler attached to mouth of insects. 2. palate
Palpt (n)- soft palm of the hand

Pamper (v)- caress, coddle, indulge, spoil
Pampre (n)- decorative ornament of grape leaves around a column

Pan (n)- 1. pot, container, cooking vessel. 2. search for gold
Pan (pr.n)- Gr. Myth. - God of flocks and shepherds
Panne (n)- soft velvet with flattened pile

Panade (n)- 1. bread crumbs boiled in liquid and flavored. 2. large knife or dagger
Pannade (n)- Archaic - the curvet of a horse

Panary (adj)- pertaining to bread
Pannary (n)- obs. - place where bread is stored

P

Pandar (n)- person who provides means to help ambitions of another
Pander (n)- procurer, pimp, go between in sexual intrigue

Pane (n)- window glass, glass panel, light
Pain (n)- suffering, hurt, ache, twinge, discomfort
Peine (n)- severe and hard punishment

Paned (adj)- having panes
Pained (adj)- tortured, ached, twinged

Panel (n)- 1. jury, docket, roster. 2. section of a wall
Pannel (n)- 1. rustic saddle. 2. stomach of a hawk

Panical (adj)- panic - sudden fear
Panicle (n)- tuft on plants
Pannicle (n)- obs. - brain pan or skull

Pannade (n)- Archaic - the curvet of a horse
Panade (n)- 1. bread crumbs boiled in liquid and flavored. 2. large knife or dagger

Pannam (n)- obs. - bread
Pannum (n)- dried rootstock of various ferns of the genus dryopertis

Panne- see Pan

Pannicle- see Panical, Panicle

Pantalets (n-pl)- long drawers with frills at bottom of each leg
Pantalettes (n-pl)- separate frills to attach to legs of women's drawers

Pantaloon (pr.n)- name of character in Italian comedy
Pantalon (n)- trousers and hose in one garment

Pappous (adj)- Botany - downy, bristly, as in dandelion and thistle
Pappus (n)- Greek - Old man or grandfather

Paque (n)- Archaic (also prounounced pasch). Passover or Easter
Pack (n)- 1. group, bunch, quantity, number. 2. deck of cards
Pac (n)- 1. moccasin. 2. heavy boot worn by loggers

Par (adj)- equal, draw, tie, equivalent, even terms
Parr (n)- young of the salmon and codfish
Parr (pr.n)- Catherine. Sixth wife of Henry VIII

Para (n)- 1. Hindu - hog deer. 2. New Zealand - scabbard fish
Parah (n)- East Indian measure of weight
Parra (n)- 1. Zool. - Jacana. 2. West Indian timber tree

P

Parc (n)- den, enclosure, fold
Park (n)- tract of land set aside for recreation, gardens, sports

Parca (pr.n)- Roman Relig. - a birth goddess
Parka (n)- outer garment made of skins of mammals or birds. Worn by eskimos, etc.

Parcae (n-pl)- Roman Myth. The fates
Parsee (pr.n)- Zoroastrian. Sect in India
Parsi (pr.n)- descendants of Persians who settled in India

Pardi (adv)- Archaic - once a fashionable form of profanity
Pardy (inter)- indeed, verily. By God

Pare- see Pair, Pear

Pareil (n)- obs. - equality. An equal. A mate
Parel (n)- 1. mantel piece. 2. a preparation containing eggs used to refine wine
Parral (n)- obs. - variant of apparel
Parrel (n)- Naut. - rope loop or sliding collar. Jackstay

Paring (n)- act of cutting off rind or skin
Pairing (n)- act of making a pair

Park- see Parc

Parka- see Parca

Parl (v)- speak, talk, converse
Parle (n)- discussion, parley

Parlay (v)- bet original wager plus winnings on another race or contest
Parley (n)- discussion, conference, talk

Parlor (n)- living room, front room, sitting room
Parlour (n)- British - drawing room, reception room

Parnel (n)- 1. Archaic - a priest's mistress or concubine. 2. a wanton woman, harlot
Parnell (pr.n)- 1. Charles. Advocate of home rule for Ireland. 2. suburb of Auckland, New Zealand

Parol (adj)- verbal, spoken, vocal, not written
Parole (n)- promise, word of honor pledge

Parolee (n)- person released from prison on parole
Paroli (n)- Fr. - Double stakes. In faro - a doubled bet

Parr- see Par

Parra- see Para

Parral- see Pareil, Parrel, Parel

P

Parrock (n)- small field or enclosure
Pearoc (n)- Prov. Scotch - paddock or croft

Parrs (n-pl)- young salmon or codfish
Parse (v)- to describe words grammatically

Parry (v)- dodge, shun, avoid, fence, elude, report, evade
Peri (n)- Myth - fairy or elf
Perry (n)- fermented drink made from pears

Partable (adj)- separable, as an estate or inheritance
Partible (adj)- that which may be divided or parted

Parter (n)- one who parts or separates
Parterre (n)- ground floor, parquet circle, orchestra circle

Parti (n)- person considered a matrimonial match
Party (n)- company, assembly, meeting of friends

Partible (adj)- that which may be divided or parted
Partable (adj)- separable, as an estate or inheritance

Partisan (n)- supporter, adherent, sympathizer
Partizan (n)- member of irregular troop

Parvolin (n)- small volatility
Parvoline (n)-Chem.-organic base of oily nature

Pas (n)- movement in dancing esp. in ballet
Pah (inter)- exclamation of disgust
Pa (n)- Colloq. of papa

Pasch (n)- Heb. Archaic - also spelled pask - Passover
Paque (n)- Fr. Archaic - Easter

Pasha (n)- title or rank or honor placed after a name
Pacha (n)- high civil or military officer

Passable (adj)- moderate, fair, presentable
Passible (adj)- capable of feeling or suffering

Passed (v)- passed in examination or contest, gone by
Past (adj)- 1. retired, extinct. 2. (n) - previous time, history

Paste (n)- glue, adhesive, gum, mastic
Paced (v)- strode, counted or measured, by paces

Pastil (n)- Fr. - pellet of aromatic paste for burning as a deodorant
Pastille (n)- flavored or medicated lozenge

Pastoral (adj)- rural or rustic life among shepherds
Pastorale (n)- musical composition suggesting rural theme

P

Pat (n)- 1. light tap. 2. (v) - strike gently with fingers or hand. 3. (adj) - unyielding
Patt (n)- being even, neither winning or losing. Stalemate

Pate (n)- meat or fish pie or patty
Patee or Patte (n)- Her. - a cross having arms narrow at the center

Paten (n)- plate used for bread in eucharist
Patten (n)- footwear, shoe with wooden sole
Patton (pr.n)- George Smith. U.S. General

Patena (n)- grassy area in hills in Ceylon
Patina (n)- fine crust or film on copper or bronze

Patience (n)- calm, fortitude, composure, quiet
Patients (n)- invalids, sick persons under medical or surgical care

Patrol (n)- 1. group of 8 Boy Scouts. 2. subdivision of troop
Patrole (n)- group of ships, planes used in garnering enemy information

Patt- see Pat

Patti (pr.n)- Adelina. Opera singer
Patty (n)- little pie, thin round piece

Pau (pr.n)- town in S.W. France
Po (pr.n)- river in No. Italy
Poe (pr.n)- Edgar Allan. Poet and writer
Pow (n)- Scot. and Eng. - the head, the poll

Pauk (n)- obs. - Eng. - a small lobster
Pawk (n)- Scot. - impertinent person

Paul- see Pall, Pawl

Paum- see Palm

Pause (n)- temporary stop, lull, suspension, respite
Paws (n)- feet of animals with nails and claws

Pavais (n)- medieval shield covering whole body
Pave (n)- Fr.- setting gems so closely together no metal shows

Pavan (n)- stately dance in 16th century
Paven or Pavin (n)- Italian paduan dance

Paver (n)- one who lays pavements
Pavier (n)- a rammer used in laying pavements

Pavese (n)- Ital. - shield used in medieval warfare
Pavis (n)- a companion archer

P

Pavilion (n)- 1. external ear. 2. flag, colors, ensign or a banner
Pavillion (v)- to furnish or cover with tents

Pawk- see Pawk

Pawl- see Pall, Paul

Paws- see Pause

Pax (pr.n)- Roman myth. Goddess of peace
Packs (v)- 1. crams, binds. 2. parcels, packages. 3. crowds, throngs

Pay (n)- 1. salary, wages, fee. 2. (v) - refund, redeem. 3. suffer, be punished
Pais (n)- Law- the people from among whom a jury is taken
Pe (n)- 1. 17th letter of Hebrew alphabet. Numerical value is 80. 2. Brazilian or Portugal measure of weight
Pei (pr.n)- river in China

Pe - see Pay

Pea (n)- small round vegetable
Pee (v)- 1. to look at with one eye. 2. (n) - tip of the fluke of an anchor. 3. slang - urinate

Peace (n)- 1. freedom from commotion or war. 2. quiet, tranquility
Pece (n)- obs. - a wine cup or other drinking vessel
Pees (n)- roe of a fish
Piece (n)- 1. fragment, portion, part. 2. (v) - patch, repair, mend, unite

Peachy (adj)- resembling a peach, esp. in looks and color
Peechi (n)- Burchell's zebra

Peak (n)- 1. point, spire, cone, steeple, crest. 2. (v) - tip, bulge, rise above
Peek (n)- peep, glimpse, glance.
Peke (pr.n)- slang - dim. for Pekingese Chinese dog
Pique (n)- 1. grudge, offense, resentment. 2. (v) - arouse, excite, incite

Peaker (n)- logging - the top log of a load
Peeker (n)- 1. a flat chisel used by Cornish miners. 2. looker

Peal (v)- ring, resound, echo, blow, bugle
Peel (v)- pare, strip off skin, bark or rind

Pealer (n)- Archaic - an appealer
Peeler (n)- 1. one that peels or strips. 2. slang - a stripper

Pealing (v)- tolling, roaring, resounding
Peeling (v)- shedding, flaking, scaling, molting

P

Pean (n)- Her. - one of the furs, the ground being sable and the spots and tufts
Peen (n)- hammer

Pear (n)- edible fruit
Pare (v)- peel, skin, shell, strip
Pair (n)- brace, team, couple, duo

Pearl (n)- something precious or choice. Treasure, gem
Pirl (v)- 1. Eng. Dial. - to spin as a top. 2. twist or twine as hair in making fishlines
Purl (v)- 1. flow with murmuring sound, ripple, whirl. 2. knitting stitch

Pearled (adj)- set with pearls or nacre. Formed into pearls
Purled (v)- decorated with a border, fringe or embroidery

Pearoc (n)- Scot. - paddock or croft
Parrock (n)- small field or enclosure

Peart (adj)- Eng. Dial. - brisk, lively, quick, nimble
Pert (adj)- saucy, bold, impertinent, brash

Pease (n)- plural of pea - vegetables
Peise (n)- obs. - measure of weight. A weight in a clock

Peat (n)- dried block of turf used as a fuel
Pete (pr.n)- 1. masculine name - dim. of Peter. 2. slang - a safe (underworld usage)

Pece- see Peace, Pees, Piece

Pech (n)- Scot. and Eng. Dial. - heavy sigh, pant, heavy breath
Peck (n)- 1. dry measure. 2. (v)- strike with a beak. 3. slang - eat nibblingly

Pedal (n)- lever worked by foot, treadle
Peddle (v)- sell, market, retail, dispense

Peddar (n)- Scot. - hawker. Retail street dealer
Pedder (n)- Brit. - peddler

Peddlery (n)- trade or goods of a peddler
Pedlary (n)- obs. - trifling, trickery

Pee (v)- 1. obs. - to look at with one eye. 2. (n) - tip of fluke of an anchor. 3. slang - urinate
Pea (n)- small round vegetable

Peechi- see Peachy

Peek- see Peak, Pique, Peke

P

Peeker (n)- a flat chisel used by Cornish miners
Peaker (n)- the top log of a load

Peel (v)- pare, strip off skin, bark or rind
Peal (v)- ring, resound, echo, bugle

Peele (n)- the reebok - a South African antelope
Pele (pr.n)- Hawaiian Goddess supposed to inhabit the crater of Kilavea
Pelee (n)- volcano on island of Martinique

Peeler (n)- 1. one that peels or strips. 2. slang - a stripper
Pealer (n)- obs. - an appealer

Peeling (v)- shedding, flaking, scaling, molting
Pealing (v)- tolling, roaring, resounding

Peen (n)- hammer
Pean (n)- Her. - one of the furs, the ground being sable and the spots and tufts

Peeps (n)- 1. chirps, cheeps, tweets, 2. (v) - peers, peeks
Pepys (pr.n)- Samuel. English diarist

Peer (n)- 1. equal, mate, match. 2. Nobleman, aristocrat, lord
Pier (n)- dock, jetty, wharf, quay

Peerie (n)- Scot. - a peg top
Peery (adj)- inquisitive, suspicious

Pei- see Pay, Pe, Pais

Peine- see Pain, Pane

Peise (n)- a measure of weight. A weight in a clock
Pease (n)- plural of pea - vegetables

Peke- see Peak, Pique, Peek

Pele- see Peele, Pelee

Pelisse (n)- furred long cloak with arm openings
Police (n)- organized civil force to maintain order, enforce laws

Pen (n)- 1. female swan. 2. enclosure of animals. 3. instrument for writing with ink
Penn (pr.n)- William. Founded colony of Pennsylvania

Pence (n)- British plural of penny
Pens (n-pl)- 1. female swans. 2. animal enclosures

Pencel (n)- Archaic - small pennon as at head of a lance
Fencil (n)- writing material, lead, chalk, marker
Pensile (adj)- building a hanging nest

P

Pendant (n)- ornament, necklace, lavaliere, necklet
Pendent (adj)- overhanging, suspended, jutting

Pend (v)- to be undecided, wait. Hang in balance, be unsettled
Penned (v)- enclosed, caged, confined

Penitence (n)- regret, remorse, sorrow, pangs of conscience
Penitents (n-pl)- repentants, prodigals, pilgrims

Penk (n)- minnow, fish
Pink (n)- 1. light rose color. 2. plant. 3. vessel with narrow stern as fishing boat

Penned- see Pend

Peon- see Paeon, Paean

Pepys (pr.n)- Samuel. English diarist
Peeps (n)- 1. chirps, cheeps, tweets. 2. (v) - peers, peeks, glances

Per (prep)- through, by, by means of
Purr (v)- sound expressing satisfaction, hum, coo
Purre (n)- Eng. Dial. - a dunlin (bird) in winter plummage

Perry- see Parry, Peri

Perse (n)- grayish blue color
Purse (v)- 1. pucker, frown, wrinkle. 2. (n) - handbag, pocket book, wallet

Persue (n)- hunting - the track of a wounded beast
Pursue (v)- follow, seek, chase

Pert- see Peart

Pes (n)- the footlike part. Ancient Roman measure
Pess (n)- Eng. Dial. - a hassock, esp. one used in church

Pete- see Peat

Peter (pr.n)- 1. masculine name. 2. Bibl. - one of the twelve apostles also called Simon. 3. slang - (v) - to become exhausted. 4. slang - (n) - knockout drops
Petre (n)- saltpeter, nitre

Petit (adj)- Fr. now used in law - of small importance
Petty (adj)- trivial, unimportant, small, minor

Pew (n)- benches with backs fixed in rows in a church
Pu (n)- Chinese measure of weight
Pue (v)- obs. - to make a chirp or low whistle as birds

Pharaoh (n)- ancient Egyptian king
Faro (n)- gambling game of cards

P

Pharm (n)- pharmacy, pharmaceutic
Farm (n)- tract of land devoted to agriculture

Phase (n)- situation, condition, aspect
Faze (v)- worry, discomfort, disturb, embarrass
Fays (n)- fairies, elves, sprites

Pheer (n)- Scot. - companion
Fear (n)- dread, fright, alarm, panic

Pheese (v)- fume, fret
Fees (n)- pay for professional service
Feaze (v)- frighten, beat, punish

Phew (inter)- exclamation of disgust, impatience, surprise
Feu (n)- Scot. Law - fee
Few (adj)- rare, not many, scant, hardly any

Phi (n)- 21st letter of Greek alphabet
Fie (inter)- exclamation expressing disgust

Phial (n)- vial, container, bottle, flask
File (n)- 1. walk in a line. 2. march in a file. 3. smooth with a file
Faille (n)- ribbed silk or rayon fabric

Philip (pr.n)- 1. male name. 2. one of several Kings of France
Fillip (n)- 1. stroke, blow, knock. 2. (v) - stimulate, spur, urge

Philter (n)- 1. love charm. 2. magic potion to induce love
Filter (n)- 1. sieve, strainer, screen. 2. (v) - purify, refine

Phiz (n)- 1. facial expression. 2. face, visage
Phizz (adj)- hissing noise
Fizz (n)- bubbling, froth, fizzle

Phlegm (n)- mucus secreted in respiratory passages
Fleam (n)- Eng. Dial. - a mill stream

Phlox (n)- showy flower of various colors
Flocks (n)- herds, round-ups, litters, schools

Phrase (n)- word-group, parts of a sentence, passage
Frays (n-pl)- 1. quarrels, brawls, fights. 2. (v) - ravels, tatters
Fraise (n)- 1. a small milling cutter. 2. a ruff for the neck

Phyfe (pr.n)- Duncan. Furniture maker
Fife (n)- musical instrument

Pi (n)- 1. jumbled mixture of printing type. 2. 16th letter of Greek alphabet
Pie (n)- pastry, dessert, sweets, tarts
Pye (n)- Brit. Dial. - woodpecker, magpie

P

Pice (n)- small coin in India
Pies (n-pl)- pastries, tarts, desserts

Pick (v)- 1. select, choose, harvest, reap. 2. eat like a bird. 3. peck
Pic (n)- linear measure used in Turkey

Picked (v)- specially chosen or selected
Pict (pr.n)- race of people formerly inhabited Britain and Scotland

Picks (n)- axes, tools, implements
Pix (n-pl)- slang - motion pictures
Pyx (v)- 1. test coins for fitness. 2. (n) - box in which Host is kept

Picnic (n)- party, excursion, junket, lunch, supper
Pyknic (adj)- compact, solid

Pict (pr.n)- race of people formerly inhabited Britain and Scotland
Picked (v)- specially chosen or selected

Pie- see Pi, Pye

Piece (n)- 1. fragment, portion, part. 2. (v) - patch, repair, mend, unite
Pees (n)- roe of a fish
Pece (n)- obs. - a wine cup or other drinking vessel
Peace (n)- freedom from commotion or war. Quiet, tranquility

Pier (n)- dock. jetty, wharf, quay
Peer (n)- 1. equal, mate, match. 2. nobleman, aristocrat, lord

Pik- see Peak, Pique, Peke, Peek

Pike (n)- 1. long pole with metal tip. 2. long snouted fish
Pyke (v)- 1. Scot. - to pick. 2. Hindu - foot soldier, police officer

Pilate (pr.n)- Pontius. Roman governor
Pilot (n)- 1. airman, flyer. 2. steersman, wheelman. 3. conductor, guide

Pilau (n)- Oriental dish of rice, meat, and spices
Pillow (n)- bag or case of soft material used as support for head during rest or sleep

Pile (n)- 1. mass, heap, quantity. 2. structure, building. 3. hemorrhoid
Pyle (n)- Scot. - a grain of chaff

P

Pink (n)- 1. light rose color. 2. plant. 3. vessel with narrow stern - as a fishing boat
Penk (n)- minnow, fish

Pillow- see Pilau

Pique- see Peak, Peke, Peek

Pirl- see Pearl, Purl

Pistil (n)- Bot. - ovule bearing or seed. Bearing organ of a flower
Pistol (n)- revolver, automatic, repeater, gun

Pit (n)- 1. hole or cavity in ground. 2. stone of a fruit
Pitt (pr.n)- William. British prime minister

Place (n)- 1. portion of space, area, site, district. 2. position
Plaice (n)- flat fish, flounder

Plack (n)- small coin formerly current in Scotland
Plaque (n)- thin piece of metal, clay, etc. used on wall for ornament

Plain (adj)- 1. clear, distinct, manifest. 2. (n) - meadow, plateau
Plane (n)- 1. aircraft. 2. tool, trowel. 3. degree, status, position

Plait (n)- 1. braid, pigtail. 2. (v) - fold, pleat, gather
Plate (n)- 1. shallow dish, platter. 2. (v) - coat with a fine film of metal overlay

Planch (n)- obs. - plank, board, slab
Planche (n)- a flat shoe for a mule

Planchet (n)- flat piece of metal, esp. disk ready to be stamped
Planchette (n)- 1. a circumferentor - a horizontal compass. 2. a tire circle

Plane- see Plain

Plaque- see Plack

Plat (n)- plan, map, chart esp. of a townsite or the like
Platt (n)- mining - space widened to permit wagon to pass or ore to be deposited

Plate- see Plait

Playable (adj)- capable of or suitable for being played or played on
Pleyable (adj)- Scot. - debatable

Pleas (n-pl)- excuses, apologies, supplication, prayers
Please (v)- satisfy, gratify, make happy

P

Pliers (n-pl) - small pincers with long jaws, nippers, tongs
Plyers (n-pl) - 1. utilizers, users, workers. 2. puts to use

Plook (n) - Scot. - small knob to make exact measure of liquid
Plouk (n) - Eng. Dial. - a pimple

Plot (n) - secret scheme, conspiracy
Plott (v) - Eng. Dial. - to pluck, fleece

Plum (n) - fruit with a stone - damson, greengage, prune
Plumb (n) - 1. a plummet, a plumb bob. 2. sinker

Po (pr.n) - river in No. Italy
Poe (pr.n) - Edgar Allan. U.S. poet and writer
Pow (n) - Scot. and Eng. - the head, the poll
Pau (pr.n) - town in S.W. France

Pocks (n) - obs. - eruptive disease of sheep
Pox (n) - Med. - any disease characterized by pustules as small pox, syphilis

Poke (v) - 1. thrust, push, bag, or sack. 2. bonnet with a brim
Polk (pr.n) - James Knox - 11th president of U.S. 1845-1849

Poi (n) - Hawaiian - article of food prepared from the taro root
Poy (n) - projecting gallery or terrace with a railing on a house

Polar (adj) - opposite in character or action, opposed, contrary
Poler (n) - 1. extortioner. 2. one who poles a boat
Poller (n) - 1. Barber, one who shaves or shears persons. 2. one who registers voters. 3. pillager, plunderer

Polayn (n) - old armor - piece protecting the knee
Poulaine (n) - 1. long pointed toe of the crakow. 2. a pike

Pole (n) - staff, rod, stick, post, mast
Pole (pr.n) - native or inhabitant of Poland
Poll (v) - 1. tabulate, count noses, canvas. 2. vote, ballet
Polle (n) - measure of land in Ireland of fifty or sixty acres

Poley (adj) - Brit. Dial. - having no horns
Poly (n) - plant, evergreen shrub

Poller - see Polar, Poler

Police (v) - keep watch, regulate, control, guard, protect
Pelisse (n) - furred long cloak with arm openings

Polk - see Poke

Poll - see Pole, Polle

Poly - see Poley

P

Pood (n)- Russian weight equal to 36 lbs. avoirdupois
Poohed (inter)- scoffed, ridiculed, expressed contempt

Pool (n)- 1. small pond, reservoir, swimming pool. 2. (v) - merge, unite, combine
Poule (n)- position or figure in a square dance
Pul (n)- Persian copper coin

Populace (n)- people, crowd, multitude, public
Populous (adj)- dense, thronged, teeming, well populated

Pore (n)- 1. hole, small opening, outlet, orifice. 2. meditate, ponder
Pour (v)- decant, spill, pour out, lade out, tap

Poring (v)- viewing, examining, inspecting, peering
Pouring (v)- raining, showering, flooding

Porphyre (n)- kind of a purple serpent of India
Porphyry (n)- rock consisting of feldspar crystals. Purple groundmass

Port (n)- 1. harbor, haven, dock, seaport. 2. demeanor, bearing
Porte (n)- Ottoman Turkish court and government

Portoir (n)- one that bears the branch of a vine
Portor (n)- marble from Spezia, Italy

Postal (adj)- pertaining to post office, mail service, postal arrangements
Postel (n)- a post as of a gate or door

Postil (v)- 1. to annotate or gloss. 2. write comments
Postille (n)- explanatory marginal notes in Bible

Pot (n) - 1. metallic or earthern vessel used for many purposes as a coffee pot, cooking pot. 2. slang- marijuana. 3. carburetor
Pott (n)- size of paper approx. 13 x 16

Potail (n)- India - variant of patel - headman of a village
Potale (n)- refuse from a grain distillery used to fatten swine

Poter (n)- Archaic - a drinker, toper
Potter (n)- one whose occupation is to make earthern or metal pots

Pouce (n)- dust from flax
Pous (n)- ancient Greek measure

Poulaine (n)- 1. long pointed toe of the crakow. 2. a pike
Polayn (n)- old armor - piece protecting the knee

Poule- see Pool, Pul

P

Pour (v)- decant, spill, pour out, tap, lade out
Pore (n)- 1. small opening, hole, outlet. 2. meditate, ponder

Pouring (v)- raining, showering, flooding
Poring (v)- gaping, viewing, inspecting, peering

Pous (n)- ancient Greek measure
Pouce (n)- dust from flax

Pox (n)- medicine - any disease characterized by pustules as smallpox, syphillis
Pocks (n)- eruptive disease of sheep

Poy (n)- projecting gallery or terrace with a railing on house
Poi (n)- Hawaiian - article of food prepared from taro root

Praam (n)- Nautical - flat bottomed boat used in Holland & Baltic
Pram (n)- 1. a milkman's handcart. 2. short for perambulator - baby carriage

Praise (v)- 1. laud, extol, approve. 2. (n) - honor, glory, congratulations
Prase (n)- translucent quartz of leek green color
Prays (v)- 1. implores, entreats. 2. communes with God
Preys (n.pl)- plunders, loots, pillages, pickings, spoils

Pray (v)- solicit, entreat, beseech, beg, appeal to
Prey (n)- game, quarry, victim, kill

Prays- see Praise, Preys, Prase

Precedent (n)- prior instance, practice, usage, pattern
President (n)- chief executive, presider, chief official

Precedence (n)- preference, seniority, rank, status
Presidence (n)- rare - presidency
Presidents (n.pl) - plural of president

Precious (adj)- 1. expensive, priceless, of great worth. 2. beloved, darling
Prescious (adj)- obs. - having fore-knowledge

Precisian (n)- prig, martinet, stickler, puritan
Precision (n)- accuracy, exactness, authenticity

Presence (n)- appearance, existence, life, being
Presents (n.pl)- gifts, offerings, bequests

Prescious- see Precious

President- see Precedent

Presidence- see Precedence, Presidents

P

Pressed (v)- 1. forced, compelled. 2. ironed. 3. embraced
Prest (adj)- 1. ready, prompt. 2. neat, proper

Prey (n)- game, quarry, victim, kill
Pray (v)- solicit, entreat, beseech, beg, appeal to

Preys - see Praise, Prays, Prase

Priam (pr.n)- Greek Myth. - last King of Troy
Priame (n)- obs. - small fish resembling a smelt

Pride (n)- self esteem, conceit, egotism, ambition
Pried (v)- past tense of pry. Snooped

Priced (v)- set a price on. Valued
Prist (adj)- Archaic - worthy, noble, valiant

Prier or Pryer(n)- one who looks or searches curiously
Prior (adj)- 1. earlier, previous, former. 2. monk, priest, holy man

Pries (n.pl)- raises, opens or moves by force of leverage
Prize (n)- 1. premium, reward, trophy. 2. (v) - esteem, value highly

Primer (n)- 1. school book, first reader, textbook. 2. undercoating
Primmer (adj)- more proper, precise, stiffly neat

Prince (n)- ruler, sovereign, son of the king, royal heir
Prints (n.pl)- 1. impresses, engraves. 2. newsprint. 3. snapshots, photos

Princess (n)- wife of prince, queen, duchess, ruler
Princes (n.pl)- plural of prince

Principal (n)- 1. headmaster, dean. 2. (adj) - chief, leading, prime. 3. capital sum, fund, invested money
Principle (n)- 1. belief, origin, source, fundamental, beginning. 2. doctrine, belief

Prints - see Prince

Prior - see Prier

Prist - see Priced

Prize (n)- 1. premium, reward, trophy. 2. (v) - esteem, value highly
Pries (n.pl)- raises. Opens or moves by force of leverage

Professed (adj)- openly declared, avowed, acknowledged
Profest (v)- to make a pretense of. To pretend

P

Proficience (n)- expertness, adeptness, well-skilled
Proficients (n.pl)- ones well advanced in business, art, science, etc.

Profit (n)- 1. gain, earnings, net. 2. (v)- serve, help, contribute
Prophet (n)- one who speaks for God. Oracle, disciple, saint

Prog (v) Brit. - search for food or plunder. Forage
Progue (v)- Scot. - to poke, prod. A goad

Prominence (n)- conspicuousness, protuberance
Prominents (n.pl)- moths - so called because larva has a hump or prominence on its back

Propene (n)- Chem. - propylene
Propine (n)- 1. Scot. - a gift, especially of money for drink. 2. Chem. - allylene

Prophecy (n)- forecasting, prognosis, foretelling
Prophesy (v)- predict, indicate, omen, forbode

Prophet - see Profit

Pros (n.pl)- 1. consideration, arguments. 2. votes for something. 3. professionals
Prose (n)- language written without meter or rhyme

Prospecter (n)- 1. looking forward, anticipation. 2. foresights
Prospector (n)- one who searches, explores for minerals & oils

Protean (adj)- assuming different forms and characters
Protein (n)- substance thought to be essential component of all organic bodies

Psalm (n)- sacred or solemn song, hymn, song of praise
Salm (n)- unit of weight in Malta

Psalter (n)- book of Psalms. Hymn book
Salter (n)- 1. one who salts food. 2. dealer in salt

Psaltery (n)- ancient musical instrument with numerous strings
Saltery (n)- salt works

Pshaw (interj)- expression of contempt, impatience
Shaw (pr.n)- George Bernard. Irish dramatist

P

Psi (n)- 1. 23rd letter of Greek alphabet. 2. pounds per square inch
Sigh (n)- 1. deep audible breath, moan, sob, wail. 2. (v) - grieve for, bemoan
Seye (n)- Scot. - armhole of a garment into which the sleeve is set
Sye (n)- Scot & Eng. Dial. - a scythe
Sie (v)- Eng. & Scot. 1. sink, fall, descend. 2. sift. 3. drift
Cy- 1. Chem. symbol frequently used for the cyanogen group CN. 2. Abbrev. for currency used in stock market tapes.

Psora (n)- Med. - scabies, itch
Sora (n)- small short billed bird

Prunell (n)- a milled cashmere
Prunelle (n)- small yellow dried plum packed without skin

Psychosis (n)- severe form of mental affection or disease
Sycosis (n)- inflammatory disease of hair follicles

Pteris (n)- Bot. - large genus of coarse ferns
Terrace (n)- raised level space as of houses, lawns - having sloping sides

Pu - see Pew, Pue

Puffed (adj)- caused to puff by exertion or shortness of breath
Puft (adj)- gathered in puffs as a sleeve

Puisne (adj)- 1. Law - younger, inferior in rank. 2. junior or associate
Puny (adj)- weak, small, feeble development

Pul - see Pool, Poule

Pumped (v)- raised with a pump, drew water, air
Pumpt (adj)- out of breath, winded

Puny - see Puisne

Puree (n)- thick soup or vegetables, boiled or strained
Purree (n)- Hindu - Indian yellow

Purl - see Pearl, Pirl

Purled (v)- decorated with a border, fringe or embroidery
Pearled (adj)- set with pearls or nacre. Formed into pearls

Purr (v)- sound expressing satisfaction, hum, coo
Purre (n)- a dunlin (bird) in winter plummage
Per (prep)- through, by, by means of

Purree - see Puree

Purse - see Perse

150

P

Pursue - see Persue

Put (n)- obs. 1. any short thing; short thick woman. 2. dwarf
Putt (v)- golf - strike ball with a putter when playing a short distance from the hole

Puttee (n)- gaiter wrapped around leg used by soldiers, walkers, riders.
Putty (n)- whiting mixed with linseed oil for filling cracks, securing panes of glass

Pye - see Pi, Pie

Pyke - see Pike

Pyknic - see Picnic

Pyle - see Pile

Pyr (n)- unit of light intensity
Pyre (n)- pile arranged for burning dead body

Pyrrol (n)- fiery
Pyrrole (n)- Chem. - a colorless liquid C_4H_5N

Pyx - see Picks

–Q–

Quab (n)- young bird without feathers
Quob (v)- obs. - tremble, throb

Quad (n)- quadrangle. Geom. - plane figure
Quod (n)- slang - prison

Quaere (v)- 1. inquire. 2. inserted in reports - as in law
Query (v)- express doubt, question

Quaich (n)- Scot. - cup or bowl
Quake (n)- shaking or tremor

Quaint (adj)- pleasingly odd & antique
Quient (v)- obs. - p.p. of quench

Quart (n)- cards - a sequence of 4 cards
Quarte (n)- fencing- the fourth of eight defensive positions
Carte (n)- 1. menu - a la carte. 2. map or chart
Cart (n)- 1. wagon, push cart. 2. (v) - transport, carry, haul

Quarts (n.pl)- measure of capacity
Quartz (n)- silicon, dioxide, mineral

Quay (n)- dock, anchorage, pier, wharf
Key (n)- 1. opener, latch key, opening device. 2. pass, safe conduct
Kae (n)- Scot. - Jack Daw

Quean (n)- minx, slut, hussy, trollop, harridan
Queen (n)- female monarch, wife of a king, royal consort

Queens (n.pl)- plural of Queen
Queens (pr.n)- borough and county in New York

Querpo (n)- obs - undressed, unclad
Cuerpo (n)- the body. Form of the body

Query - see Quaere

Queue (n)- 1. pigtail. 2. waiting line
Kew (pr.n)- village on Thames, England
Cue (n)- clue, hint, intimation

Quient (v)- obs. - p.p. of quench
Quaint (adj)- pleasingly odd and antique

Quiescence (n)- repose, quiet, rest, calm, silence
Quiescents (n.pl)- silent letters, not sounded

Quire (n)- paper measure. 24 sheets of paper
Choir (n)- company of church singers

Q

Quitter (n)- 1. metal - slag from tin smelting. 2. matter from a sore, pus.
Quittor (n)- a disease of the feet of horses, asses and other solipeds

Quoif (n)- Dial. - commotion, turmoil
Coif (v)- to gather into a circular form. Wind into a ring

Quoin (n)- wedge of wood or metal
Coin (n)- mint, money, issue, make
Coign (n)- projecting corner

-R-

Ra (pr.n)- Egyptian sun god
Ray (n)- 1. line of light, gleam, beam. 2. variety of fish
Re (n)- Music - syllable used for second note of scale
Wray (v)- betray, reveal, disclose

Rabat (n)- polishing material made from imperfectly baked potters clay
Rabatte (v)- to beat down, lower

Rabbet (n)- cut a groove, joint, unite
Rabbit (n)- long eared mammal, hare, bunny, cottontail

Rabbi (n)- 1. Jewish master, teacher. 2. learned doctors of the law ordained in Palestine
Rabi (n)- Arabic - spring

Rach (n)- Scot. - a dog that hunts by scent
Ratch (n)- Eng. Dial. - race - a white mark

Rack (v)- harass, torture, distress, torment, pain
Wrack (n)- 1. seaweed or other marine plant cast on shore. 2. weeds

Racket (n)- loud noise, hubbub, fracas, din, tumult
Rackett (n)- music - old wind instrument of double bassoon kind, no keys
Racquet (n)- light bat with nylon, catgut, etc. for tennis, badminton

Racks (n.pl)- instruments of torture. Wheel, thumbscrew, boot
Rax (v)- 1. stretch or strain oneself. 2. reach or hand to a person
Wracks (n.pl)- wrecks or wreckage cast ashore

Racquet- see Rackett, Racket

Rade - see Raid, Rayed

Radical (adj)- extreme, insurgent, leftist, ultra
Radicle (n)- 1. rootlike, beginning of nerve vein. 2. diminutive root

Raff (n)- 1. timber, lumber. 2. refuse, trash. 3. worthless fellow
Raffe (n)- Naut. - triangular sail on American lake schooners

Raid (n)- invade, pillage, plunder, assail, march upon
Rayed (adj)- Botany - radiate. Striped
Rade (n)- Scot. - road, raid

Raik (n)- 1. a course or journey. 2. (v) - wander, stroll
Rake (v)- 1. lead a dissolute life. 2. (n)- tool, implement with teeth, hoe

R

Raiker (n)- Scot. - a vagabond
Raker (n)- man or machine who rakes hay or grain

Rail (n)- bar fixed horizontally for support. Fence, railing
Rale (n)- abnormal sound in chest, wheeze, rattle

Raim (v)- Archaic - ransom, plunder
Rame (n)- Scot. - a repeated wail or cry

Rain (v)- shower, drizzle, sprinkle, pour
Rane (n)- Scot. - jargon of sounds; long-continued cry or clamor
Reign (v)- sit on throne, wear a crown, rule, dominate
Rein (v)- check, restrain, control, guide

Rains (n.pl)- cloudbursts, downpours, rains, storms
Reigns (n.pl)- royalty, kinghood, monarchy, powers
Reins (n.pl)- confinement, restraint, harness, leads

Raise (v)- 1. elevate, heave, hoist, lift, pull up. 2. originate, start. 3. stir up, arouse
Rase (v)- erase, rub out, obliterate
Raze (v)- scrape, grate, graze, abrade
Rays (n.pl)- plural of ray - flashes, flames, flickers

Raised (n)- 1. made in low relief, embossed. 2. made light with yeast. 3. excited, awakened
Razed (adj)- Archaic - striped in a pattern

Raiser (n)- 1. breeder of stock. 2. procurer of funds
Razor (n)- sharp edge instrument for shaving face

Raja (n)- honorary title conferred on Hindus
Rajah (n)- Indian prince, monarch, ruler, emir

Rake - see Raik

Raker - see Raiker

Rale - see Rail

Rame - see Raim

Ramee (n)- fine fiber resembling that of cotton
Ramie (n)- Asiatic plant with rodlike stems

Ramose (adj)- bearing many branches
Ramous (adj)- tree-shaped

Ramp (n)- slope or ascent, inclined or sloping plane
Wramp (n)- Brit. Dial. - sprain

Rancor (n)- spite, hate, animosity, venom
Ranker (adj)- British soldier in the ranks

R

Ranee (n)- wife of a king, rajah, prince
Rani (n)- princess

Rang (v)- gave forth a clear sound as a bell
Wrang (n)- Scot. - wrong

Ranker - see Rancor

Rap (n)- 1. trifle, least bit, mite, straw. 2. communication 3. slang - knock
Wrap (v)- 1. make fast. 2. enclose, encase, conceal, hide, cover

Rapped (v)- knocked, clipped, tapped, buffeted
Rapt (adj)- engrossed, absorbed, spell bound
Wrapped (v)- encased, covered, concealed

Rapper (n)- person who raps
Wrapper (n)- 1. envelope, container, casing. 2. dressing gown, robe

Rapt - see Rapped, Wrapped

Rase - see Raise, Rays, Raze

Rasse (n)- a civet native to China and East Indies
Wrasse (n)- edible, marine, usually brilliantly colored fish

Rat (n)- rodent of the genus mus
Wrat (n)- Scot. - a wart

Ratan (v)- to punish with rattan cane
Rattan (n)- palm used in making wicker work or chair seat

Rath (n)- hill, mount, fortress
Rathe (adj)- poetic - quickly, promptly, eager
Wrath (n)- rage, anger, fury, spleen

Raven (v)- to seize forcibly
Ravin (n)- obs. - ravenous
Ravine (n)- prey or plunder

Ray - see Ra, Re, Wray

Raya (n)- an East Indian broadbill
Rayah (n)- a person not a Mohammedan forced to pay tax to the ottoman porte

Rayed - see Raid, Rade

Raze - see Raise

Razed - see Raised

Razor - see Raiser

R

Re (prep) - in the case of, with reference to
Ree (n) - an overflow of the river
Rhee (pr.n) - Syngman. President of Korea 1948-1960

Reach (v) - stretch out, extend, to pass to another
Recche (v) - obs. - to go, pursue one's way

Read (v) - get the meaning of something by interpreting the signs
Reed (n) - 1. straight stalk of grass, twig, blade. 2. musical instrument
Rede (n) - 1. counsel, advice. 2. plan, scheme. 3. interpretation
Reid (n) - Scot. - a roadstead. Stomach

Read (adj) - versed in books, learned
Red (adj) - scarlet, blood-colored, reddish, blushing
Redd (v) - Scot. - put in order, make tidy

Reader (n) - 1. elementary book. 2. one who reads books, lessons or prayers
Reeder (n) - reed-covered frame to protect drying China clay

Ready (adj) - equipped, prepared, in readiness, set
Reddy (adj) - Brit. Dial. - tidy up, neat up

Reak (n) - a seaweed or rush. Trick
Reek (n) - stench, stink, strong unpleasant smell
Wreak (v) - execute, inflict

Reaks (n-pl) - tricks, pranks
Reeks (n-pl) - fumes, exhausts, vapors
Wreaks (v) - carries out promptings of ill humor on a victim

Real (adj) - 1. actual, in existence. 2. solid, material, tangible
Reel (n) - rotary device, spool, bobbin, axis.

Ream (n) - 1. quantity of paper. Bale or pkg. of paper. 2. (v) - enlarge a hole
Reem (n) - 1. Biblical - wild ox, unicorn. 2. (v) - moan

Reams (n) - Colloq. - a large quantity. Lots, many, much
Rheims (pr.n) - city in France

Reap (n) - 1. harvest. 2. (v) - clear a crop
Reep (n) obs. - to cut grain with sickle, scythe, reaping machine

Reaper (n) - one that reaps - man or machine
Reeper (n) - Indian - strip of wood used as a batten or lathe

Reave (v) - steal, rob. Take away by stealth or violence
Reeve (n) - Canada - president of council or village. British - overseer

R

Rebait (v)- to bait as a hook again
Rebate (v)- make a discount from a sum due. Deduct from

Rebec (n)- stringed instrument, earliest known of viol class
Rebeck (v)- to beckon back

Recche (v)- obs. - to go. Pursue one's way
Reach (v)- to stretch out, extend. To pass to another

Recede (v)- abate, wane, fade, depart, ebb
Reseed (v)- propagates itself by self sown seed

Receipt (v)- cancel, nullify, acknowledge payment in writing
Reseat (v)- seat or set again. Place in position or office

Recent (adj)- new, novel, late, fresh. Not long past
Resent (v)- fly into a rage, lose one's temper, fume

Reck (v)- Archaic - to have care or concern. Heed
Wreck (v)- destroy, demolish, ruin

Red - see Read, Redd

Reddy - see Ready

Rede - see Read, Reed, Reid

Reeder - see Reader

Reef (n)- chain of rocks laying at or near surface of water. Shoal
Reif (n)- Archaic - robbery, plunder

Reek - see Reak, Wreak

Reel (v)- 1. stagger, sway. 2. a lively dance
Real (adj)- true, authentic, genuine, actual

Reem (v)- 1. moan, lament. 2. (n) - Biblical - wild ox, unicorn
Ream (v)- 1. enlarge a hole. 2. (n) - quantity of paper

Reep - see Reap

Reeper - see Reeper

Reeve - see Reave

Refrain (n)- 1. musical setting of a verse or a phrase of a song. 2. (v)- abstain
Refrane (n)- Scot. - restraint

Regester (n)- a registrar. An official recorder
Register (n)- record, archives, roll, annals, chronicle

Reheat (v)- to heat again
Rehete (v)- obs. - cheer, encourage, refresh

R

Reif - see Reef

Reign (n)- rule, authority, power, privilege
Rein (v)- cause to stop or slow down - as with a horse
Rane (n)- Scot. - Jargon of sounds. Long continued cry or clamor
Rain (n)- water falling to earth in drops condensed from moisture in the air

Reigns (n.pl)- years in power, time of authority
Reins (n.pl)- regulation, guidance, supervision
Rains (n.pl)- floods, mist, deluge

Reina (n)- Spanish Queen
Rena (n)- small deepwater rockfish

Relater (n)- narrator, recounter
Relator (n)- Law - one who institutes a special proceeding by relating of information

Releaser (n)- one that releases
Releasor (n)- one by whom a release is given

Remark (n)- observation, comment, casual expression
Remarque (n)- etching and engraving

Renovater (n)- renewer, repairer
Renovator (n)- a nozzle attachment for suction pipe of vacuum cleaner

Repost (v)- to mail again
Riposte (n)- 1. fencing-a quick return thrust. 2. repartee, quick retort.

Reseat - see Receipt

Reseed - see Recede

Resent (v)- dislike, be angry, be offended, be provoked
Recent (adj)- up to date, untried, modern, new

Residence (n)- house, lodging, abode, dwelling
Residents (n.pl)- dwellers, occupants, inhabitants

Rest (v)- sleep, repose, nap, doze, lie down
Wrest (v)- pull, jerk. Force by violent twist

Retch (v)- heave, vomit, strain
Wretch (n)- poor creature, vagabond, outcast, sufferer

Review (v)- criticize, comment upon, revise, analyze
Revue (n)- musical show with songs, skits, dances

Reviver (n)- 1. renovator, restorer. 2. slang - a stimulant
Revivor (n)- Eng. law - revival of a suit which is abated

R

Rhee (pr.n)- Syngman. President of Korea 1948-1960
Re (n)- music - syllable used for second note of scale

Rheims - see Reams

Rheum (n)- cold, catarrh, rhinitis
Room (n)- berth, lodging place, apartment, chamber

Rhodes (pr.n)- Cecil. Brit. colonial capitalist
Roads (n-pl)- boulevards, avenues, highways, paths

Rhone (pr.n)- river flowing into the Mediterranean
Rown or Rowan (v)- propelled by oars
Roan (n)- horse having mixture of gray and bay. Color
Roanne (pr.n)- city in France

Rhos (n-pl)- plural of Greek letter rho
Rose (n)- 1. color. 2. flower. 3. cut stone. 4. feminine name. 5. (v) p.p. of rise
Rows (n-pl)- 1. processions, series, files, ranks, queues. 2. method of cultivating crops
Roes (n-pl)- deer or fish

Rhumb (n)- point of the compass
Rum (n)- alcoholic liquor distilled from molasses, sugar cane. 2. Brit. - queer, old-fashioned

Rhyme (n)- song, verse, poetry
Rime (n)- crevice, crack, fissure, breach

Rig (v)- 1. to furnish with gear, fit or equip. 2. Naut. - to fit with sails and tackling
Wrig (n)- 1. feeblest member of a litter or brood. 2. puny child

Rigger (n)- 1. protective scaffold used in construction to catch tools. 2. one who works with housing tackle or rigging ships
Rigor (n)- 1. rigidity, stiffness, cold. 2. mathematical precision

Right (adv)- 1. toward the right hand - not left. 2. starboard
Rite (n)- formal religious ceremony, worship, sacrament
Write (v)- author, compose, describe, narrate
Wright (n)- workman, creator, one who makes or constructs

Righter (n)- one who does justice or redresses wrong
Writer (n)- one who writes or has written. Penman, scribe

Rigor- see Rigger

Rill (n)- small channel or brook. Streamlet
Rille (n)- Astron. - long narrow valleys on surface of moon

Rime- see Rhyme

R

Rind (n)- skin coating, husk, bark, shell, peel
Rynd (n)- iron piece across hole to support millstone

Rine (n)- 1. obs. - rind. 2. Brit. - a ditch
Rhine (pr.n)- river flowing through Germany

Ring (n)- 1. circlet, hoop. 2. arena, prize ring. 3. peal of bells
Wring (v)- squeeze, compress, wrest, twist violently

Ringer (n)- 1. person that rings a bell. 2. strong resemblance to another
Wringer (n)- apparatus which forces water out by pressure

Riot (n)- revolt, mutiny, rebellion, uprising
Ryot (n)- India - peasant. Cultivator of the soil

Ripe (adj)- mature, mellow, completed growth
Rype (n)- Danish - ptarmigan - species of grouse

Riposte-see Repost

Rite- see Right, Wright, Write

Roach (n)- 1. cockroach - bug. 2. European fish. 3. (v) trim mane of a horse to stand up
Roche (n)- French obs. - a rock

Road (n)- pathway, street, avenue, highway
Rode (v)- did ride
Roed (adj)- full of roe, as a fish
Rowed (v)- 1. propelled with oars. Did row. 2. arranged in or containing rows

Roads- see Rhodes

Roam (v)- wander, stray, travel about, prowl
Rome (pr.n)- capital of Italy

Roan (n)- 1. color. 2. animal having mixture of gray and bay
Rown (v)- propelled by oars
Rhone (pr.n)- river flowing into the Mediterranean
Roanne (pr.n)- city in France

Robbin (n)- package in which pepper and other commodities are exported from East Indies
Robin (n)- small, red breasted warble like bird

Roc (n)- Arabian and Persian legend - fabulous bird of prey
Rock (n)- 1. large mass of stone. 2. move or sway back and forth
Rok (n)- slang - South Korean - from the initials of "Republic of Korea"

Roche- see Roach

R

Rock- see Roc, Rok

Rocket (n)- bomb signal, firework, weapon
Rockett (n)- member of worlds largest chorus line at Radio City Music Hall
Roquette (n)- European plant, like spinach, eaten as a salad

Rode- see Road, Rowed, Roed

Roe (n)- 1. female of the red deer. 2. egg or spawn of fish
Row (n)- file, rank line, tier, column

Roes- see Rhos, Rose, Rows

Rok- see Roc, Rock

Role (n)- 1. character represented by an actor, impersonation. 2. work, function, duty
Roll (n)- 1. bundle, document, record, register, list. 2. (v)- turn, rotate, revolve, swing

Roll- see Role

Rome- see Roam

Rondeau (n)- Music - verse form, composition of lively, cheerful character
Rondo (n)- gambling game played by rolling balls on the table, the house receives commission on all bets

Rood (n)- 1. English measure of length. 2. cross upon which Jesus was crucified
Rude (adj)- unpolished, uncouth, ignorant, insolent, impolite
Rued (v)- regretted, repented, was sorry, wished undone

Roof (n)- Arch. - the outer cover on top of any building or house
Rufe (n)- Scot. - pause, rest, piece, quiet

Rookie (n)- raw recruit in Army or any other service
Rooky (adj)- full of or frequented by black crows

Room (n)- expanse, scope, capacity, leeway, range
Rheum (n)- watery discharge from nose, eyes, mouth

Roomer (n)- lodger, boarder
Rumor (v)- to tell, report, spread as gossip, hearsay

Roon (n)- 1. Scot. - border, shred. 2. Ir.- treasure, darling
Rune (n)- any alphabet formerly used by Teutonic peoples about 3rd century

Roop (n)- Scot. 1. shout, hoarseness. 2. cold. 3. a disease of poultry
Roup (v)- Scot. - to sell at auction. A sale by outcry

R

Roose- see Rues, Ruse

Root (n)- 1. cause, rationale, reason, origin, motive. 2. plant, bulb
Route (n)- 1. road, way or course traveled. 2. military - order specifying course of travel

Roquette- see Rocket, Rockette

Rose (n)- 1. fragrant flower with prickly stem. 2. name. 3. cut-stone. 4. color. 5. (v)- past tense of rise
Roes (n-pl)- 1. small agile European and Asiatic deer. 2. fish
Rows (n-pl)- 1. method of cultivating crops in drills or rows. 2. processions, files, racks, series
Rhos (n-pl)- plural of Greek letter rho

Roset (n)- French - a painters red color
Rosette (n)- Bot. - a circular cluster of leaves, petals

Rote (n)- 1. routine, repetition. 2. fixed course of procedure
Wrote (v)- past tense of write. Did write

Rough (adj)- 1. crude, coarse. 2. not mild, harsh, not gentle. 3. bumpy, not level
Ruff (v)- 1. plait, ruffle. 2. wrinkle, disorder. 3. high frilled collar
Ruffe (n)- European perch

Roup- see Roop

Rouse (v)- stimulate, excite, agitate, incite, stir up
Rows (n)- noisy quarrels, disputes, disturbances

Rout (v)- drive off, vanquish, put to flight, defeat, overthrow, ruin
Route (n)- 1. regular set of customers as paper or milk route. 2. baseball - pitch entire game

Route- see Root

Route- see Rout

Row (v)- propel a boat on water by using oars
Roe (n)- eggs or spawn of fishes. 2. female of the red deer

Rowed- see Road, Rode, Roed

Rows- see Rose, Roes, Rhos

Rows (n-pl)- commotions, noisy disputes, quarrels
Rouse (v)- waken, call, get up, raise, shake

Rud (n)- ruddy color - redness. Complexion
Rudd (n)- fresh water fish

R

Rude (adj)- coarse, vulgar, discourteous, bad mannered
Rued (v)- mourned, was contrite, regretted, deplored
Rood (n)- 1. originally the cross on which Jesus was crucified. 2. English measure of length

Rues (v)- sorrows over, repents, wishes undone, mopes
Ruse (n)- trick, dodge, wile, subterfuge, sham
Roose (n)- Scot. - praise

Rufe (n)- Scot. - pause, rest, piece, quiet
Roof (n)- Arch. - the outer cover on top of any building or house

Ruff (n)- 1. high frilled collar. 2. wrinkle, disorder
Ruffe (n)- European perch
Rough (adj)- 1. not smooth, bumpy, not level. 2. harsh, crude

Rum (n)- 1. Brit. - queer, old fashioned. 2. alcoholic liquor
Rhumb (n)- point of the compass.

Rumor (n)- gossip, hearsay, unconfirmed story or statement
Roomer (n)- a lodger, resident, one who rooms

Run (n)- 1. go rapidly, hasten. 2. (v) - to accomplish as run for office, run a race, run a machine.
Runn (n)- India - flat land flooded during monsoon months and incrusted with salt when dry

Rune- see Roon

Rung (n)- 1. step on a ladder. 2. spoke on a wheel
Wrung (v)- twisted, squeezed or pressed out

Ruse- see Rues

Rye (n)- 1. cereal grass. 2. alcoholic liquor
Wry (adj)- crooked, distorted, out of shape, twisted

Rynd- see Rind

Rype- see Ripe

Ryot- see Riot

S

–S–

Sabal (n)- palmetto tree
Sable (n)- weasel like mammal noted for its dark brown fur
Sable (pr.n)- cape in Nova Scotia, also southern tip of Florida

Sac (n)- cyst, pouch, baglike structure, bladder
Sac (pr.n)- No. American tribe of Algonquian Indians
Sack - 1. bag, satchel, pouch. 2. pillage, waste, ravage. 3. slang - get fired. 4. slang - bed
Saque (n)- 1. loose gown for women. 2. loose fitting jacket worn by babies

Sacks (n.pl)- 1. bags, satchels. 2. plunders, pillages, loots. 3. slang - beds
Sax (n)- 1. slate makers axe, short sword, dagger. 2. slang - saxophone
Seax (n)- Her. - a long knife

Sacre (n)- obs. - a sacred solemnity. The consecration
Saker (n)- Zool. - a falcon

Sad (adj)- sorrowful, dejected, depressed, cheerless
Sadd (n)- dam, waste water

Sae (adj)- Scottish form of so
Say (v)- express in words, declare, reply, answer
Sey (v)- Scot. - advance, arrive

Sail (v)- 1. travel in a vessel, pass by water, cruise, boat, yacht. 2. (n)- canvas, cloth for catching wind
Sale (n)- transfer of goods for money or credit, act of selling, discount, rebate

Sailer (n)- a vessel propelled by sail or sails
Sailor (n)- seaman, mariner, enlisted man in navy, seafaring man

Sain (v)- safeguard by prayer, bless
Sane (adj)- rational, normal, lucid, sound in mind
Seine (n)- fishing net which hangs vertically in the water. Catch fish with a net
Seine (pr.n)- river flowing through France

Sais (n)- Hindu, India - a groom
Sice (n)- number six at dice

Saith (v)- Archaic or poetic - third person sing, of say
Seth (pr.n)- 1. third son of Adam. 2. male name

Saker- see Sacre

Sale- see Sail

S

Sallee (n)- any of several Australian acacias. Flowering shrubs
Sallie (v) obs. - to start suddenly. Leap or rush out
Sally (n)- 1. European house wren. 2. feminine name

Salloo (n)- east Indian Red twilled cotton or calico
Sallu (n)- Biblical - exaltation

Salm (n)- 1. unit of weight in Malta. 2. a star
Psalm (n)- sacred or solemn song, hymn, song of praise

Salma (n)- measure of capacity in Italy, Sicily, etc.
Salmah (n)- Biblical - garment

Salt (n)- colorless white crystal known chemically as sodium chloride
Sault (v)- obs. - leap, tumble, jump

Saltee (n)- Eng. slang - a penny
Saltie (n)- European flat fish
Salty (adj)- 1. somewhat salt. 2. (adj)- slang - angry, upset

Salter (n)- 1. one who deals in salt. 2. one who salts food
Psalter (n)- book of Psalms, hymn book

Saltery (n)- salt works
Psaltery (n)- ancient musical instrument with numerous strings

Saltier (n) Her. - a cross formed by a bend dexter and a bend sinister
Saltire (n)- a leap or a jump

Salut (n)- health, welfare, safety
Salute (v)- 1. to greet, hail. 2. (n) - ceremony expressing good will, respect

Salver (n)- 1. tray, platter, plate. 2. waiter
Salvor (n)- one who salves or helps salvage a ship or cargo

Sam (n)- 1. slang - member of native American party with an illusion to Uncle Sam. 2. Abbrev. - surface to air missile
Samm (n)- to soften and moisten leather throughout

Sambuk (n)- small kind of Arab Dhow
Sambuke (n)- ancient stringed instrument of Syrian or Egyptian origin

Same (adj)- one and same thing. Identical
Sejm (n)- obs. - Polish assembly. Lower House of Parliament 1922

S

Samoyed (n)- Mongolian people, hunters and fishers, closely allied to the Lapps
Samoyede (n)- breed of dog, native to Siberia, used as sled dogs and herding reindeer

Sane- see Sain, Seine,

Saque- see Sac, Sack

Sarcel (n)- falconry - outer joint of a wing of a hawk
Sarcelle (n)- Teal - river duck

Sargent (n)- a palm of the Florida keys and Bahamas
Sergeant (n)- non-commissioned Army officer - rank above corporal

Sasin (n)- common antelope of India
Sasine (n)- Scots. law - seizing or possession of Feudal property

Sass (v)- slang - impudent or disrespectful talk
Sasse (n)- sluice, canal, or lock on navigable river

Satinet (n)- kind of thin satin or imitation satin
Satinette (n)- breed of fancy pigeon allied to the owl

Satiric (adj)- fond of indulging in satire
Satyric (adj)- pertaining to satyrs

Satle (v)- Eng. and Scot. - to settle
Sattle (n)- merchandising sailing vessel in 17th century

Saturater (n)- one who or that which saturates
Saturator (n)- apparatus for supplying moist air to rooms

Satyric- see Satiric

Saul (pr.n)- 1. Masc. name. 2. 1st King of Israel. 3. Hebrew name for Apostle Paul
Saule (v)- obs. - to satiate

Sault (v)- obs. - to leap, jump, tumble
Salt (n)- colorless white crystal known chemically as sodium chloride

Saurel (n)- salt water food fish
Sorel (n)- buck (male deer) in 3rd year
Sorrel (n)- 1. various plants having succulent leaves used in salads and sauces. 2. reddish brown color.

Saury (n)- sharp snouted fish of the Atlantic
Sorry (adj)- 1. feeling regret, remorseful, contrite, repentant. 2. sad, pathetic

S

Savanna (n)- variety of West Indian fiddlewood tree
Savannah (n)- grassland in tropical region with scattered trees
Savannah (pr.n)- major city in state of Georgia

Saver (v)- one who saves
Savor (v)- season, flavor, tempt the appetite
Savour (n)- Brit. - relish, enjoy with appreciation

Sax- see Sacks, Seax

Say (v)- utter, pronounce, speak. Express in words
Sey (v)- Scot. - advance, arrive
Sae (adv)- Scottish form of so

Scail (v)- Scot. - to disperse, separate
Scale (n)- 1. weight, balance. 2. Astron. - sign or constellation Libra - the balance
Skale (v)- Eng. - spill, spatter

Scald (n)- 1. burn caused by hot liquid or steam. 2. (v)- to heat almost to the boiling point
Scalled (n)- scabby disease of the skin
Scauld (v)- Scot. - scold, berate
Skald (adj)- 1. affected with scall. 2. (n) - ancient Norse poet and singer, reciter

Scar (n)- mark left by a healed wound, sore or burn
Scaur (n)- Scot. - cliff, precipice

Scarf (n)- long broad piece of material worn about head, shoulders, neck, waist
Scarfe (n)- cormorant - aquatic bird

Scarp (n)- a steep descent
Scarpe (n)- Her. - a diminutive of the bend sinister - half its width

Scary (adj)- easily scared, timid. Alarming
Skerry (n)- 1. a rocky isle. 2. kind of potato

Scat (inter)- 1. go away, begone, scram. 2. (v) - slang - to sing Scat (jazz). 3. to drive fast
Scatt (n)- land tax in the Shetland Islands
Sceatt (n)- early Anglo-Saxon coin of silver, rarely gold
Skat (n)- card game played with 32 cards

Scath (n)- injury, harm, destruction
Scathe (v)- blast, wither, denounce fiercely

Scend (v)- Naut. - to be heaved upward by a swell
Send (v)- transmit, radio, televise, telegraph

S

Scene (n)- location, setting, region, surroundings
Seen (v)- p.p. of see. Manifest, understood
Sene (adj)- Archaic - wise, sensible, discreet

Scent (n)- 1. perfume, aroma, bouquet, fragrance. 2. track, trail, nose
Sent (v)- caused to go
Cent (n)- penny, coin. U.S. monetary unit

Scents (n-pl)- inhales, gets wind of, smells, detects
Cents (n-pl)- more than one cent. Coins
Cense (v)- perfume with incense
Sense (v)- 1. discover, regard, become aware of. 2. recognize

Schal (n)- catfish from the river Nile
Shall (v)- will, would

Schout (n)- bailiff in former Dutch colonies of America
Scout (v)- 1. investigate, search. 2. (n)- pioneer, watchman. 3. member of Boy or Girl Scouts.

Scilly (pr.n)- group of small isles, part of Cornwall in England
Silly (adj)- unwise, foolish, stupid, indiscreet

Scion (n)- 1. descendant, heir, offspring, successor, son. 2. twig, branch
Sion (n)- mount in Jerusalem

Scoat (n)- Brit. Dial. - a prop or a stay
Scote (n)- placing an obstacle or block to prevent rolling

Scoot (v)- Scot. and Eng. - shoot or squirt forth as water from a hose
Scout (n)- 1. Eng. Dial. - razor-billed auk. 2. a high rock
Scute (n)- 1. old French gold coin. 2. small shield or buckle

Scot (pr.n)- one of a Gaelic people. Native of Scotland
Scott (n)- defective piece of lumber, lowest grade

Scout- see Schout

Scrat (n)- Hermaphrodite. Biol. - an individual having both male and female reproductive organs
Skratt (v)- Eng. and Scot. - scratch

Screw (n)- a solid cylinder grooved, an advancing spiral on its surface
Scroo (n)- Scot. - stack. Haycock

Scull (n)- 1. light racing boat for one or more rowers. 2. (n) oar
Skull (n)- 1. bony framework of head enclosing and protecting the brain. Cranium, pate. 2. slang - intellectual, brain

S

Sculptor (n)- modeler, carver, artist, designer
Sculpture (v)- chisel, carve, fashion, mold, cast

Scut (n)- to dock an animal's tail
Scute (n)- Zool. - a thin plate or scale - scutelium

Scye (n)- Scot. - armhole of a garment into which sleeve is set

Sie (v)- Eng. and Scot. 1. sink, fall, descend. 2. sift. 3. drift
Sigh (n)- 1. moan, whine, wail. 2. deep audible breath
Sye (n)- Eng. and Scot. - scythe
Psi (n)- 1. pounds per square inch. 2. 23rd letter of Greek alphabet

Sea (n)- 1. deep sea, ocean, ship route, high seas. 2. multitude, abundance, mass quantity
See (v)- 1. get knowledge through the eyes. Perceive visually. 2. comprehend, understand
Sí (adv)- Italian and Spanish for yes
Cie (n)- French - company
Cee (n)- 1. obs. - 16th part of a penny. 2. certain quantity of beer

Seal (v)- 1. secure, fasten, bolt, lock. 2. endorse, approve. 3. sign one's signature
Seel (v)- 1. close the eyes. 2. to blind
Sele (n)- Eng. and Scot. - a time, a season, an occasion
Ciel (n)- furniture - a canopy or tester
Ceil (n)- overlay wall with plaster, wood, etc.

Sealing (v)- securing, closing, fastening. Attaching together
Seeling (v)- p.p. of seel. Closing the eyes
Ceiling (n)- overhead of a room. Topside, interior, lining of a room

Seam (n)- joint, weld, junction, closure, suture, fissure
Seem (v)- look, exhibit, appear to be, show
Seme (n)- obs. - load, burden

Seamed (v)- cracked open, became fissured
Seemed (v)- appeared, became, gave impression of being

Seamen (n)- sailors, mariners
Semen (n)- fluid which carries male sperm

Sear (v)- 1. dry, parch, scorch, burn. 2. (n) - catch in a gunlock
Seer (n)- prophet, crystal gazer, fortune teller
Sere (adj)- 1. withered, shriveled. 2. separate, different
Ser (n)- unit of weight in India
Cere (v)- coat or cover with wax

Seax- see Sacks, Sax

S

Seas (n-pl)- 1. large bodies of water. Plural of sea. 2. multitudes, abundance
Sees (v)- 1. discerns objects, colors by using eyes. 2. comprehends, understands
Seize (v)- impound, intercept, confiscate, usurp

Sec (adj)- Fr. - dry - used of wines and opposed to brut
Seck (adj)- unprofitable, barren - said of rents

See- see Sea, Sí, Cie, Cee

Sects (n-pl)- 1. religious denominations that have broken from established church. 2. groups under a common leadership
Sex (n)- 1. gender - masculine or feminine. 2. allurement, magnetism

Seed (n)- 1. germ, spore, egg, sperm. 2. progeny, offspring
Cede (v)- yield, concede, surrender, hand over

Seeder (n)- person or apparatus for sowing seeds
Cedar (n)- evergreen tree
Ceder (n)- yielder, conceder, resigner, releaser

Seek (v)- to go in search or quest of. Nose out, hunt, explore
Sikh (pr.n)- member of religious sect in Northern India

Seel- see Seal, Sele, Ciel, Ceil

Seeling- see Sealing

Seem- see Seam, Seme

Seen (adj)- 1. observed, skillful. 2. manifest, understood
Sene (adj)- wise, sensible, discreet
Scene (n)- 1. picture, vista, show, view. 2. division of a play, act

Seer- see Sear, Sere, Ser, Cere

Sees- see Seas, Seize

Seg (n) obs. - a nobleman, a knight
Segg (n) Scot. - a boar, bull or ram castrated at maturity
Segge (n)- cuttlefish

Seignor (n)- lord and master, ruler, overlord, chief
Senior (adj)- older, first born, elder

Seine- see Sain, Sane

Seize- see Seas, Seas

Sejm (n)- Polish assembly. Lower house of Parliament 1922
Same (adj)- equal, similiar, like, identical

S

Sell (v)- dispose of for a price, market, vend, peddle
Cell (n)- small compartment, cage, jail

Seme- see Seam

Seller (n)- trader, merchant, shopkeeper, vender, retailer
Cellar (n)- basement, vault, subterranean room

Semen (n)- fluid which carries the male sperm
Seamen (n)- sailors, mariners

Senate (pr.n)- United States Senate
Senate (n)- governing body, state council, legislative body
Sennet (n)- 1. signal of entrance or exit, sounded on a horn. 2. the barracuda
Sennight (n)- Archaic - seven days and seven nights
Sennit (n)- 1. Naut. - flat braid cordage used on shipboard. 2. Chem. - pinite

Send (v)- dispatch, guide, send forth, deliver, consign
Scend (v)- Naut. - to be heaved upward by a swell

Senior (n)- superior, master, higher rank, more experienced
Seigner (n)- aristocrat, peer, blue blood, nobleman, lord

Sennet- see Senate

Sense (n)- 1. common sense, grasp, sharpness of mind, understanding. 2. recognize, become aware of
Scents (n.pl)- detects, smells, gets wind of, inhales
Cents (n.pl)- more than one cent. Coins
Cense (v)- perfume with incense

Sent (v)- caused to go
Cent (n)- penny, coin. U.S. monetary unit
Scent (v)- 1. perceive by smell, breathe, inhale. 2. track, trail, nose

Sentience (n)- capacity for sensation or feeling
Sentients (adj)- feels power of perception by senses, mind

Septain (n)- obs. - stanza of seven verses
Septane (n)- heptane (liquid hydrocarbon contained in petroleum)

Sequence (n)- succession, order, continued or connected series
Sequents (n.pl)- following logically or naturally, consecutive

Ser- see Sear, Sere, Seer Cere

Serf (n)- bondman, slave, helot, in fuedal servitude
Surf (n)- breaking waves, ground swell, whitecaps, spray

S

Serge (n)- twilled worsted cloth used for suits and linings
Surge (v)- 1. flock, swarm, mass. 2. swell, swirl, roll along. 3. rise and fall

Sergeant (n)- non commissioned officer - rank above corporal
Sargent (n)- a palm of the Florida Keys and Bahamas

Serial (adj)- anything published or broadcast at regular intervals
Cereal (n)- breakfast food made of grain

Serious (adj)- grave aspect, solemn disposition, critical, severe
Sirius (n)- dog star in canis major. Brightest star in the heaven
Cereus (adj)- plant bearing fragrant flowers opening at night
Cerous (adj)- chemical containing cerium

Serpet (n)- a kind of rush. A basket made of serpet
Serpette (n)- a pruning knife with a curved blade

Serrate (n)- notched, like the edge of a saw. Toothed
Cirrate (adj)- 1. having ringlets. 2. zool. - bearing cirri
Cerrate (n)- 1. ointment, salve. 2. waxed

Serviteur (n)- glass making - a man who fashions body of articles finished by workmen
Servitor (n)- one who serves, an attendant, a serving man

Session (n)- meeting, seance, assembly, council, court
Cession (n)- surrender, yielding, granting

Setaceous (adj)- bristly - coarse hair
Cetaceous (adj)- species of whale

Seth- see Saith

Sew (v)- fasten stitches, join by thread and needle by hand or machine
So (adv)- then, therefore, hence, whence
Soe (n)- large cask, large wooden tub
Sow (v)- scatter seed for purpose of growth

Sewer (n)- 1. one who or that which sews. 2. larva of a moth
Sower (n)- one who or that which sows

Sewer (n)- artificial conduit for carrying waste material & refuse
Suer (n)- summoner, impeacher, prosecuter, one who sues

Sex (n)- 1. males or females (men or women) collectively. 2. allurement, magnetism
Sects (n.pl)- 1. group or people having common leadership. 2. denominations that have broken from the established church

S

Sexed (adj)- belonging to sex. Having sex
Sext (n)- 1. Music - a sixth. 2. Eccl. - one of the canonical hours

Sey- see Sae, Say

Sha (n)- the corial - wild sheep of India
Shah (n)- king, sovereign, prince

Shad (n)- kind of fish
Shadd (n) mining - rounded stones containing tin or ore lying on surface indicating a vein

Shagreen (n)- 1. back of a horse. 2. rough skin of a shark
Chagrin (n)- humiliation, shame, despair, dismay

Shail (n)- obs. - a kind of scarecrow
Shale (n)- rock resembling slate

Shaird (n)- Scot. - fragment, piece
Shared (v)- apportioned, divided, partook

Shaitan (n)- among Mohammedans - an evil spirit, a devil
Sheitan (n)- India - a dust storm

Shake (n)- tremulous motion, quiver, jounce, sway
Sheik (n)- 1. highest dignitary of respect. 2. Arab chief

Shale- see Shail

Shall- see Shal

Shanty (n)- shed, shack, cabin, cottage, hovel
Chanty or Chantey (n)- a sailor's song

Shared (v)- apportioned, divided, partook
Shaired (n)- Scot. - fragment, piece

Shark (n)- large voracious, destructive fish
Chark (n)- 1. fire drill or fire churn. 2. small Russian glass or cup

Shays (pr.n) Daniel. Leader of Shay's Rebellion in Massachusetts
Chaise (n)- light open carriage usually with hood

Shear (v)- trim, fleece, cut with scissors, crop
Sheer (adj)- 1. upright, plumb, steep. 2. swerve, veer. 3. thin material, veil

She (n)- 1. a woman. 2. animal or person of female sex
Shee (n)- obs. - Irish fairy folk

Sheer- see Shear

S

Sheik (n)- highest dignitary of respect. Arab chief - also pronounced chic
Shake (n)- quiver, tremulous motion, jounce, sway

Sheik (n)- Arab chief. Highest functioning dignitary of respect - also pronounced shake
Chic (n)- 1. stylish, attractive, in style. 2. (adj) - fashionable

Shela (n)- fine muslin or silk
Shelah (n)- a clan name

Shide (n)- obs. - thin board, plank
Shied (v)- p.p. of shy

Shier (n)- a horse that shies or startles easily
Shire (n)- Brit. - division of land, counties
Shyer (adj)- more timid, bashful or more shy

Shinny (v)- climb by use of shins - chiefly with up
Shinney (n)- a game of hockey informally played by schoolboys, etc.

Shir (n)- Persian tiger
Shirr (v)- 1. bake eggs in buttered shallow dish with crumbs. 2. (v)- draw up or gather cloth
Sure (adj)- undoubting, positive, persuaded, convinced, confident

Sho (n)- Japanese measure of weight
Show (v)- 1. direct, guide. 2. prove, explain. 3. to exhibit

Shoad (v)- Brit. mining - loose collection of minerals separated from the vein
Shode (v)- obs. - a parting, a separation
Showed (v)- 1. put on display. 2. made an entrance, an appearance

Shoal (n)- school or assemblage of fish
Shole (n)- props supporting ship in dry dock

Shoar (n)- Brit. - a prop, temporary support
Shore (n)- pillar, support, foundation, mainstay

Shoat (n)- young hog
Shote (n)- worthless fellow

Shock (n)- impact, sudden violent blow, concussion, attack
Shough (n)- dog with shaggy hair

Shode- see Shoad, Showed

S

Shoe (n)- external covering for the foot. Sandal, loafer, boot
Shoo (interj)- exclamation to drive away. Slang - scat, begone, beat it
Shu (n)- Egypt. Relig. - a solar diety
Shue (n)- Tibetan deer

Shole- see Shoal

Shone (v)- past tense of shine. Gave forth light. Was radiant
Shown (v)- past participle of show. Expose or present to view

Shool (v)- Scot. - to shovel
Shul (n)- Synagogue

Shoo- see Shoe, Shu, Shue

Shoot (n)- 1. match contest at games of shooting. 2. bot. - twig, new growth
Shute (n)- flume, artificial channel
Chute (n)- 1. a fall, slanting trough. 2. rapids, waterfall

Shophar or Shofar (n)- curved rams horn used in Jewish religious services
Choffer (n) Scot. - portable heater or chafing dish
Chauffeur (n)- paid, licensed driver of private motor car

Shore- see Shoar

Shote- see Shoat

Shot (n)- 1. missile weapon, projectile. 2. small variety of trout
Shott (n)- shallow saline lake in the closed basins of North Africa

Shough- see Shock

Show (v)- 1. direct, guide. 2. prove, explain. 3. to exhibit
Sho (n)- Japanese measure of weight

Showed- see Shoad, Shode

Shown (v)- exhibit for view, sale or inspection
Shone (v)- past tense of shine. Gave forth light, was radiant

Shu- see Shoe, Shoo, Shue

Shul (n)- Synagogue
Shool (v)- Scot. - to shovel

Shute- see Shoot, Chute

Shyer- see Shier, Shire

176

S

Sí (adv)- Italian or Spanish for yes
See (v)- get knowledge through the eyes. Perceive vision
Sea (n)- ocean, deep sea - high seas, ship routes
Cie (n)- French - company
Cee (n)- 1. obs. - 16th part of a penny. 2. certain quantity of beer

Sibilous (n)- sibilant, hissing
Sibilus (n)- small flute in teaching song birds

Sic (adv)- 1. so or thus, it is so. 2. (v)- slang - to attack
Sick (adj)- unwell, ill, ailing, indisposed, bedridden
Sike (n)- Scot and Eng. - small stream, brook, rill

Sice (n)- number six at dice
Sais (n)- India - a groom

Side (adj)- 1. flanking, being at or on one side. 2. lateral. 3. aspect, phase
Sighed (v)- 1. moaned, fretted over, deplored. 2. bewailed, grieved for

Sider (n)- one who sides with a person or party. Adherent
Cider (n)- juice of apples used for drinking

Sie (v)- 1. obs. - sink, fall, descend. 2. drip, trickle. 3. sift
Sigh (n)- moan, deep audible breath, whine, wail
Sye (n)- Scot. and Eng. - a scythe
Scye (n)- Scot. - armhole of a garment into which a sleeve is set
Psi (n)- 1. pounds per square inch. 2. 23rd letter of Greek alphabet
Cy- 1. Chem. symbol frequently used for the cyanogen group CN. 2. Abbrev. for currency used in stock market tape

Sighed- see Side

Sigher (n)- one who sighs
Sire (n)- 1. father, procreator. 2. stud animal. 3. term addressing a king

Sighs (v)- 1. yearns, longs. 2. lets out one's breath audibly
Size (n)- scope, largeness, proportions, capacity, volume

Sight (n)- 1. vision, eyesight. 2. view, appearance
Site (n)- position, location, area, situation
Cite (v)- mention, summon, quote, enumerate

S

Sign (n)- 1. proof, mark, identification. 2. signature, trademark. 3. omen, wonder
Sine (n)- 1. mathematical ratio. 2. (prep) - Latin - sans, without
Syne (adv)- Eng. and Scot. - since. "Auld Lange Syne"

Signet (n)- official seal, stamp, small seal
Cygnet (n)- young swan

Sike (n) Eng. - ditch, drain, trench
Syke (n) Her. - a fountain

Sike- see Sic, Sick

Sikh- see Seek

Sile (n)- Scot. - spawn or fry of a fish. A young herring
Sill (n)- 1. basis or foundation of a thing. 2. horizontal piece of lumber

Silicious (n)- containing silica
Cilicious (v)- hairlike process

Silkie (n)- 1. a seal. 2. breed of domestic fowl
Silky (adj)- made of silk, smooth and soft

Sill- see Sile

Silly- see Scilly

Simar (n)- Archaic - undergarment of chemise
Cymar (n)- loose robe for women

Simba (n)- African Swahili name for lion
Cymba (n)- Zool. - a boat shaped sponge spicule

Simball (n)- New England slang - kind of doughnut
Symbol (n)- sign, emblem, mark, brand
Cymbol (n)- musical instrument
Simbal (n)- obs. - confectionary or cake

Simon (pr.n)- 1. Apostle Peter. 2. masc. name
Cimon (n)- Athenian general

Sind (n)- Eng. Dial. - a rinsing. A drink to wash down solid food
Sinned (n)- erred, transgressed. Inequity

Sine- see Sign, Syne

Single (adj.)- solitary, sole, one, separate
Cingle (n)- girth for horses

S

Sink (v)- 1. subside, drop, wane. 2. kitchen receptacle attached to drain
Cinque (n)- a five on dice or cards
Sync (v)- slang - synchronize

Sinned- see Sind

Sion or Zion (n)- Mount in Jerusalem
Scion (n)- 1. twig, graft. 2. son, descendant, heir, offspring

Sioux (n.pl)- Dakota tribe of North American Indians
Sou (n)- small French coin
Sough (v)- make a rustling or murmuring sound
Sue (v)- 1. serve with a writ, summon, prefer a claim. 2. implore, plead. 3. prosecute, indict
Sue (pr.n)- 1. Eugene, French writer. 2. Fem. name

Sir (n)- respectful title. Man of rank, lord, master
Sur (n)- 1. mullet, red. 2. above, upon, over

Sire- see Sigher

Sirius- see Serious, Cereus, Cerous

Sis (n)- 1. sister, girl, sweetheart. 2. slang - cowardly, weak, effeminate
Siss (v)- pl. of sithe - journey, travel

Sis (n)- Six - highest number on a die. Cast of six in dicing
Syce (n)- India - groom

Sist (n) Scot. - cite, summon, bring into court
Cyst (n)- saclike structure containing fluid
Cist (n)- box or chest containing sacred utensils

Sit (v)- 1. perch, roost, convene. 2. slang - be situated
Cit (n)- city person, cited. Slang for citizen

Site- see Sight, Cite

Sizar (n)- Cambridge or Dublin student who is exempted from college fees & charges
Sizer (n)- instrument or contrivance with which to size articles

Size (n)- dimensions, volume, bulk, scope, measurement
Sighs (v)- 1. yearns, longs. 2. lets out one's breath audibly

Skald - see Scald, Scauld, Scalled

Skale - see Scale, Scail

Skat - see Scat, Scatt

Skait (n)- Scot. - old horse, wizened creature
Skate (n)- 1. roller skate, ice skate. 2. food fish. 3. (v) slang - avoid paying creditor. 4. cheap skate

S

Skee - see Ski

Skerry (n)- Scot.- 1. a rocky isle. 2. kind of potato
Scary (adj)- easily scared, timid, alarming

Skil (n)- candlefish - Alaska
Skill (v)- export, be dexterous, be knowing

Ski (n)- long, narrow wooden snow-shoe
Skee (n)- 1. slang - whiskey. 2. underworld use for opium

Skite (v)- Scot. - slip, slide or scoot
Skyte (n)- quick, sharp, slap

Skratt (v)- obs. - Eng. and Scot. - scratch. Toil, drudge
Scrat (n)- hermaphrodite. Biol. - an individual having both male and female reproductive organs

Skull (n)- 1. top of the head, cranium, pate. 2. slang - intellectual, brain
Scull (n)- 1. light racing boat for one or more rowers. 2. oar

Sky (n)- upper atmosphere. Heavens. Firmament
Skye (pr.n)- 1. isle - inner Hebrides. 2. Terrier (dog)

Skyte (n)- quick, sharp, slap
Skite (v)- Scot. - slip, slide, scoot

Slae (n)- Scot. - the blackthorn, sloe
Slay (v)- murder, massacre, execute, exterminate, kill
Sleigh (n)- sled, cutter, sledge, runner
Sley (n)- 1. weaver's tool. 2. guideways of knitting machine. 3. reed of a loom

Slack (adj)- loose, relaxed, inactive, slow, lax
Slak (n)- obs.- 1. beating, blow, defeat. 2. slaughter

Slain (v)- p.p. of slay. Murdered, killed
Slane (n)- Eng. Dial. - kind of long handled spade

Slait (n)- Scot. - a sheep walk. A familiar walk
Slate (n)- 1. fine grained grayish rock. shale. 2. politics - list of candidates

Slak - see Slack

Slane - see Slain

Slate - see Slait

Sleave (v)- divide or separate into filaments as silk
Sleeve (n)- part of the garment that covers the arms

Sleigh - see Slay, Sley, Slae

S

Sleight (n)- 1. tricks, deceit, device, hoax. 2. dexterity, cunning
Slight (adj)- 1. petty, trivial, foolish, unimportant, meager. 2. tiny, little, wee

Slew (n)- 1. large group or number. Multitude. 2. p.p. of slay
Slough (n)- march, bog, swamp, mire, quagmire, quicksand
Slue (n)- swing around, turn on its own axis. Twist

Slight - see Sleight

Slipe (n)- unscoured skin wool
Slype (n)- Arch. - narrow passage in certain English cathedrals

Sloak (n)- Scot.- 1. drink, draft. 2. a bog. 3. (v) - quench
Sloke (n)- Scot. - slime or scum in water

Sloan (adj)- Scot and Eng. - lazy, worthless, sly
Slone (n)- Eng. - a sloe

Sloe (n)- shrub or small tree with dark, purple fruit
Slow (v)- 1. delay, rein, control, brake. 2. keep back. 3. not fast

Sloke - see Sloak

Slone - see Sloan

Slough - see Slew

Slow - see Sloe

Slue - see Slew

Slype (n)- Arch - narrow passage in certain English Cathedrals
Slipe (n)- unscoured skin wool

Smear (n)- 1. soil, stain, smudge. 2. (v) - libel, slander. 3. slang - bribe
Smeir (n)- potters slip glaze

Smerk (adj)- Brit. Dial. - spruce, neat
Smirk (n)- complacent, conceited smile

Smit (n)- slang - combination of smog and particles of manure in the air
Smitt (n)- Scot. - fine clay used for marking sheep

Snacket (n)- Brit. - door latch
Snacot (n)- pipe fish

Sneeze (n)- sudden violent audible expiration through the nose
Snese (v)- obs. - to pierce

Snoter (adj)- prudent, wise
Snotter (n)- Naut. - loop or ring of rope or metal

S

So (adv)- therefore, hence, accordingly
Soe (n)- a large cask. A large wooden tub
Sow (v)- plant seed, capable of producing a crop
Sew (v)- hem, baste, stitch, secure with thread

Soak (v)- immerse, flood, saturate. Keep or lie in liquid
Soke (n)- Eng. law - territorial jurisdiction of a court

Soal (n)- Brit. - a dirty pool
Soale (n)- obs. - sole of the foot
Sol (n)- monetary unit of Peru. Silver coin
Sole (n)- 1. marine flat fish. 2. underpart of shoe, boot, foot
Solle (v)- go about on All Saints Day singing and begging for soul cakes

Soul (n)- essence, principle of life, spirit, immortal part
Soule (adj)- sullen desolate
Sowl (n)- contracted from. Eng. Dial. - relish, sauce
Sowle (v)- to pull by the ears

Soap (n)- 1. cleansing agent. 2. slang - flattery - soft soap
Sope (n)- Eng. Dial - sup, gulp

Soar (n)- glide at height, fly, plane, be high, hover
Sore (n)- 1. painful, festered, aching. 2. inflamed

Soared (v)- flew, extended upward, towered, planed, ascended
Sword (n)- sharp bladed weapon, rapier, sword, cutlass

Soc (n)- Siam - measure of weight
Sock (n)- 1. hose, stocking. 2. (v) - hit, beat

Soccer (n)- form of football in which use of arms or hands is prohibited
Socker (v)- one who hits, esp. with a fist

Socks (n)- 1. stockings, hosiery. 2. (v) - hits with force. 3. Brit. Dial - plow shares
Sox (n)- short hosiery

Soke - see Soak

Sol - see Soal

Solar (adj)- pertaining to the sun
Soler (n)- one who soles shoes, boots

Sold (v)- exchanged goods or services for money
Soled (v)- furnished shoe with a new sole
Souled (adj)- having a soul or feeling

Soler (n)- loft, garret, upper chamber
Soller (n)- mining - platform in a shaft

S

Some (adj)- specified or certain quantity or amount. A few, any
Sum (n)- 1. all, total, whole amount. 2. quantity of money. 3. (v) - compute, calculate, addition

Son (n)- offspring, male child, lineal descendant
Sun (n)- source of light. Central star of solar system
Sunn (n)- 1. East Indian shrub. 2. innerbark fiber used for making rope

Sonny (n)- little son. Used in addressing any young boy
Sunni (n)- member of one of two great sects of Moslems
Sunny (adj)- 1. happy, genial, smiling, cheerful, joyous. 2. warm, summery, abounding in sunshine

Soot (n)- fine particles of black carbon substance due to combination of coal, wood
Suit (n)- set of garments, clothes, attire, wearing apparel, outfit

Sope (n)- Eng. Dial. - sup, gulp
Soap (n)- 1. a cleansing agent. 2. slang - flattery, soft-soap

Sophi (n)- former title of Kings of Persia
Sophy (pr.n)- 1. Fem. name, dim. of Sophia, Sophie. 2. (n) - obs. - philosophy

Sora (n)- small billed bird
Psora (n)- Med. - scabies, itch

Sore (n)- irritated, bitter, painful, aching
Soar (v)- fly upward, rise, climb, wing, tower

Sorrel (adj)- 1. reddish brown color. 2. (n)- plant whose leaves are used for salad and sauces
Sorel (n)- buck (male deer) in third year
Saurel (n)- small marine salt water fish

Sorry (adj)- 1. sad, pathetic. 2. feeling regret, contrite, repentant
Saury (n)- sharp snouted fish of the Atlantic

Sough - see Sioux, Sou, Sue

Soul - see Soal, Sole, Sol

Souled - see Soled, Sold

Soup (n)- 1. liquid food made by boiling meat and or vegetables. 2. slang - dynamite, nitro
Supe (n)- slang - supercharge, superintendent

Sousa (pr.n)- John Philip. U.S. composer and band conductor
Susa (pr.n)- ruined city in W. Iran

S

Sous (n)- Eng. Dial. - a half penny, a sou
Souse (n)- 1. liquid used for pickling. 2. a drunkard
Sowce (n)- obs. - a pounding blow

Sow (v)- scatter seed over land for growth
Soe (n)- large cask, large wooden tub
So (adv)- therefore, also, likewise, more or less
Sew (v)- baste, embroider, fasten with stitches, bind, hem

Sowce - see Sous, Souse

Sower (n)- one who or that which sows seed
Sewer (n)- 1. larva of a moth. 2. one who used needle and thread

Sox (n-pl)- short hosiery
Socks (n)- 1. stockings, hosiery. 2. Brit. Dial. - plow shares. 3. (v) - hits with force

Spae (v)- Scand. - foretell or prophecy
Spay (v)- 1. remove ovaries from female animal. 2. male red deer in his 3rd year

Spall (n)- chip or splinter as of stone or ore
Spawl (v)- Archaic - spit, expectorate

Sparse (adj)- thinly scattered or distributed. Scanty
Spars (n)- 1. Naut. - stout poles used as masts. 2. women enlisted in U.S. Coast Guard

Spate (n)- sudden overwhelming, outpouring
Speight (n)- woodpecker

Spawl - see Spall

Spay - see Spae

Speak (v)- talk, say, tell, converse, utter
Speke (n)- a cave

Spear (n)- 1. long sharp pointed weapon, lance, javelin, harpoon. 2. Bot. - sprout, germinate. 3. (v) - penetrate pierce, puncture
Speer (v)- 1. Scottish - inquire, question. 2. (n) - Eng. - a chimney post
Spere (n)- Eng. - to ask in marriage

Speel (v)- Scottish - to climb. Spindle
Spiel (n)- 1. play, game. 2. (v) - talk, speak, orate

Speer - see Spear, Spere

Speight - see Spate

S

Speiss (n)- one or more metallic arsenides obtained by smelting certain ores
Spice (n)- dried vegetable substance as clove, cinnamon, etc. to season food

Speke - see Speak

Speld (v)- Scot. - to spread open, extend
Spelled (v)- 1. read letter by letter, formed words. 2. allowed an interval of rest, relieved another in work or duty

Spere - see Spear, Speer

Spice - see Speiss

Spiel - see Speel

Spight (n)- British Dial. - vex, offend
Spite (n)- contempt, scorn, humiliate, grudge

Spiritual (adj)- consisting of spirit, unearthly, ethereal, super natural
Spirituel (adj)- clever, subtle, witty, wise, tactful, discreet

Spite - see Spight

Spits (n-pl)- ejects saliva from the mouth
Spitz (n)- small dog with long hair, pointed muzzle and ears

Spoom (v)- Naut. - to drive steadily and swiftly as before a strong wind
Spume (v)- to froth, foam

Sprew (n)- Pathology - tropical disease. Thrush, psilosis
Sprue (n)- opening or passage through which molten metal is poured into a mold

Spright (n)- obs. - ghost, spirit, apparition
Sprite (n)- 1. life, vital essence. 2. beach crab. 3. short arrow

Sprue - see Sprew

Spume - see Spoom

Spur (n)- a goad to action, impel, urge
Spurre (n)- Scot. - the common tern

Stade (n)- 1. obs. - a stadium. 2. furlong. 3. surname
Staid (adj)- settled or sedate character, sober, steady
Stayed (v)- dwelt, resided, took up quarters, lived, remained

Staff (n)- stick, pole, rod, crutch, cane, cudgel
Staph (adj)- often used as in staph infection, bacteria, from noun staphyloccus

S

Staid - see Stade, Stayed

Staik (n)- Scot. - butcher's meat
Stake (n)- 1. pointed stick, pole, post. 2. that which is wagered - kitty, ante, bet
Steak (n)- slice of meat or fish - cut thick for broiling or frying

Stain (n)- blemish, tarnish, flaw, splotch, soil, spot
Stane (n)- Scot and Eng. Dial. - stone

Stains (n-pl)- spots, soils, flaws, tarnishes
Staines (pr.n)- town near Windsor, Eng.

Stair (n)- one step of a flight of stairs
Stare (v)- look intently, rivet eyes upon, watch, eye

Stake- see Steak, Staik

Stamen (n)- Botany - male reproductive organ in flowers
Stamin (n)- obs. - variety of coarse woolen cloth

Stanch (adj)- firm, steadfast in principle, adherence, loyalty
Staunch (v)- stop the flow of liquid especially blood from a wound

Stane- see Stain

Stap (n)- Archaic - a stave of a cask or tub
Staup (v)- Eng. and Scot. - to walk awkwardly, walk with difficulty

Staph (adj)- often used as in "staph" infection, bacteria, from noun staphyloccus
Staff (n)- stick, pole, rod, crutch, cane, cudgel

Star (n)- 1. heavenly body other than moon, comets, etc. 2. asterisk. 3. slang - headline attraction, first class
Starr (n)- Eng. - sedge, beach grass
Starre (v)- to quarrel

Stare- see Stair

Stater (n)- Greek standard of money and weight
Stator (n)- Electrical - stationary parts of a dynamo

Stationary (adj)- having a fixed position, not movable, riveted
Stationery (n)- writing materials, paper, pens, ink, clips, etc.

Staup- see Stap

Stayed- see Stade, Staid

S

Steak (n)- large slice of beef or fish or hamburger for broiling, frying
Stake (n)- 1. that which is wagered. Kitty, ante, jackpot, bet. 2. pointed stick, pole, rod, peg
Staik (n)- Scot. - butcher's meat

Steal (v)- pilfer, rob, pinch, shoplift. Take dishonestly
Steel (v)- 1. harden, strengthen, inflexible. 2. (n) hard, tough metal. 3 (n)- sword, dagger, knife
Stele (n)- Archeol. - upright slab or pillar of stone bearing an inscription

Stealer (n)- a thief. One who steals
Steeler (n)- one who steels or overlays with steel

Steam (n)- mist formed by condensation of water. Visible vapor
Steem (v & n)- 1. - obs. - esteem, value. 2. gleam, flame

Stean (n)- wall of brick, stone, cement used as lining of well, cistern, pool
Steen (n)- 1. slang - cardinal number from 13 to 19. 2. any large number

Stearn (n)- Eng. - European starling
Stern (adj)- 1. firm, strict, immovable, resolute, cruel. 2. (n)- rear part of anything e.g. ship, backside, tail, rudder

Steek (v)- Eng. - to pierce, prick
Steik (n)- Scot. - a stitch, as a loop in knitting. Thread

Steel - see Steal, Stele

Steem- see Steam

Steen- see Stean

Steer (n)- 1. any male of beef cattle. 2. (v) - guide, direct, pilot, navigate
Stere (n)- cubic meter or 35.3156 cubic feet. Sometimes used to measure cordwood

Stele- see Steal, Steel

Step (n)- move or go by using the feet, walk, tread, stride, pace
Steppe (n)- extensive plain, prairie, flat, level, tundra

Sterling (n)- British money of account, as of gold and silver as pounds sterling, sterling plate
Stirling (pr.n)- royal burgh in central Scotland

Stere- see Steer

Stern- see Stearn

S

Stich (n)- row, verse, line
Stick (v)- to cleave, remain in same place, cling, adhere

Sticks (n-pl)- branches, twigs, long pieces of wood, switch, pole
Styx (pr.n)- Greek Myth. River of lower world over which souls of the dead were ferried

Stile (n)- series of steps for going up or down in getting over a fence or wall
Style (n)- fashion, mode, vogue, contemporary taste, fad

Stir (v)- move, excite, agitate, rouse, provoke, mix around
Styr (pr.n)- river in USSR formerly in Poland

Stirling (pr.n)- royal burgh in central Scotland
Sterling (n)- British money of account, as of gold and silver as pounds sterling, sterling plate

Stoep (n)- South African - porch or veranda
Stoop (n)- 1. act of bending, nod, droop, bows, salaam, kneel. 2. raised entrance
Stoup (n)- Scot.- 1. a pail or bucket. 2. drinking vessel as cups or tankards. 3. basin for holy water
Stupe (n)- 1. Med. - soft material used in dressing a wound. 2. slang - a stupid person

Storey (n)- Brit. set of rooms on same floor or level of bldg.
Story (n)- tale, narrative, fiction, account, fable, yarn, epic

Storeys (n-pl)- Brit. storeys or floors of a building
Stories (-pl)- 1. fictitious literary compositions or prose. 2. fibs, falseheads

Story- see Storey

Stoup- see Stoep, Stoop, Stupe

Stow (v)- pack or store away in orderly, compact manner
Stowe (pr.n)- Harriet Beecher. American author

Straight (adj)- without a curve or bend. Direct, plumb, erect, in alignment
Strait (n)- 1. narrow passage of water, canal, narrows, inlet. 2. distress, plight

Straighten (v)- become or make straight, align, correct
Straiten (v)- 1. financial difficulties, put in a hole, bankrupt. 2. restrict in range, limit, confine

Strait- see Straight

Straiten- see Straighten

S

Streak (n)- 1. long narrow band, mark, vein. 2. (v) - flash, go rapidly
Streek (v)- obs. - commence, begin

Strut (v)- walk with a vain pompous bearing, swagger
Strutte (v)- obs. - to swell, bulge out

Stub (n)- 1. short remaining piece of pencil, candle, cigar. 2. a stump
Stubb (n)- fog dog - luminous spot sometimes seen in fog near the horizon

Stupe- see Stoep, Stoop, Stoup

Sty (n)- 1. a pen for pigs. 2. foul depraved place
Stye (n)- small inflamed swelling of a gland on the rim of eyelid

Style (n)- manner of expression, mode, language, form
Stile (n)- series of steps for getting over a fence or wall

Stymie (v)- slang - impede, frustrate, foil
Stymy (n)- Golf - bring ball into position

Styr- see Stir

Styx- see Sticks

Subbase (n)- Arch. - lowest part of the base
Subbass (n)- Music - pedal producing lowest tones of an organ

Subtiler (adj)- more cunning, craftier, wilier
Subtler (adj)- comparative of subtle. Adroit, quick
Sutler (n)- do dirty work, peddle, soil, sully, mean word

Subtle (adj)- 1. crafty, wily, cunning, sly. 2. diplomatic. 3. clever, expert, adroit
Suttle (n)- to carry on the business of a sutler

Succor (n)- helping hand, aid, subsidy, accomodation. Relief, assistance
Sucker (n)- 1. branch, twig, sprout, tendril. 2. lollypop. 3. mouth, aperture. 4. slang - victim, dupe

Sucker- see Succor

Suds (n-pl)- soapy water, lather, foamy
Sudds (n-pl)- floating vegetable matter which often obstructs navigation in the white Nile

Sue (v)- 1. institute process in law against. 2. prosecute, indict. 3. petition, beg
Sue (pr.n)- 1. Eugene. French novelist. 2. female name
Sioux (-pl)- Dakota tribe of No. American Indians
Sou (n)- French monetary unit
Sough (v)- to make a rustling or murmuring sound

S

Suede (n)- kid or other leather finished on flesh side with soft nap

Swayed (v)- influenced, controlled, ruled, dominated

Suer- see Sewer

Suisse (n)- French - porter of a large house
Swiss (pr.n)- native or inhabitant of Switzerland

Suit (v)- 1. fit, agree, concur. 2. please, gratify, satisfy
Soot (n)- fine particles of black substance due to combustion of coal, wood, oil

Suite (n)- company of followers, convoy, following, entourage
Sweet (adj)- candied, sugary, honeyed, pleasing to the taste

Sum (v)- 1. addition, calculate, add together, compute, account. 2. quantity of money. 3. all, total
Some (adj)- approximately, not far from, near, almost, more or less

Sun (n)- day star, orbit of the day, luminary. Source of light
Sunn (n)- 1. tall East Indian shrub. 2. inner bark fiber used for making ropes
Son (n)- male descendant, male child, scion, junior

Sundae (n)- ice cream with syrup, whipped cream and chopped nuts poured over it
Sunday (n)- 1. Sabbath, Lord's day. 2. first day of week. 3. day of worship, day of rest

Sunni (n)- member of one of two great sects of Moslems
Sunny (adj)- 1. abounding in sunshine, warm, hot, unclouded, summery. 2. happy, joyous, smiling
Sonny (n)- little son. Used in addressing any young boy in a familiar manner

Supe- see Soup

Superintendence (n)- supervision, overseeing, inspecting, regulation, control
Superintendents (n) inspectors, foremen, supervisors

Sur (n)- 1. mullet, red. 2. above, upon, over
Sir (n)- 1. respectful title. 2. man of rank, lord, master

Sura (n)- a chapter of the Koran
Surah (n)- soft twilled fabric of silk or rayon
Surra (n)- Vet. - infectious disease of horses, camels, elephants, dogs

Surcle (n)- obs. - Bot. - a little shoot, a sucker
Circle (n)- ring, encircle, sphere, orb, girdle

S

Sure (adj)- free from doubt, certain, confident, positive
Shirr (v)- 1. to draw up or gather cloth on parallel threads. 2. cook. Bake eggs with crumbs
Shir (n)- Persian tiger

Surf (n)- swell of the sea
Serf (n)- peasant, clod, bondman, slave, in servitude

Surge (n)- rush, sweep, swell, rising, ascension, deluge
Serge (n)- twilled fabric of wool, cotton, silk

Surt (pr.n)- Norse myth - fire demon
Syrt (n)- quicksand. Bog

Surra- see Sura, Surah

Sus (n)- genus of swine, now restricted to European wild boar
Suss (n)- Eng. and Scot - mess, slop, muddle, swill

Susa (pr.n)- ruined city in West Iran
Sousa (pr.n)- John Philip. U.S. composer and band conductor

Sutler- see Subtiler, Subtler

Suttle (v)- to carry on the business of a sutler
Subtle (adj)- 1. clever, expert, adroit, quick. 2. diplomatic. 3. crafty, wily, sly

Swain (n)- 1. boyfriend, suitor, beau, lover, wooer, admirer. 2. farmer, rustic, boor
Sweyne (pr.n)- King of Denmark - 1014

Swalloe (n)- trepang or sea slug
Swallow (v)- absorb, ingest, gulp. Take into the stomach through the throat

Swap (v)- give and take, interchange, drive a bargain, dicker
Swop (v)- strike hands in bargaining

Swayed (v)- lurched, reeled, waved, vibrated, swung
Suede (n)- tanned leather, kid or calf, having flesh side buffed into a nap

Swear (v)- 1. to make a promise, threat, vow. 2. slang - to use profane language
Sweer (adj)- Scot. and Eng. - oppressive, difficult, grevious

Sweet (n)- honey, molasses, sugar, syrup, saccharine
Suite (n)- retinue, train of attendants, cortege, staff

Sweyne- see Swain

Swiss- see Suisse

S

Swop (v)- strike hands in bargaining
Swap (v)- exchange one thing for another, trade, barter, reciprocate

Sword (n)- symbol of military power, destruction by sword, combat, slaughter
Soared (v)- flew, extended, rose to higher level, wafted

Sye- see Sie, Sigh, Scye, Psi, Cy

Sycosis (n)- inflamed condition of skin involving hair follicles
Psychosis (n)- any severe, major form of mental affection or disease

Symbol (n)- sign, emblem, mark, brand
Simball (n)- New England slang - kind of doughnut
Cymbal (n)- musical instrument
Cimbal (n)- obs. - kind of confectionery or cake

Syke- see Sike

Sync (v- to synchronize
Sink (v)- 1. subside, drop, wane. 2. kitchen receptacle attached to drain
Cinque (n)- number five on cards and dice

Syne (adv)- Eng. and Scottish - since. "Auld Lang Syne"
Sign (n)- proof, mark, identification, signature, trademark
Sine (n)- 1. mathematical ratio. 2. (prep) Latin - sans, without

Sypher (v)- over lap edges of planks to form a smoother joint
Cipher (n)- 1. zero, naught, nothing. 2. write in code, secret writing

Syrt (n)- quicksand, bog
Surt (pr.n)- Norse myth - fire demon

T

Ta (adj)- Eng. Dial. - one

Taa (n)- Chinese or Japanese pagoda

Tab (n)- 1. flap, tag, label, ticket, stub. 2. slang - unpaid bill. IOU

Tabb (n)- Brit. Dial. - a strap on a shoe

Tabaco (pr.n)- province in Luzon, Philippines

Tabacco (n)- West Indies - pipe or tube smoked by Caribbean Indians

Tabby (n)- 1. domestic cat. 2. slang - old maid or ill-natured gossiping woman

Taby (n)- Archaic - thick strong kind of taffeta silk

Tac (n)- Old English Law - kind of customary payment by a tenant

Tack (v)- 1. fasten lightly, baste, combine. 2. (n) - sharp pointed pin, nail, brad. 3. direction, course

Tach (n)- slang - tachometer

Tace (n)- Scot. - a suit of armor

Tass (n)- Scot. Dial. - drinking cup, goblet, also its contents

Tach (v)- Eng. and Scot. Dial. - fasten, attach

Tache (n)- obs. - touchwood, tinder

Tacked (v)- secured by fastening, sewed, basted, nailed, stitched

Tact (n)- perception, intuition, acumen, wisdom, prudence

Tackey or Tacky (n)- ill conditioned or neglected horse; also a person in a like state

Tacky (adj)- sticky, adhesive as of glue, paste, paint

Tacks (n)- short, sharp pointed pins, thumb tacks, small nails, brads

Tax (n)- 1. tariff, tribute, duty, toll. 2. payment of money to the government. 3. appraise, assess

Tact- see Tacked

Tael- see Tail, Tale

Taen (contr.)- poetic - taken

Tane (n)- Scot. - one preceded by and followed by the other

Tain (n)- thin tin plate, also foil for mirrors

Tahr (n)- wild goat of the Himalayas

Tar (n)- 1. dark, thick, sticky liquid with pungent odor. 2. sailor, seaman

Tarr (v)- Eng. Dial. - tease, incite, irritate

T

Tai (n)- Thai
Tie (v)- 1. bind or make fast with string, cord or rope. 2. (n) - draw, stalemate. 3. cravat, ascot
Tye (n)- 1. Naut. - a rope by which a yard is hoisted. 2. case or casket for jewels

Taikun (n)- title applied by foreigners to former shogun of Japan
Tycoon (n)- 1. wealthy, powerful industrialist. 2. baron, mogul, nabob

Tail (n)- 1. rear end of animal's body, as an appendage. 2. slang - buttocks. 3. tuxedo. 4. follow someone
Taille (n)- tally, feudal tax imposed by kind or lord
Tale (n)- narrative, story, recital, report
Tael (n)- Oriental unit of weight and monetary unit

Tailer (n)- blue fish, herring
Tailor (n)- 1. one who cuts and makes men or women's garments. 2. bird, tailor bird
Taler (n)- obs. - one who tells stories or tales

Taily (adj)- having or growing tails, as grain
Tailye (n)- Scot. Law - entail or deed of entail

Taimyr (pr.n)- peninsula in No. USSR
Timer (n)- 1. a device for measuring time as stopwatch. 2. one who measures or records time

Tain- see Taen, Tane

Taintor (n)- Eng. Dial. - a dyer
Taintour (n)- obs. - witness against one accused of a crime

Tait (n)- Australian marsupial
Tate (n)- Scot. and Eng. - small piece of something, as wool or hay, a lock of hair

Taiver (v)- obs. - to roam
Taver (v)- Scot. - to babble

Tale- see Tail

Tambor (n)- a swell fish. Red rock fish of California
Tambour (n)- 1. bass drum. 2. fortification, stockade to defend the exterior.

Tane- see Taen, Tain

Tang (n)- strong flavor, sharpness, pungency, spice, bite
Tangue (n)- a tenrec, tailless hedge-hog like animal

T

Taper (n)- 1. diminish, lessen, narrow gradually. 2. candle
Tapir (n)- stout bodied mammal with flexible snout from tropical America

Tapet (n)- worked or figured cloth, carpet. Hangings, tapestry
Tappet (n)- machinery - lever moved by some other piece as a cam

Tar- see Tahr, Tarr

Tare (n)- 1. injurious weed, as the darnel. 2. deduction made from gross weight
Tear (n)- 1. rupture, split, break, cut. 2. slang - carousel, spree. 3. violent outburst, rage

Tarie (n)- Gaelic - a call to arms, esp. a fiery cross used as a signal
Tarry (v)- wait, loiter, abide, delay
Terry (n)- loop formed in making cloth in which loops are uncut

Tarry- see Tarie

Tars (n-pl)- sailors, seamen
Tarse (n)- a silken material from Tartary, Asia

Tass (n)- Scot. - a drinking cup, goblet and its contents
Tace (n)- a suit or armor

Tat (n)- native East Indian pony
Tatt (v)- Eng. Dial. - entangle, confuse

Tate (n)- Scot and Eng. Dial. - small piece of something, as wool or hay, lock of hair
Tait (n)- Australian marsupial

Tau (n)- 1. Her. - taucross. 2. toadfish. 3. 19th letter of Greek alphabet
Taw (v)- 1. make skins into leather. 2. (n) - fancy marble, game of marbles

Taught (v)- p.p. of teach, gave lessons, provided knowledge
Taut (adj)- 1. inflexible, tense, rigid, hard. 2. orderly, neat, ship shape

Taupe (n)- color of moleskin. Dark brownish gray
Tope (v)- 1. drink alcoholic beverage to excess. 2. (n) - small shark. 3. building containing Buddhist Shrine

Taurus (n)- second sign of the zodiac. The bull
Torus (n)- Botany - part of a plant on which floral leaves grow

Taut- see Taught

Taver- see Taiver

T

Taw- see Tau

Taws (n-pl)- 1. marbles, shooters. 2. (v) - softens skins of sheep, goats, etc.

Tawse (n)- leather strap with thongs or slit end, used for punishment

Tax - 1. appraise, assess, charge. 2. audit, tribute. 3. payment of money to Gov't

Tacks (n)- short, sharp pointed pins, thumb tacks, small nails, brads

Tchick (n)- sound made by pressing tongue against roof of mouth. Cluck

Chick (n)- 1. young chicken or bird. 2. slang - attractive young girl or woman

Tea (n)- 1. dried and prepared leaves of a shrub used for a beverage. 2. slang - marijuana

Tee (n)- pin to mount a golf ball on. Shaped like a "T"

Ti (n)- 1. palm like plant. 2. 7th note of diatonic scale

Teach (v)- to give instruction to, inform, counsel, guide

Teache (n)- sugar manuf. - series of boilers or evaporating pans

Teaed (n)- slang - often with "up" - under the influence of marijuana

Teed (v)- golf - often with "up" - placed the ball on the tee

Teal (n)- 1. small fresh water duck. 2. grayish blue color

Teel (v)- to plant, bury

Teil (n)- linden or lime tree

Team (n)- 1. persons associated in joint actions or a ball team. 2. animals harnessed together. 3. span

Teem (v)- 1. be pregnant, product offspring. 2. abound or swarm

Tear (n)- 1. rupture, split, break, cut. 2. slang - carousel, spree. 3. violent outburst, rage

Tare (n)- 1. injurious weed as the darnel. 2. deduction made from gross weight

Tear (n)- 1. drop of fluid from the eye. 2. weep, cry. 3. symbol of grief

Teer (v)- 1. Eng. Dial. - to daub, plaster. 2. to stir up colors in block calico painting

Tier (n)- 1. row or rank one above other. 2. layer, line, file, queue

T

Teas (n)- 1. Brit. - light meals in late afternoons. 2. receptions or social gatherings in afternoon.
Tease (v)- irritate, vex, plague, torment. bother
Tees (v)- places a golf ball on a tee

Teat (n)- protuberance on breast or udder through which milk is drawn. Nipple
Teet (n)- Scot. - peep, pry, spy

Tee- see Tea, Ti

Teed- see Teaed

Teem- see Team

Teenes (n-pl)- obs. - injuries, grief, anger
Teens (n-pl)- years between thirteen and nineteen inclusive

Teer- see Tear, Tier

Tees- see Tease, Teas

Teet- see Teat

Teler (n)- 1. obs. - linen draper. 2. linen cloth worn as part of a woman's head dress
Teller (n)- 1. informer, narrator, describer. 2. bank clerk who receives and pays out money

Temse or Tems. (n)- 1. sieve. 2. (v) - to sift
Thames (pr.n)- river in England

Tenner (n)- 1. slang - ten dollar bill. 2. ten year prison sentence
Tenor (n)- 1. tendency, trend, character. 2. adult male voice, singer, vocalist

Tens (n-pl)- cardinal number. Sets of this many people or things
Tense (adj)- nervous, taut, up tight, high strung
Tents (n-pl)- portable shelters of canvas supported by poles

Terce (n)- a third or third part
Terse (adj)- 1. wiped or rubbed, polished, smoothed. 2. concise, succinct
Turse (v)- 1. Scot. - to carry hastily. 2. to truss, pack up or off

Term (n)- limit, boundary, time, season, condition
Turm (n)- trouper, company, squadron as of horsemen

T

Tern (n)- 1. member of the gull family. 2. sea swallow. 3. three winning numbers drawn together in a lottery
Terne (n)- thin steel or iron plate coated with an alloy
Turn (v)- 1. rotate, revolve, bend, fold. 2. (n) - deflect, curve. 3. opportunity, act, deed

Ternary (adj)- three, triple, treble, triplicate
Ternery (n)- a place where terns breed
Turnery (n)- art of forming solid substance into other forms by means of a lathe

Terne- see Tern, Turn

Terpene (n)- Chem. - terebene, turpentine
Terpine (n)- Chem. - white crystalline substance, derivative of menthane

Terrace (n)- raised level as of a lawn or houses having sloping sides
Pteris (n)- Bot. - large genus of coarse ferns

Terrain (n)- tract of ground or region
Terrene (adj)- 1. pertaining to the earth. 2. worldly, mundane
Terrine (n)- 1. a tureen. 2. kind of a stew

Terry- see Tarie, Tarry

Terse- see Terce, Turce

Testae (n-pl)- Bot. - outer, usually hard coats of seeds
Teste (n)- a witness. Witnessing a clause which expresses date of issue
Testy (adj)- impatient, irritated, headstrong

Tew- see To, Too, Two

Thallous (adj)- Chem. - containing thallium
Thallus (n)- Bot. - member of plant family. Shoot, branch, frond

Thames (pr.n)- river in England
Temse or Tems (n)- 1. sieve. 2. (v) - to sift

Thane (n)- warrior, companion of English Kings before conquest
Thegn (n)- Scot. - an Earl's son or chief of a clan holding land for the king

The (adj)- adjective sometimes used to a particular person or thing
Thee (pro)- used in place of "thou" by Quakers. Thyself

T

Thead (n)- Eng. Dial. - a vessel. Wicker strainer used by brewers

Thede (n)- obs. - a people, nation. Also a country

Theam or Team- see Theme

Theave (n)- a sheep. Ewe of the first year
Thieve (v)- to take by theft, purloin, steal

Thede- see Thead

Thegn- see Thane

Their (adj)- 1. belonging to them. 2. **(pron)**- possessive of they
There (adv)- 1. at that place. Yonder to that point. 2. (n) - that place. 3. (adj) - slang - skillful, competent
There - function word to introduce a sentence, "There isn't anybody at their house"
They're (contr)- they are

Theme (n)- subject, topic, text. Discourse, logic
Theam or Team (n)- Old English Law - the right to hold court

Therefor (adv)- for that, for this, for it
Therefore (adv)- consequently, as a result, for that reason

Therm (n)- 1. a hot bath, pool of water. 2. Physics - the greater calorie
Thurm (n)- cabinet making - to work with saw and chisel against the grain

They're- see Their, There

Thieve- see Theave

Tho (n)- Tonkin native
Though (adv)- although, however, if

Thorn (pr.n)- city in Poland
Torn (v)- pulled apart, ripped, broken

Thos (n)- genus of dogs including several species of jackals. 2. people of Northern Tonkin
Those (pro)- plural of that, this

Thoth (pr.n)- Egypt. Myth. - God of learning, wisdom and magic
Toat (n)- handle of a joiner's plane
Tote (v)- 1. carry or haul in the arms or on the back. Transport. 2. slang - to total. 3. (n) - horse racing - electronic totalizator

Threap (v)- Scot. - rebuke, scold, reproach
Threep (v)- Eng. - argue, dispute, wrangle

T

Threw (v)- cast, tossed, flung, hurled. Past tense of throw
Through (prep)- in one end, side or surface and out the other. Among, by way of, around

Thro (adj)- 1. obs. - stubborn, rigid. 2. averse, reluctant
Throe (n)- spasm of pain, cramp, agony, convulsion, torture
Throw (v)- 1. cast, pitch, toss, fling, hurl. 2. venture, risk. 3. (n) - spread, coverlet. 4. action of a person who throws

Throne (n)- chair of state, royal seat, monarch or Pope's chair
Thrown (n)- 1. silk in filament form. 2. (adj)- pitched, hurled, unseated

Through- see Threw

Throw- see Thro, Throe

Thrown- see Throne

Thurm (n)- cabinet making - to work with saw and chisel against the grain
Therm (n)- 1. a hot bath, pool of water. 2. Physics - the greater calorie

Thyme (n)- low shrub with aromatic leaves used for seasoning
Time (n)- 1. era, cycle, decade, age. 2. vacant time, leisure, ease. 3. (v) - measure, record duration of

Thurse (n)- obs. - demon, wicked spirit
Thyrse (n)- Bot. - a thyrsus (lilac, horse-chestnut, etc.)

Ti (n)- 1. seventh note of the diatonic scale. 2. palm like plant
Tee (n)- pin to mount a golf ball on. Shaped like a "T"
Tea (n)- dried leaves of a shrub used for a beverage. Slang - marijuana

Tic (n)- involuntary repeated spasmodic contraction of a muscle
Tick (n)- 1. large group of wingless, bloodsucking insects or mites. 2. sound

Tide (n)- 1. times, season, opportunity. 2. alternate rise and fall of surface of oceans, seas
Tied (v)- 1. connected, bound, joined. 2. stalemate

Tie (v)- 1. bind or make with string, cord. 2. (n) - draw, stalemate. 3. cravat, ascot
Tye (n)- 1. Naut. - a rope by which a yard is hoisted. 2. case for jewels
Tai (pr.n)- Thai

Tied- see Tide

T

Tier (n)- 1. layer, line, row, file, queue. 2. (v) - arrange in tiers
Teer (v)- Eng. Dial. - to daub, plaster. To stir up colors in block calico painting
Tear (n)- 1. a symbol of grief. 2. water from the eye. 3. weep, cry

Tier- see Tire, Tyre

Tierce (n)- 1. third. 2. cask larger than a barrel. 3. a position in fencing
Tiers (n-pl)- rows, layers, lines
Tears (n-pl)- symbols of grief. Cries, weeps

Tight (adj)- 1. closely held together. 2. firm, compact, close
Tite (adv)- Brit. Dial. - fast, quickly, soon

Tighter (adj)- stretched to full extent, taut.
Titer (n)- Chemistry - standard of strength of solution determined by titration

Tike (n)- 1. obs. - a tick or mite. 2. country bumpkin. 3. eccentric person
Tyke (n)- small, lively, mischievous child

Til (n)- a plant with small edible seeds. Sesame
Till (n)- 1. cash register, money drawer. 2. (v)- cultivate the ground, hoe, sow

Tiler (n)- 1. one who makes or lays tiles. 2. doorkeeper in a free Mason's lodge
Tyler (pr.n)- John. President of United States-1841

Timball or Tymbal (n)- kettle drum - Moorish drum
Timbale (n)- minced meat, fish, and vegetable cooked in small mold

Timber (n)- lumber, beams, wood for building, timberland
Timbre (n)- Music - pitch, resonance, quality of sound

Time (v)- 1. measure, keep time, record the duration of. 2. (n)- era, cycle, decade, age. 3. leisure, ease, vacant time
Thyme (n)- low shrub with aromatic leaves used for seasoning

Timer- see Taimyr

Tind (v)- Scot. and Eng. - to kindle, set on fire
Tined (n)- slender projecting part, forked, pronged

Tine (n)- 1. sharp, projecting point or prong as in a fork. 2. Med. - tuberculin test performed upon the skin
Tyne (pr.n)- river in England

T

Tipe (n)- Eng. Dial. - trap for catching mice, rabbits, etc.
Type (n)- 1. mark or impression, sign, emblem. 2. (v)- to represent, to typewrite

Tire (v)- 1. overtax, exert, weary, exhaust, fatigue, overdo. 2. (n) - part of a wheel. 3. rubber tube filled with air
Tier (n)- childs apron or pinafore
Tyer (n)- one who ties
Tyre (n)- preparation of milk and rice used for food in West Indies
Tyre (pr.n)- ancient seaport of Phonecia, now Lebanon. Great city of Antiquity
Tyr (pr.n)- son of Odin, God of war and victory. His name is given to Tuesday

Tite- see Tight

Titer- see Tighter

To (prep)- until, onto, on, as far as, towards
Too (adv)- more than enough, overly, also. Extremely. In addition, besides
Two (adj)- 1. more than one. 2. (n) - number between one and three
Tew (v)- Brit. Dial. 1. beat or press leather, hemp, soften or render pliable. 2. work hard, strive

Toad (n)- a tailess jumping amphibian resembling a frog
Tode (n)- 1. rude sled for hauling logs. 2. (v) - to haul logs with a tode
Toed (adj)- 1. having a toe or toes. 2. carpentry - nail driven in oblique manner
Towed (v)- pulled by force. Dragged

Toady (n)- a fawning flatterer. Sycophant
Todi (n)- small West-Indian bird related to American Kingfisher

Toar (n)- Eng. Dial. - long coarse grass left on pastures throughout the winter
Tor (n)- hill, rocky eminence. Tower, turret
Tore (v)- pulled apart or in pieces by force

Toat (n)- handle of a joiner's plane
Tote (v)- 1. carry or haul in arms or back. Transport. 2. slang - to total. 3. (n) - horse racing - electronic totalizator
Thoth (pr.n)- Egypt. Myth. - God of wisdom, learning and music

Tocsin (n)- signal of distress, SOS, warning, signal, siren, flare
Toxin (n)- any organic poisons produced in dead or living organisms

T

Tode- see Toad, Tode, Towed

Todi- see Toady

Toe (n)- in man - one of the terminal members or digits of the foot
Tow (v)- to drag or pull (boat or car) by means of a rope or chain
Tou (n)- Chinese liquid measure

Toed- see Toad, Tode, Towed

Told (v)- narrated, related, gave an account of. Communicated, informed
Toled (v)- Archaic - allured, attracted, decoyed
Tolled (v)- 1. rang (churchbell, etc.) slowly with regular, repeated strokes. 2. taxed

Tole (v)- Archaic - to draw with a lure, attract, decoy, entice
Toll (n)- 1. act or sound of ringing a bell. 2. tax or fee. 3. (v) - Eng. Law - to vacate, annul

Toled- see Told, Tolled

Toler (n)- Dial. - a dog trained to decoy ducks
Toller (n)- one who tolls a bell

Toll- see Tole

Tolled- see Told

Toller- see Toler

Tomb (n)- 1. a grave for the dead. 2. (v) to place in a tomb, bury, inter
Toom (v)- Brit. and Scot Dial. - 1. evacuate, empty. 2. (n) - a dumping ground
Tum (n)- Egypt. Relig. - sun god regarded as creator of the world

Ton (n)- unit of weight equal to 2000 pounds avoirdupois
Tun (n)- large cask for holding liquids, especially wines, beer, ale

Tongue (n)- 1. movable muscular structure attached to floor of mouth. 2. language. 3. slang - a lawyer, mouthpiece
Tung (adj)- poisonous oil from seeds of Chinese Tung tree

Too- see To, Tew, Two

Tool (n)- instrument, implement, utensil, machine, equipment, gear
Toul (pr.n)- town in N.E. France
Tulle (n)- fine silk or rayon used in millinery or dress making

T

Toom- see Tomb

Toon (n)- wood of reddish brown color used in India for cabinet work

Tune (n)- 1. melody, air. 2. agreement in pitch, unison and harmony

Tooter (n)- of a horn - one who causes a horn to sound by blowing

Tutor (n)- teacher, private instructor, coach, counselor, professor

Tope (n)- 1. small shark found along European coast. 2. building containing Buddhist shrine. 3. (v)- drink alcoholic liquor to excess

Taupe (n)- dark gray tinged with brown

Tor- see Toar, Tore

Tora (n)- African antelope

Torah (n)- Judaism - learning law, instruction. Whole body of Jewish religious literature

Torfel (v)- Scot. - to pine away, to die

Torfle (v)- Eng. Dial. - to toss about, overexert

Torn (v)- 1. ripped, left ragged. 2. distressed greatly

Thorn (pr.n)- city in Poland

Tors (n-pl)- rocky pinnacles, towers

Torse (n)- 1. Her. - a wreath used for support of a crest. 2. Geom. - a developable

Torus (n)- Botany - part of a plant on which floral leaves grow

Taurus (n)- second sign of Zodiac. The bull

Tote- see Toat

Tou- see Toe, Tow

Toucan (n)- fruit eating picarian bird of tropical America

Tucan (n)- Mexican rodent. Pocket gopher

Tough (adj)- 1. strong, sturdy, hardy, firm, athletic. 2. ruffian

Tuff (n)- porous rock, accumulation of ashes at crater of volcano

Toul- see Tool, Tulle

Toupee (n)- small wig for covering bald spot

Toupet (n)- crested or tufted titmouse

T

Tour (n)- 1. journey, excursion, trip, circuit. 2. travel from place to place
Tours (pr.n)- city in W. France on Loire River
Tur (n)- caucasian wild goat
Turr (n)- music - a Burmese three stringed viol

Toured (v)- traveled, journeyed. Went from place to place
Turd (n)- slang - ordure, dung, filth

Tournay (n)- printed worsted fabric for upholstery
Tourne (adj)- Her. - regardant
Tournee (n)- card game - a play in the game of skat

Tow- see Toe Tou

Towed (v)- pulled by force. Dragged
Toed (adj)- 1. having toes. 2. carpentry - drove nail in oblique manner
Tode (n)- rude sled for hauling logs
Toad (n)- tailess, jumping amphibian resembling a frog

Toxin (n)- any organic poisons produced in living or dead organisms
Tocsin (n)- signal of distress, warning, siren, SOS

Tracked (v)- tread, traveled, followed, pursued until caught
Tract (n)- 1. pamphlet or leaflet. 2. expanse of land, area

Traik (v)- Eng. Dial. - wander with fatigue. Misfortune
Trake (n)- Scot. - flesh of sheep that died from disease

Trail (v)- 1. follow, lag behind. 2. hunt by tracking
Treille (n)- 1. lace making - a netground. 2. Heraldry- a lattice

Traipse (v)- slang - wander, walk or trudge about idly
Trapes (n)- Eng. Dial. - a slattern. A gadabout

Trake- see Traik

Transience (n)- transient state. Short duration, impermanence
Transients (n) - temporary lodgers, roomers, boarders

Trapes- see Traipse

Travois (n)- 1. primitive vehicle used by No. American Indians. 2. sled used by lumbermen in logging
Travoy (v)- to drag or skid

Tray (n)- coaster, server, salver, waiter
Trey (n)- card, domino or die having 3 spots or 3 pips

T

Treadle (n)- lever or pedal moved by foot and connected to a small crank of a machine

Treddle (n)- Brit. Dial. - dung of sheep or hares

Treaties (n)- international compacts, agreements, alliances, pacts

Treatise (n)- thesis, essay, composition, dissertation, writing

Treddle- see Treadle

Treille- see Trail

Trew (v)- Scot. - to believe, trust. Tribute.

True (adj)- 1. loyal, not false, faithful, honest. 2. real, genuine

Trews- see Truce, Trousse

Trey- see Tray

Tride (adj)- short and quick, fleet

Tried (adj)- 1. p.p. of try. 2. proved, tested. 3. reliable.

Trier (n)- one who tries. One who experiments or tests anything

Trior (n)- person appointed by law to try challenges of jurors

Troche (n)- medicated lozenge, usually circular

Trochee (n)- a metrical foot comprising two syllables - one long and one short

Trolley (v)- 1. convey or travel by trolley car. 2. mining - small truck used underground

Trolly (n)- Eng. and Scot. - slang - a trollop, sloven. Loose woman

Troolie or Trooly (n)- ubussu palm, Brazilian palm

Truly (adv)- 1. sincerely, honestly. 2. in truth, in reality. 3. exactly.

Troop (n)- 1. great number, multitude, throng. 2. company, squad, crew

Troupe (n)- members of theatrical company. Band of players, actors, singers

Trooper (n)- cavalryman, mounted policeman, state policeman

Trouper (n)- actor of long experience

Troupe- see Troop

Trouper- see Trooper

Trousse- see Truce

T

Truce (n)- 1. pledge. 2. pause or respite. 3. temporary suspension of warfare by agreement
Trews (n-pl)- close fitting tartan trousers worn by certain Scottish regiments
Trousse (n)- receptacle or case containing small implements

True (adj)- 1. loyal, faithful, honest. 2. not false. 3. real, genuine
Trew (v)- Scot. - to believe, trust. Tribute

Truly (adv)- see Troolie

Trussed (v)- 1. supported, sustained, upheld, compressed. 2. bandaged, splinted
Trust (n)- 1. combination of companies, corporations, cartel, syndicate. 2. (v) - depend on, confide in, rely on

Trust- see Trussed

Trustee (n)- anyone who holds property for the benefit of another
Trusty (adj)- reliable, deserving confidence

Tucan (n)- Mexican rodent, pocket gopher
Toucan (n)- fruit eating picarian bird of tropical America

Tuff (n)- porous rock, accumulation of ashes at crater of volcano
Tough (adj)- 1. strong, hard, resistant, firm. 2. robust, hardy. 3. ruffian

Tuile (n)- Fr. - a tile
Tuille (n)- armor. - one of two hinged plates before the thigh

Tulle- see Tool

Tully (n)- Geology - minor subdivision of American upper Devonian
Tuly (n)- obs. - a scarlet dye or color

Tum- see Tomb, Toom

Tun (n)- large cask for holding liquids, esp. wine, beer, ale
Ton (n)- unit of weight equal to 2000 lbs. avoirdupois

Tuna (n)- 1. the tunny, ocean fish. 2. West Indian prickly pear
Tunna (n)- dry and liquid measure of weight in Sweden and Norway

Tune (n)- 1. melody, air. 2. agreement in pitch, unison and harmony
Toon (n)- wood of reddish brown color used in India for cabinet work

T

Tung (adj)- poisonous oil from seeds of Chinese tung tree
Tongue (n)- 1. movable, muscular structure attached to floor of mouth. 2. language. 3. slang - attorney, mouthpiece

Tunna- see Tuna

Tur- see Tour, Tours, Turr

Turd (n)- slang - filth, ordure, dung
Toured (v)- traveled, journey

Turkey (n)- large fowl, wild or domesticated. Its flesh is prized as food
Turkey (pr.n)- Republic in West Asia and Southeast Europe
Turki (adj)- pertaining to Turkish people or their language

Turm (n)- 1. troop or squadron as of horsemen. 2. company
Term (n)- limit, boundary, time, season, condition

Turn (v)- 1. rotate, revolve, fold, twist. 2. (n) - deflect, curve. 3. opportunity, deed, act
Terne (n)- thin iron or steel plate coated with an alloy of tin or lead
Tern (n)- 1. member of gull family. 2. sea swallow. 3. three winning numbers drawn together

Turnery (n)- art of forming solid substance into other forms by means of a lathe
Ternery (n)- a place where terns breed
Ternary (adj)- three, triple, treble, triplicate

Turse (v)- Scot. - to carry hastily. To truss, pack up or off
Terse (adj)- 1. wiped or rubbed, polished or smoothed. 2. concise, terse, succinct
Terce (n)- a third or a third part

Tuskar (n)- Scot. - a turf cutter. A peat spade
Tusker (n)- elephant or wild boar. Having large tusks

Tutor (n)- trainer, private instructor, educator, teacher
Tooter (n)- of a horn - one causes a horn to sound by blowing

Tutti (adj)- Music - all. All the voices and instruments together
Tutty (n)- impure oxide of zinc used chiefly as a polishing powder

Twerp (n)- slang - an objectionable male
Twirp (n)- slang - insignificant, peculiar, weird

T

Two (n)- 1. number between one and three. 2. (adj)- more than one
Too (adv)- also, besides, as well as. Very, extremely
To (prep)- until, onto, towards, as far as
Tew (v)- Brit. Dial. - beat or press leather, hemp, soften or render pliable

Tycoon (n)- wealthy, powerful, industrialist. Baron, mogul, nabob
Taikun (n)- title applied by foreigners to former shogun of Japan

Tye (n)- 1. Naut. - a rope by which a yard is hoisted. 2. case or casket for jewels
Tie (v)- 1. bind or make fast with string, cord or rope. 2. (n) - draw, stalemate. 3. cravat, ascot.
Tai (pr.n)- Thai

Tyke (n)- small lively mischievous child
Tike (n)- 1. obs. - a tick or mite. 2. country bumpkin. 3. eccentric person

Tyler (pr.n)- John. President of the United States 1841
Tiler (n)- 1. one who makes or lays tile. 2. doorkeeper in a free mason's lodge

Tymbal or Timbal (n)- Moorish drum, kettle drum
Timbale (n)- minced, chopped food cooked in a small mold

Tyne (pr.n)- river in England
Tine (n)- 1. sharp projecting point or prong as in a fork. 2. Med - tuberculin test performed on skin.

Type (n)- 1. mark, impression, sign, emblem. 2. (v)- to typewrite, to represent
Tipe (n)- Eng. - trap for catching mice, rabbits, etc.

Tyr, Tyre- see Tire, Tier, Tyer

U

–U–

Uhlan (n)- Polish mounted officer usually armed with a lance
Ulan (n)- cavalry man in former German army

Unceded (adj)- not yielded, not granted, not surrendered
Unseeded (adj)- not sown with seeds.

Unde (adj)- Her. - wavy, undulating
Undy (n)- slang- woman's underwear, under pant, unmentionable, skivvy, panty

Undo (v)- annul, defeat, retract, cancel, lose, unfasten
Undue (adj)- 1. not yet payable. 2. improper, unsuitable

Unlade (v)- unload. Discharge the load or cargo
Unlaid (adj)- untwisted as a rope

Unseeded- see Unceded

Ure (n)- 1. obs. - use, practice. 2. a bull
Your (pr.n)- possessive of you.
You're (contr)- contraction of you are

Urn (n)- vase especially with foot or pedestal ewer, pot, samovar
Earn (v)- 1. gain by labor or service. 2. make money. 3. merit
Erne (n)- a sea eagle

Use (v)- put into service, utilize, employ, operate
Ewes (n-pl)- plural of ewe. Female sheep
Yews (n-pl)- evergreen trees

–V–

Vail (v)– 1. Archaic - caused to descend or sink lower. 2. take off or doff hat in submission
Vale (n)– valley, glen, dell, glade, gully, ravine
Veil (v)– 1. conceal, disguise, hide, mask, camouflage. 2. thin material to hide face

Vain (adj)– 1. conceited, self-important, haughty, proud. 2. useless, trivial
Vane (n)– weathercock, wind indicator, wind gauge
Vein (n)– 1. blood vessel, nerve, artery, aorta, capillary. 2. prevailing spirit, nature, humor

Vale– see Vail, Veil

Vane– see Vain, Vein

Vary (v)– change, alter, reconstruct, modify, diversify
Very (adj)– 1. actual, genuine, real, true, correct. 2. extremely

Vassal (n)– feudal servant
Vasal (n)– Anat.-duct

Veil– see Vail, Vale

Vein– see Vain, Vane

Venous (adj)– pertaining to or of the nature of a vein or veins
Venus (pr.n)– 1. Astro.- a planet. 2. Roman goddess of love

Versed (adj)– expert, competent, at home with, adept, skilled
Verst (n)– Russian measure of length

Very– see vary

Vi (pr.n)– Fem. name, dim. for Violet, Vivian
Vie (n)– strive in competition or rivalry with another

Vial (n)– small bottle, phial, cruet, decanter, carafe
Vile (adj)– foul, disgraceful, sinful, disgusting
Viol (n)– bowed musical stringed instrument

Vice (n)– 1. a sin. 2. wickedness, evil habit, depraved. 3. weekness, failing
Vise (n)– 1. a press. 2. a tool for holding or gripping

Villain (n)– rascal, knave, scoundrel, scamp, rogue
Villein (n)– peasant, class of half free persons under feudal system

Villous (adj)– covered with soft hairs which are not interwoven
Villus (n)– minute wormlike processes on certain animal membranes

Vise– see Vice

W

—W—

Wa (n)- member of Indo-Chinese tribe
Wah (n)- the panda

Waaf (n)- Gr. Brit. - a member of Women's Auxiliary Air Force
Waff (n)- Scot. and Engl. Dial. - 1. vagrant or vagabond. 2. waving motion

Wac (pr.n)- member of Woman's Army Corp.
Wack (n)- Scot. - clammy, moist, damp
Whack (n)- sharp, resounding blow

Wacke (n)- gravel stone, soft rock of fine texture
Wacky or Whacky (adj)- irrational, eccentric. Slang - nutty, crazy

Wacks (n-pl)- slang - loonies, erratic or irrational persons
Wacs (pr.n)- plural of Wac. Members of Women's Army Corp.
Wax (n)- 1. yellow substance secreted by bees. 2. (v)- rub, polish. 3. increase, expand
Whacks (v)- strikes with sharp blows. Beats

Wad (n)- 1. small soft mass. Lump or compact mass. 2. slang - money, wealth
Wadd (n)- ore of manganese combined with oxides. Brit. - graphite

Wade (v)- walk through water, ford, go across on foot
Wayed (v)- 1. broken or trained to the road, said of horses. 2. frequented
Weighed (v)- 1. measured on a scale. 2. considered carefully

Wae- see Way, Weigh, Whey

Waff- see Waaf

Wah- see Wa

Wail (v)- 1. cry, bewail, lament, weep, grieve audibly, sob. 2. dirge
Wale (n)- 1. welt, mark or skin, streak. 2. fabric - weave, texture, feel
Whale (n)- large sea mammal noted for its oil, bone, flesh. Behemoth, grampus

Wailer (n)- in some countries, a professional mourner
Waler (n)- horse from Australia and New South Wales
Whaler (n)- 1. a whaling ship. 2. whale man

Wails (v)- cries, weeps, grieves, laments
Wales (pr.n)- division of Great Britain

W

Wain (n)- 1. Astron. - a constellation, Charle's Wain. 2. cart or wagon. 3. (v)- convey, fetch
Wane (n)- ebb, decline, decrease, recession, falling off

Wair- see Ware, Where, Wear

Waist (n)- waistline, middle part of the body, bodice
Waste (v)- 1. devastate, spoil, despoil. 2. decay, perish, use up, consume

Waister (n)- Naut. - unskilled seaman doing odd jobs in waist of ship
Waster (n)- spend thrift, prodigal, wastrel, bum

Wait (v)- loiter, pause, remain inactive, linger, hang fire
Weight (n)- pressure, load, heaviness, burden, gravity

Waive (v)- surrender, give up, abandon, remit, forego
Wave (n)- 1. whitecap, swell, roller, surf, tide. 2. flutter, sway, vibrate
Wave (pr.n)- member of Woman's Naval Reserve

Waiver (n)- Law - relinquishment of some rights, claim or privilege
Waver (v)- 1. become unsteady, falter, stagger. 2. be undecided

Wake (v)- 1. arouse from slumber. 2. excite
Wayke (adv)- Scot. - weak

Wale- see Wail, Whale

Wald (n)- power, rule, sway
Walled (adj)- 1. enclosed, shut off. 2. divided with a wall

Waler- see Wailer, Whaler

Walk (v)- step, stride, stroll, saunter, amble
Wok (n)- large pan with rounded bottom used by Chinese for fast cooking

Wall (n)- 1. upright structure, fence, enclosure. 2. cliff, precipice, bulwark
Waul (v)- cry as a cat. Squall

Walled- see Wald

Wane (n)- decline, downgrade, decrease
Wain (n)- 1. wagon or cart. 2. Astron. - constellation Charles's Wain. (v) - convey, fetch

Want (n)- 1. deficiency, lack, need, poverty. 2. desire, crave
Wont (adj)- custom, practice, habit

Wap (v)- Eng. and Scot. - wrap, fold up, bind
Wapp (n)- Naut. - a fair leader

W

War (n)- 1. act or state of hostility. 2. enmity, strife, conflict. 3. active military operations
Wore (v)- past tense of wear. Had on, carried on person

Ward (n)- 1. city district. 2. guardianship of child or incompetent person. 3. (v)- turn aside, avert
Warred (v)- waged, fought war. combat, shed blood

Ware (n)- merchandise. Anything to be sold
Wear (v)- 1. put on a covering for the body, don, gown. 2. carry, bear, exhibit
Where (adv)- at what place? At which place? Whither?
Wair (n)- 1. Brit. and Scot. - expend, waste, squander. 2. carpentry - a piece of plank

Warn (v)- give notice, notify, forewarn, caution
Worn (adj)- 1. used up, shabby, seedy, broken down. 2. tired, exhausted, beat

Warp (v)- turn, twist or be twisted out of shape
Wharp (n)- Eng. - fine sand from river Trent, used in polishing

Warred- see Ward

Wart (n)- fungous growth. Small hard elevation of the skin
Wort (n)- liquid prepared with malt. After fermenting becomes beer, ale

Wary (adj)- vigilant, alert, cautious, careful, on one's guard
Weri (n)- 1. New Zealand caterpillar (aweto). 2. a fibrous root
Wherry (n)- 1. light rowboat. 2. racing scull for one person

Waste (v)- 1. use up, consume, exhaust, run through. 2. decay, despoil
Waist (n)- part of body between ribs and hips, middle, bodice

Waster (n)- spendthrift, idler, loafer, wastrel, bum
Waister (n)- Naut. - unskilled seaman doing odd jobs in waist of ship

Wat (n)- Scot.- 1. a person of importance. A manor fellow. 2. a hare
Watt (n)- unit of electrical power
What (pro)- used in asking for identity, quality, quantity
Whatt (adj)- Scot. - whittle
Wot (v)- Archaic - to know, to wit, namely, that is to say

Water (n)- 1. H^2O. Transparent and tasteless liquid. 2. bath, shower. 3. (v) - irrigate, moisten, douse, wet
Watter (n)- having a specified wattage

W

Waterie (n)- a pied wagtail (bird)
Watery (adj)- wet, containing or discharging water, tearful

Watter- see Water

Wave- see Waive

Waver (v)- 1. be undecided. 2. become unsteady, falter, stagger, stumble
Waiver (n)- formal written statement relinquishing rights, claims

Waul (v)- cry as a cat. Squall
Wall (n)- 1. cliff, precipice, bluff. 2. upright structure, fence, enclosure

Wax- see Wacks, Wacs, Whacks

Way (n)- 1. path, road, street, highway. 2. manner, mode, fashion, method
Weigh (v)- 1. ascertain weight by scale. 2. consider carefully, ponder
Wey (n)- English unit of weight or measure
Whey (n)- thin watery part of milk separated from heavy part as in cheese making
Wae (n)- Scot. and Eng.- sorrow, woe

Wayed (v)- 1. broken or trained to the road, said of horses. 2. frequented
Weighed (n)- 1. measured on a scale. 2. considered carefully
Wade (v)- walk through water, go across on foot, ford

Wayer (n)- 1. horse pond. 2. (v) - to water a horse, plunge a horse in water
Weigher (n)- one that weighs. An officer who tests weights

Wayke- see Wake

We (pro)- ourselves. Our, ours. Plural of I
Wee (adj)- little, tiny, very small, miniature, petite
Wie (n)- 1. obs. - noble knight. 2. person, creature

Weak (adj)- not strong, feeble, exhausted. Fragile
Week (n)- period of seven successive days
Weke (adj)- obs. - moisture, wet

W

Weal (n)- 1. profit, prosperity, well being. 2. mark, wale, ridge, lump
Weel (n)- snare or trap for fish
Weele (n)- welfare
Weile (n)- choice
Wele (n)- happiness
We'll (contr)- contraction of we will
Wheal (n)- 1. pimple, pustule. 2. burning, itching, red swelling of the skin
Wheel (n)- 1. tricycle, bicycle, cycle. 2. (v) - revolve, turn, rotate, roll
Wiel (n)- pool, eddy

Weald- see Wield

Wean (v)- accustom (child or animal) to food other than mother's milk
Ween (v)- 1. to think or suppose, opine, presume. 2. hope, expectation

Wear (v)- 1. carry, bear, exhibit. 2. put on a covering for the body, don, gown
Where (adv)- at which place? At what place? Whither?
Ware (n)- merchandise. Anything to be sold. Commodity
Wair (n)- 1. Brit. and Scot. - expend, waste, squander. 2. carpentry - a piece of plank

Weary (adj)- tired, fatigued, tiresome
Wheary (n)- Scot. - European bold crest (small bird)

Weasel (n)- cunning, flesh eating mammal related to stoats and marten
Weazel (n)- thin, weasen

Weather (n)- meteorology, climate, atmospheric conditions
Wether (n)- a castrated ram
Whether (conj)- in case, in the event of, supposing that, if

Weave (n)- knit, loom, interlace, entwine, braid
We've- contraction of we have

Weaver (n)- 1. one whose occupation is weaving cloth. 2. a weaver bird
Weever (n)- small marine fish common in British waters

We'd (contr)- contraction of we would, we had, we should
Wede (v)- 1. obs. - to fade, vanish. 2. (n) - madness
Weed (n)- 1. useless, troublesome plant. 2. mourning band or garment
Weid (n)- Scot. - sudden illness which attacks women in childbirth

W

Wee- see We

Week- see Weak

Weel- see Weal, Wheel, We'll

Ween (v)- 1. to think or suppose, opine, presume. 2. hope, expectation
Wean (v)- accustom (child or animal) to food other than mother's milk

Weet- see Wit, Whit

Weever- see Weaver

Weid- see We'd, Weed, Wede

Weigh (v)- 1. ascertain weight by means of a scale. 2. consider carefully, ponder
Wey (n)- English unit of weight
Whey (n)- watery part of milk separated from thicker part as in cheese making
Way (n)- 1. path, road, highway, street. 2. manner, mode, method, fashion
Wae (n)- Scot. and Brit. - sorrow, woe

Weighed (v)- 1. measured on a scale. 2. considered carefully
Wayed (v)- 1. broken or trained to the road, said of horses. 2. frequented
Wade (v)- walk through water, ford, go across of foot

Weigher (n)- one that weighs. An officer who tests weights
Wayer (n)- 1. horse pond. 2. (v) - to water a horse, plunge a horse in water

Weight (n)- pressure, load, heaviness, burden, gravity
Wait (v)- loiter, pause, remain inactive, linger, hang fire

Weir- see Wer

Weke- see Weak, Week

Welch (v)- slang - cheat, evade payment, swindle
Welsh (pr.n)- inhabitant of Wales, also language

Weld (n)- 1. fuse metal by heat and compression. 2. plant yielding yellow dye
Welled (v)- poured forth, gushed, sprung up

Welk (v)- Scot. and Eng. Dial. - fade, dry up. Decrease, wane
Whelk (n)- marine gastropod (snail, slug) used as food in Europe

W

We'll- see Weal, Wheel, Wiel

Welled- see Weld

Wells (n)- deep holes to tap under ground supplies of oil, water, gas
Wels (n)- sheat fish

Welm (n)- spring, fountain
Welme (v)- obs. - to reverse
Whelm (v)- Eng. Dial. - turn upside down, overturn, upset

Welsh- see Welch

Wen (n)- 1. cyst. Benign tumor. 2. painful swelling
When (adv)- at what time. As soon as. How soon? While

Wer (v)- 1. to defend. 2. (n) - man, husband, warrior
We're- contraction of we are
Weir (n)- 1. dam in the river. 2. sluice, obstruction, flood gate

Were (v)- plural of was. Past tense of to be
Whir (n)- buzzing or whirring sound made by bird's wings. Swishing sound

Weri- see Wary, Wherry

Wet (adj)- 1. soaked, wringing, damp, rainy, sloppy. 2. (n)- water, moisture, dew
Whet (v)- 1. arouse, stimulate, excite, goad, spur. 2. hone, sharpen by friction, grind

Wether- see Weather, Whether

We've- contraction of we have
Weave (v)- interlace, knit, braid, intertwine, design

Whack (n)- sharp, resounding blow
Wack (n)- Scot. - clammy, moist, damp
Wac (pr.n)- member of Woman's Army Corp.

Whacky or Wacky (adj)- irrational, eccentric. Slang - nutty, crazy
Wacke (n)- gravel stone, soft rock of fine texture

Whacks- see Wacks, Wax, Wacs

Whale (n)- large sea mammal noted for its oil, bone, flesh. Behemoth, grampus
Wail (v)- cry, bewail, lament, seep, grieve audibly, sob
Wale (n)- welt, mark on skin, streak. Fabric - weave, texture, feel

W

Whaler (n)- a whaling ship, a whaleman
Wailer (n)- in some countries, a professional mourner
Waler (n)- horse from Australia or South Wales

Wharp (n)- Eng. - fine sand from river Trent used in polishing
Warp (v)- turn, twist or be twisted out of shape

What (pro)- used in asking for identity, quality, quantity
Whatt (adj)- Scot. - whittle
Wot (v)- Archaic - to know, to wit, namely, that is to say
Watt (n)- unit of electrical power
Wat (n)- Scot. - 1. a person of importance. A manor fellow. 2. a hare

Wheal, Wheel- see Weal, We'll, Wiel

Wheary- see Weary

Whelk- see Welk

Whelm- see Welm

When (adv)- at what time. As soon as. How soon? While
Wen (n)- 1. cyst. Benign skin tumor. 2. painful swelling

Where- see Ware, Wear

Wherry- see Wary, Weri

Whet (v)- 1. hone, sharpen by friction, grind, strop. 2. arouse, stimulate, excite, goad
Wet (n)- 1. water, moisture, downpour, dew. 2. (adj) - soaked, wringing, damp, rainy

Whether (conj)- if, allowing for, in case, provided if
Wether (n)- castrated ram
Weather (n)- atmospheric conditions, climate, mercury

Whewer (n)- the European widgeon (duck)
Wooer (n)- one who woos. A suitor

Whey- see Way, Weigh, Wey

Which (pro)- 1. interrog.- what person or thing. 2.(adj)- what kind
Witch (v)- 1. captivate, put under a spell, charm, enchant. 2. (n) - sorceress, siren, vampire
Wych or Witch (n)- Elm or hazel tree e.g. wych hazel, wych elm

Whicker (v)- Eng.-cry or call of a horse, neigh, whinny
Wicker (n)- slender plant twig used for baskets, chairs, furniture

W

Whig- see Wig, Wigg

While (conj)- 1. although, as long as, even if. 2. (n) - time, span, term, space of time
Wile (n)- 1. trick, ruse, deceit, fraud, cheat, doubledealing. 2. lure, guile

Whin- see Win, Wynn

Whine (v)- whimper, mewl, cry, bewail, moan, fret
Wine (n)- fermented juice of grapes, fruits or plants used as an alcoholic beverage

Whip (v)- to punish by whipping, beat, flog. Strike with a lash, whip or rod
Wip (v)- Scot. and Eng. Dial. - twist, coil

Whir (v)- swishing, whizzing. Whirring sound as made by birds wings
Were (v)- past tense of to be, plural of was

Whish (v)- to move or make with a swish. A swishing sound
Wish (v)- desire, yen, long for, covet, want

Whist (n)- 1. card game. 2. (inter) - to be quiet, make no noise
Wist (v)- thought, knew, past tense of to wit

Whit- see Wit, Weet

White (n)- 1. member of caucasian race. 2. (adj) - colorless, pale, very blonde, ashen
Wite (n)- Scot. - blame or censure. Punishment or penalty
Wight (n)- 1. person, thing. 2. creature, animal

Whither (adv)- to what place, where, used to introduce questions
Wither (v)- lose moisture, shrivel, die, deteriorate

Whoa (imperative)- stop, stay, wait a minute (also pronounced woe)
Ho (inter)- exclamation of surprise
Hoe (n)- 1. dig, scrape, weed. 2. long handled tool

Whoa (inter.)- stop, especially a command to a horse (also pronounced ho)
Wogh (n)- obs. - error, harm, injustice
Woe (n)- sorrow, misery, suffering, trouble, misfortune

Whole (n)- everything, all, intact
Hole (n)- opening, aperture, breach

Wholly (adv)- entirely, altogether, fully
Holy (adj)- sacred, hallowed, blessed
Holey (adj)- full of holes

W

Whoop (v)- yell, shout, holler, cry out loud
Hoop (n)- band, ring, circlet, wheel
Houp (n)- Scot. - a mouthful of drink

Whore (n)- prostitute
Hor (n)- Biblical - mountain
Hore (adj)- 1. moldy, musty. 2. (n) - obs. - dirt, mud
Hors- French- out of
Hoar (adj)- 1. gray or white with age. 2. frost, rime

Whored (v)- corrupted, seduced, debauched
Hoard (v)- accumulate, stockpile, stowaway, amass
Horde (n)- crowd, multitude, tribe

Who's- contraction of who is
Whose (pro)- possessive of who or which

Why (adv)- for what reason? To what purpose? On what account?
Wye (n)- electrical - three phase circuit arrangement like letter Y
Wye (pr.n)- river in England

Whys (n-pl)- reasons, causes, motives
Wise (adj)- prudent, sensible, discreet, learned, sage
Wyes (n-pl)- electrical - three phase circuit arrangement as in letter Y

Wick (n)- twisted threads in candle, lamp that absorbs fuel and when lighted burns with a small steady flame
Wicke (adj)- obs. - wicked, bad, foul, mean

Wicker (n)- slender pliant twig - used for baskets, chairs, furniture
Whicker (v)- Eng. - cry or call of a horse, neigh, whinny

Wie- see We

Wield (v)- utilize, use, control, handle, manage
Weald (n)- forest, woods, open country
Weald (pr.n)- district of Kent, Surrey and Essex, England

Wig (n)- toupee, artificial covering of the hair, peruke, hairpiece
Wigg (n)- Scot. and Eng. Dial. - raised seed cake or a currant bun
Whig (pr.n)- member of a political party

Wight- see White, Wite

Wild (adj)- untamed, undomesticated, savage, lawless
Wilde (pr.n)- Oscar. British dramatist, poet, novelist
Wiled (n)- lure, beguiled

221

W

Wile (n)- 1. double dealing, trick, ruse, deceit, cheat. 2. lure, guile
While (n)- 1. time, span, term, space of time. 2. (conj) - although, as long as, even if
Win (v)- achieve, attain, get, acquire, earn
Whin (n)- evergreen shrub with yellow flowers, gorse, furze
Wynn (n)- kind of timber truck or carriage
Wyn (n)- old English alphabet, one of the runes adopted into the Anglo-Saxon

Wind (v)- curl, coil, twist, reel, crank, entwine
Wined (v)- supplied, entertained or treated to wine
Wynd (n)- Scot. - narrow lane or alley

Wine (n)- fermented juice of grapes, fruits, plants used as alcoholic beverage
Whine (v)- complain, wail, murmur, mewl, cry, fret

Wined- see Wind, Wynd

Wip (v)- Eng. and Scot. Dial. - twist, coil
Whip (v)- to punish by whipping, beat, flog. Strike with a lash, whip, or rod

Wipe (v)- rub or pass over with a cloth. Clean or dry in this manner
Wype (n)- obs. - lapwing

Wise (adj)- informed, learned, enlightened, sage, sensible
Whys (n-pl)- reasons, causes, motives
Wyes (n-pl)- electrical - three phase circuit arrangement as in letter Y

Wish (v)- desire, yen, long for, want, crave
Whish (n)- soft whizzing sound and swish

Wist (v)- past tense of to wit, thought, knew
Whist (inter)- 1. be silent, be still. 2. (n)- card game

Wit (n)- 1. jest, repartee, sense of humor, witticism. 2. intellect, brains, reason
Whit (n)- mite, particle, iota. Drop in the bucket
Weet (n)- cry of several kinds of birds. The bird itself

Witch (n)- 1. charmer, sorceress, siren, vampire, fortune teller. 2. (v) - captivate, put under a spell
Which (pro)- 1. interrog. - what person or thing. 2. (adj)- what kind
Wych or **Witch** (n)- hazel or elm tree. Wych hazel or witch hazel

Wite- see White, Wight

222

W

With (prep)- among, amidst, beside, along with, in company, by use of
Withe (n)- branch, bough, twig, shoot, willow

Wither (v)- fade, decay, droop, wilt, dry up
Whither (adv)- used to introduce questions - to what place, where

Woe- see Whoa

Wok (n)- large rounded pan used by Chinese for fast cooking
Walk (v)- travel on foot, saunter, step, stroll

Won (v)- past tense of win. Was successful, attained, gained
One (adj)- a single unit or individual

Wont (n)- habit, use, custom, practice, routine
Want (v)- wish, long for, crave, yearn, desire

Wood (n)- forest, trees, woods, groves, brush, timberland
Would (v)- past tense of will, expressing desire

Wooer (n)- one who woos. A suitor
Whewer (n)- the European widgeon (duck)

Wore (v)- past tense of wear. Had on, carried on person
War (n)- active military operations, declared hostilities. Emnity, strife, conflict

Worn (adj)- 1. tired, exhausted, worn out, haggard, beat. 2. shabby, seedy, decayed
Warn (v)- forwarn, caution against, sound the alarm, predict

Worst (adj)- bad, evil, harmful, most inferior
Wurst (n)- sausage generally used in combination of liverwurst, weinerwurst

Wort (n)- liquid prepared with malt, after fermenting becomes, beer, ale
Wart (n)- fungous growth. Small protuberance on the skin

Wot- see Wat, What, Watt

Would (v)- past tense of will, expressing desire
Wood (n)- firewood, lumber, timber, kindling, fuel

Wrack (n)- seaweed or other marine plant on shore. Weeds
Rack (v)- harass, torture, distress, torment, pain

Wracks (n-pl)- wrecks or wreckage cast ashore
Racks (n-pl)- instruments of torture, wheel, rack, thumbscrew
Rax (v)- 1. stretch or strain oneself. 2. reach or hand to a person

W

Wramp (n)- Brit. - a sprain
Ramp (n)- a slope or ascent, inclined or sloping plane

Wrang (n)- Scot.- wrong
Rang (v)- gave forth a clear sound as a bell, or testing a coin

Wrangell (pr.n)- mountain range in Alaska
Wrangle (v)- 1. argue, dispute, altercation. 2. to tend horses

Wrapped (v)- encased, covered, concealed
Rapt (adj)- engrossed, absorbed, spellbound
Rapped (n)- knocked, clipped, tapped, buffeted

Wrapper (n)- 1. envelope, container, casing. 2. dressing gown, robe
Rapper (n)- person who raps

Wrat (n)- Scot.- a wart
Rat (n)- rodent of the genus mus

Wrath (n)- rage, anger, fury, spleen
Rathe (adj)- poetic - quickly, promptly, eager
Rath (n)- hill, mount, fortress

Wrasse (n)- edible, marine, usually brilliant colored fish
Rasse (n)- a civet native to China and East Indies

Wray (v)- betray, reveal, disclose
Re (n)- Music - syllable used for second note of scale
Ray (n)- line of light, gleam, beam
Ra (pr.n)- Egyptian Sun God

Wreak (n)- execute, inflict, revenge, vengeance
Reek (n)- stench, stink, strong, unpleasant smell
Reak (n)- obs. - a seaweed or rush

Wreaks (v)- carries out promptings of ill humors on a victim
Reeks (n-pl)- fumes, exhausts, ether, vapor
Reaks (n-pl)- obs. - tricks, pranks

Wreck (v)- destroy, demolish, ruin, raze
Reck (v)- Archaic - to have care or concern. Heed

Wrest (v)- pull, jerk, force by violent twist
Rest (v)- sleep, repose, nap, doze. Lie down

Wretch (n)- poor creature, vagabond, outcast, sufferer
Retch (v)- to heave, vomit, strain

Wrig (n)- 1. feeblest member of a litter or brood. 2. youngest child of a family or puny child
Rig (v)- Naut. - to fit with sails, tackling. To furnish with gear, fit up or equip

W

Wright- see Write, Rite, Right

Wring (v)- squeeze, compress, wrest, twist violently
Ring (n)- 1. circlet, hoop. 2. arena, prize ring. 3. peal of bells

Wringer (n)- apparatus which forces water out by pressure
Ringer (n)- 1. person that rings a bell. 2. strong resemblance to another

Write (v)- 1. pen, transcribe, scribble, record, inscribe. 2. (v)- compose, author, describe
Wright (n)- workman - mechanic used in compounds as wheelwright, shipwright
Rite (n)- baptism, christening, celebration. Religious ceremony, worship, sacrament
Right (v)- 1. set upright, make straight, put in order. 2. (adv)- toward the right hand, not the left

Writer (n)- one who writes or has written. Pen man, Scribe
Righter (n)- one who does justice or redresses wrong

Wrote (v)- past tense of write. Did write, inscribe, pen
Rote (n)- routine, repetition. Fixed course of procedure

Wrung (v)- twisted, squeezed or pressed out
Rung (n)- 1. step on a ladder. 2. spoke on a wheel

Wry (adj)- crooked, distorted, out of shape, twisted
Rye (n)- 1. cereal grass. 2. alcoholic liquor

Wurst (n)- sausage generally used in combination of liverwurst, weinerwurst
Worst (adj)- bad, evil, harmful, most inferior

Wych- see Witch, Which

Wye- see Why

Wyes- see Wise, Whys

Wynd- see Wind, Wined

Wyn- see Win

Wype (n)- obs. - lapwing
Wipe (v)- rub or pass over with a cloth. Clean or dry in this manner.

X
Y
Z

–X–

Xanthin (n)- Chem. - yellow insoluble coloring matter
Xanthine (n)- Biochem. - white compound closely related to uric acids

–Y–

Yap (n)- 1. sharp, shrill, bark or yelp. 2. peevish or noisy person
Yap (pr.n)- one of the Caroline Islands
Yapp (n)- type of bookbinding with limp leather, projecting flaps expecially used in Bibles

Yar (adj)- Eng. Dial. - acid, sour, brackish
Yarr (v)- obs. - to growl or snarl

Yeld (adj)- Scot. - barren cow, not giving milk
Yelde (v)- obs. - to shield, help
Yelled (v)- shouted, screamed, shrieked

Yew (n)- cone bearing evergreen tree
You (pro)- yourself, person to whom one is speaking or writing
Ewe (n)- female sheep

Yews (n-pl)- cone bearing evergreen trees
Use (v)- put to a purpose, utilize, manage, handle
Ewes (n-pl)- plural of female sheep

Yoke (v)- couple, connect, link, unite, join together
Yolk (n)- yellow substance of an egg

You'll - see Yule

Your (pro)- possessive, belonging to or done by you
You're - contraction of you are
Ure (n)- 1. obs. - use, practice. 2. a bull

Yule (n)- noel, Christmas
You'll - contraction of you will, you shall

–Z–

Zein (n)- genus of grasses, kind of grain
Zeine (n)- Biochem. - a protein deficient in the amino acids

Zilla (n)- Bot. - genus of thorny plants
Zillah (n)- India- district or administrative division

Zombi (n)- 1. West Africa, Haiti- voodoo cults, the deity of the python. 2. a corpse re-animated
Zombie (n)- 1. Canada- home defense Army conscript unwilling to volunteer for overseas duty. 2. tall drink made of several types of rum and fruit juices. 3. slang- so-called walking dead.

WHY THIS BOOK WAS WRITTEN

As a volunteer teacher for Dr. Laubach's method of teaching 'English as a Second Language,' I discovered that all my foreign students encountered much difficulty in dealing with words that sound alike, but that differ in meaning and spelling.....homophones or homonyms.

The postcards from young children explaining "I am going to camp in too days" and "There barber cut my hare to short and made me bawled" were cute. The shock set in when a high school senior wrote "Fore quartz make a gallon" and a college graduate thanked me for the "silver bowels." The business letter signed by the boss under "Greatfully yours" was no surprise.

It is sad when one realizes that after twelve years of schooling, a student can leave high school as a functional illiterate and that a diploma no longer guarantees minimum competence. Educators, parents and business managers have been extremely critical of the poor spelling of students and graduates. There are spelling clinics, tutors, spelling texts, teaching machines and other learning aids, except when it comes to homonyms which, authorities agree, cause the largest percentage of spelling errors.

With the exception of a few children's handbooks, no book dedicated to homonyms is available in most libraries and school systems. It was hard for me to believe there was not a single reference book devoted to these misspelled, mispronounced, troublesome, tricky and confusing word plagues.

I was forced to enlarge upon my own set of index file cards, which I had previously compiled for the purpose of entering contests, and devised a special flash card game of homonyms in order to help teach my bilingual students. I was so successful that my foreign students soon outclassed all others in reading, spelling and pronunciation. They accomplished so much in so short a time span that my colleagues (private, school and volunteer tutors) began to borrow my files and flash cards. This enormous demand prompted the research and writing of this 'Reference Guide.'

A student who consults the dictionary for the correct spelling of 'hare' and 'bawled' will realize he has made an error after reading the definitions, but the dictionary cannot help him easily find the correct spelling of 'hair' and 'bald.' In this book the student would see at a glance the difference between to, too, two; or for, fore, and four.

Geographically, people from Boston have a different pronunciation and speech pattern than a person from Brooklyn, Atlanta or Dallas. A good illustration is this excerpt from John Steinbeck's 'The Grapes of Wrath'....

"I knowed you wasn't Oklahomy folks. You talk queer kinda. This aint no blame, you understan. Ever'body says words different," said Ivy, "Arkansas folks says 'em different and Oklahomy folks says 'em different. And we seen a lady from Massachusetts, an' she said 'em differentest of all. Couldn' hardly make out what she was saying."

Pronunciation symbols are omitted as they vary from one dictionary to another, and all dictionaries are not consistent. Just as some words vary from dialect to dialect or from person to person; and as regional differences in pronunciation and vocabulary do exist; some readers will find that certain groups of words in this book are not homonymous in their sphere of experience.

For those who may feel that our use of archaic and obsolete words in this comprehensive Encyclopedia is excessive, we have also prepared a condensed and simplified version for schools, educators and students.

The substitution of one word for another, or the use of homonyms, has enabled this writer to win numerous prizes, cars, trips and even thousands of cash dollars. Variant homonyms have brought disappointment and unhappiness to puzzle fans not possessed with the proper reference books, while the use of 'sound alikes' has brought more profit and prizes to writers than any other device.

To the over 15 million crossword puzzle fans and contest fans who enjoy jingles, puns, limericks and word games; to the countless writers and linguaphiles; this Encyclopedia will be of great aid in endowing them with the 'Write Attitude.'

–Dora Newhouse–

Facts and Figures

For those amongst us who enjoy statistics, here are some facts concerning this Encyclopedia.

- 3,500 individual homonyms are listed and grouped by 'sound-alikes'. Each of the 3,500 lead words are arranged alphabetically.

- 8,000 total homonym entries appear listed and cross- referenced.

- 'Sound-Alike groups with:

Three variant spellings	400
Four variant spellings	90
Five variant spellings	15
Six variant spellings	4
Nine variant spellings (sole, wheel)	2
Fourteen variant spellings (air)	1

Letters of the alphabet with the most homonyms:

Letter S	430 words
Letter P	320 words
Letter C	300 words
Letter T	240 words
Letter B	240 words
Letter M	215 words
Letter W	200 words

There are many homonyms with 'sound-alike' words that begin with two different letters of the alphabet (ate-eight, know-no). However there are only six words that sound alike and start with THREE different letters of the alphabet (air, err, heir).

Guinness Superlatives Limited

DIRECTORS
A. J. R. Purssell, Chairman
N. D. McWhirter, Managing
E. Beedell (J. R. E. Lawton, alternate)
J. S. Anthony
A. R. McWhirter
D. F. Hoy
P. T. Cunningham

15th January, 1975

Dora Newhouse,
146 No. Rampart Blvd.,
LOS ANGELES,
California 90026,
U. S.A.

Dear Dora Newhouse,

    We were more than delighted to receive your letter of December 31st with the extraordinary compilation on the most prolific homophones. The linguaphile who furnished us with Roz will, I think, be very highly impressed *even depressed*.

    We are starting on our revision period shortly for our next edition and there are no further formalities necessary to ensure that your discovery will be included. I shall attribute it to you personally which I hope will be of some assistance in the placing of your manuscript, and as an extra token of my appreciation for your furnishing us with the superlative fruits of your mammoth study I shall send you a complimentary copy of the next edition which will incorporate this entry.

    It is quite extraordinary that we have not had a single letter advocating the claims of Sole, Air or Weal, so we must particularly congratulate you on your ingenuity and industry.

    With all best wishes.

Yours sincerely,

Norris D. McWhirter
Editor

Most Homophones. The most homophonous sound in English is **sol** which, according to the researches of Dora Newhouse of Los Angeles, has 35 meanings with 6 variant spellings: Soal, sol, sole, soul, sowl, and the verb sowle, meaning "to pull by the ears."

    From the 1976 edition of the
    Guiness Book of World Records, page 201

(Newest and latest record of the must homophonous sound is 'Air' which, according to the author's research has 14 variant spellings and 38 meanings.)

SPECIAL EXPLANATORY NOTES AND ABBREVIATIONS
used in this Reference Book

Abbr.- abbreviated, abbreviation

adj.- adjective

adv.- adverb

Afr.- Africa

Agr.- agriculture

Anat.- anatomy

Anc.- ancient

Arch.- architecture

Archaic- antiquated, out of use

Archeol.- archeology

Astrol.- astrology

Astron.- astronomy

Bibl.- Bible, biblical

Biochem.- biochemical

Biol.- biology

Bot.- botany

Brit.- British

Celt.- Celtic

Chem.- chemistry, chemical

Colloq.- colloquial

Conj.- conjunction

Contr.- contraction

Dial.- dialetic, dialect

dim.- diminutive

Eng.- England, English

e.g.- for example

esp.- especially

etc.- et cetera

Fem.- feminine

Fr.- French

Gael.- Gaelic

Gr.- Greek

Gr.Brit.- Great Britain

Her.- heraldry

inter.- interjection

Ir.- Irish

Masc.- masculine

Math.- mathematic

Med.- medical

Myth.- mythology

n- noun

Naut.- nautical

obs., obsol.- obsolete

Pl.- plural

Poet.- poetic

p.p.- past participle

pr.n- proper noun

Prep.- preposition

pro., pron- pronoun

Prov.- provincial

P.T.- past tense

Sc.,Scot.- Scotch or Scottish

Sing.- singular

v- verb

Var.- variant

Zool- zoology

REFERENCE BOOKS USED

Pronunciation, Meaning and **Etymology** for the words used in this Reference Book were taken from the following works:

The Holy Bible

The Complete Works of Shakespeare

1888- Webster's Unabridged Dictionary (Merriam Co.)

1916- Webster's New International Dictionary (Merriam Co.)

1924- Winston Simplified Dictionary (John Winston & Co.)

1933- Shorter Oxford Dictionary, Vol. 1 & 2 (Clarendon Press)

1947- Words - The New Dictionary (Grosset & Dunlap)

1948- Funk & Wagnall's Dictionary, Vol. 1 & 2 (Funk & Wagnalls)

1951- Webster 2nd International Dictionary (Merriam Co.)

1952- New Century Dictionary, Vol. 1 & 2 (Unicorn Press)

1969- American College Dictionary (Random House)

1969- Webster's Unabridged Dictionary (Rockville House)

1971- Compact Oxford Dictionary, Vol. 1 & 2 (Oxford Press)

1976- Webster's New Universal Dictionary, Unabridged (Webster's International Press)

MOST COMMON MISSPELLED AND MISUSED WORDS

Out of the thousands of words contained in this Encyclopedia we have selected a few hundred to help illustrate the difficulty encountered by children and bilinguals who must learn to read, write and speak English.

This first group of words should be mastered by children at the elementary levels. In fact many high school graduates, who we tried these words on, did not know all of these simple examples:

Aid	Beat	Cent	Die	Find
Aide	Beet	Sent	Dye	Fined
		Scent		
Ail	Better	Cereal	Do	Flea
Ale	Bettor	Serial	Dew	Flee
			Due	
Air	Blue	Chews	Do	Flew
Err	Blew	Choose	Doe	Flue
Heir			Dough	Flu
Ate	Board	Chile	Dual	Flour
Eight	Bored	Chili	Duel	Flower
		Chilly		
Alter	Brake	Cite	Ewe	For
Altar	Break	Sight	You	Fore
		Site	Yew	Four
Ant	By	Close	Eye	Foul
Aunt	Buy	Clothes	Aye	Fowl
	Bye		I	
Ball	Capital	Dam	Faint	Gate
Bawl	Capitol	Damn	Feint	Gait
Bomb	Cede	Days	Fair	Gilt
Balm	Seed	Daze	Fare	Guilt
Bare	Ceiling	Dear	Feat	Gym
Bear	Sealing	Deer	Feet	Jim
		Dere	Fete	
Base	Cell	Desert	Fir	Gnu
Bass	Sell	Dessert	Fur	Knew
				New

235

Grate	Know	Ought	Right	Steal
Great	No	Aught	Rite	Steel
			Write	
Groan	Lessen	Paced	Ring	Tail
Grown	Lesson	Paste	Wring	Tale
Hall	Loan	Pain	Role	Tea
Haul	Lone	Pane	Roll	Tee
Hair	Loose	Pair	Sail	To
Hare	Lose	Pare	Sale	Too
Herr		Pear		Two
Heal	Made	Pause	Seen	There
Heel	Maid	Paws	Scene	Their
He'll				They're
Hear	Mail	Peace	Sea	Vice
Here	Male	Piece	See	Vise
			Si	
Higher	Mall	Pedal	Seas	Way
Hire	Maul	Peddle	Sees	Weigh
			Seize	
Hoarse	Meat	Plain	Seam	Waste
Horse	Meet	Plane	Seem	Waist
	Mete			
Hole	Medal	Praise	Shoot	Where
Whole	Meddle	Prays	Chute	Wear
				Ware
Hour	Miner	Quarts	Size	Worn
Our	Minor	Quartz	Sighs	Warn
I'll	Mowed	Rain	Soared	Weight
Isle	Mode	Reign	Sword	Wait
Aisle		Rein		
It's	None	Red	Son	Weather
Its	Nun	Read	Sun	Whether
Knight	Oh	Real	Stair	Whine
Night	Owe	Reel	Stare	Wine
	Eau			
Knot	One	Rose	Steak	Would
Not	Won	Rows	Stake	Wood
		Roes		

This second group of words should be known by every high school graduate but are difficult and confusing even to the college educated. Imagine the degree of difficulty encountered by those not as fortunate:

Ascent	Confidant	Emerge	Hostel	Oral
Assent	Confident	Immerge	Hostile	Aural
Based	Council	Eruption	Impressed	Parlay
Baste	Counsel	Iruption	Imprest	Parley
Berth	Course	Fate	Ingenious	Pearl
Birth	Coarse	Fete	Ingenous	Purl
Born	Cue	Flair	Lean	Pray
Borne	Queue	Flare	Lien	Prey
Bourne		Flayer		
Braise	Descent	Foreward	Leased	Principal
Braze	Dissent	Forward	Least	Principle
Brays			Lest	
Breach	Deviser	Fort	Lightening	Rapped
Breech	Devisor	Forte	Lightning	Rapt
	Divisor			Wrapped
Bridal	Discreet	Gage	Mantel	Review
Bridle	Discrete	Gauge	Mantle	Revue
Champagne	Draft	Gibe	Meter	Stationary
Champaign	Draught	Jibe	Metre	Stationery
Choral	Ellicit	Heroin	Mold	Therefor
Coral	Illicit	Heroine	Mould	Therefore
Corol				
Complement	Elusion	Hoard	Naval	Vain
Compliment	Ilusion	Horde	Navel	Vane
		Whored		Vein

Why English Is So Hard

We'll begin with a box, and the plural is boxes.
   But the plural of ox should be oxen, not oxes.
Then one fowl is goose, but two are called geese.
   Yet the plural of moose should never be meese.
You may find a lone mouse or a whole lot of mice.
   But the plural of house is houses, not hise.
If the plural of man is always called men.
   Why shouldn't the plural of pan be called pen?
The cow in the plural may be cows or kine.
   But the plural of vow is vows, not vine.
And I speak of foot and you show me your feet,
   But I give you a boot...would a pair be called beet?
If one is a tooth and the whole set are teeth,
   Why shouldn't the plural of booth be called beeth?
If the singular is this and the plural is these,
   Should the plural of kiss be nicknamed kese?
Then one may be that, and three may be those,
   Yet the plural of hat would never be hose.
We speak of a brother, and also of brethren,
   But though we say mother, we never say methren.
The masculine pronouns are he, his and him.
   But imagine the feminine she, shis, and shim!
So our English, I think you will all agree,
   Is the trickiest language you ever did see!

                                              Anonymous